Economic Crisis and Social Integration

Comparative Regional Integration Studies

Edited by
György Széll and Woosik Moon

Vol. 1

PETER LANG
Frankfurt am Main · Berlin · Bern · Bruxelles · New York · Oxford · Wien

Yongha Kim / György Széll (eds.)

Economic Crisis and Social Integration

PETER LANG
Internationaler Verlag der Wissenschaften

Bibliographic Information published by the Deutsche Nationalbibliothek
The Deutsche Nationalbibliothek lists this publication in the Deutsche Nationalbibliografie; detailed bibliographic data is available in the internet at http://dnb.d-nb.de.

ISSN 1868-758X
ISBN 978-3-631-62059-5

www.peterlang.de

We gratefully acknowledge the support of:

Her Excellency Jeon Jae-Hee,
Minister for Health, Welfare and Family Affairs

Mr. Chung Hyung Gun,
Chairman of the National Health Insurance Corporation

Mr. Park Hae-choon,
Chairman of the National Pension Service

Table of Contents

Foreword

Yongha Kim and György Széll

The Korea Institute for Health and Social Affairs (KIHASA) was built on the merger of its two constituent predecessors, the Korea Health Development Institute and the Korea Institute for Family Planning, which was founded in 1971, and has since grown to become a power house of more than 180 well-rounded researchers and support staff, many of them economists and social scientists by training, who live and breathe some of the defining policy issues of these times, among them social security, population aging, health care, childcare and poverty.

The work we do here, which includes a large number of national surveys and statistical analyses, is the bedrock for those who shape and implement national policy to protect people's well-being from social risks as diverse as old age, disease, disability, unemployment, and other unforeseen calamities of various kinds. What we do here is thus closely bound up with people's life conditions.

In the current times where the demand for public health and social welfare is soaring as never before, the objective of our research is not only in meeting such needs, but in doing so in a fiscally sustainable and socially supportable manner and, if possible, in a way that adds to the country's national productivity. In that regard, we take as our overarching goal the pursuit of a health and welfare system that can help bring people closer to one another, make different social groups more cohesive, and reinforce the overall social fabric of the country.

We take great pride in the tradition we have of expertise, integrity and dynamism. It is this tradition in tandem with our humility of knowing that as challenges to our people's well-being continue to arise from within and without the country, we must also grow on that will keep lifting us to new heights.

In this endeavour KIHASA organised an international symposium on the economic crisis and social integration, which took place at Hotel Shilla, Seoul, on May 27-28, 2009. At the symposium took part besides researchers from KIHASA representatives from Ireland, France, England, Germany, Denmark, The Netherlands, the U.S.A., Japan and China. This book assembles most of these contributions. Although two years have passed since then, we are convinced that this volume is absolutely up to date as the economic crisis is far from overcome and social reintegration remains one of the foremost challenges in today's world.

Seoul and Osnabrück, May 2011

Foreword

0. Abstracts

1. How are Social Policies in the EU Responding to the Financial Crisis?

David Stanton, Chair of the Indicators Subgroup of the EU Social Protection Committee

The article starts by describing the process set up by the EU to monitor the consequences of the financial crisis for social integration. The EU has produced two reports summarising how the crisis is affecting social issues. It also gives an account of how areas such as the labour market and housing are being affected and the special initiatives that have been taken. The article then examines whether the responses are sustainable in a fiscal sense. The background to this are the EU's recently released medium term projections for age related social expenditure. The last step is to consider the pressures on social integration policies and therefore social expenditure that have already been at work over the last thirty years. This part of the article draws on "Growing Unequal? Income Distribution and Poverty in OECD Countries". The conclusion is that the combined pressures of the financial crisis that are essentially a response for a real economy adjustment will put a long term upward pressure on social expenditure budgets. The sustainability of these needs to raise social expenditure will be challenged, as we enter a period when populations age and as governments struggle to contain public sector deficits unseen in peace time.

2. Social Protection for the Economic Crisis: The U.S. Experience

Gary Burtless, The Brookings Institution Washington, D.C.

I. *Introduction.* A brief introduction will describe the basic rationale for the U.S. economic stimulus program and for the elements in the package that will change, temporarily or permanently, the American system of social protection. Since February 2008 the U.S. Congress has passed five major and minor pieces of legislation aimed at dealing with the financial crisis of the banks and real estate industry or with the economic fallout from that crisis. The legislation has attempted to (1) prevent the failure of major financial institutions; (2) minimize the impact of financial institution weakness on ordinary business and consumer borrowing; (3) provide immediate stimulus to consumer spending by raising after-tax household income (through temporary tax reductions or benefit increases); (4) provide temporary funds to state and local governments in order to reduce their need to boost taxes or reduce spending in the middle of a recession; (5) protect the incomes and health insurance of newly laid off workers and members of other economically vulnerable populations; and (6) provide direct federal support for infrastructure investments, for example, in the telecommunications and electric networks, transportation projects, public buildings and laboratories, and energy-saving initiatives.

II. *Magnitude of the economic downturn.* This section will briefly summarize basic information on the recession up to the spring of 2009. In what sectors did weakness first appear? How rapid and deep has been the decline in U.S. economic activity, both absolutely and in comparison with earlier post-World-War-II recessions? Because the article is focused on social protection and reforms in the unemployment and social assistance systems, the summary will concentrate on developments in household income, employment and unemployment, hours of work and wages, and household net worth. How big is the gap between actual U.S. production and potential output if the economy were operating at full employment?

III. *Elements of the U.S. government response to the financial crisis, with special reference to provisions for the social safety net.*

- *(a)* Two legislative packages provided immediate stimulus to consumer spending through temporary tax reductions to federal income tax payers and lump-sum payments to certain Americans who do not file income-tax returns.
- *(b)* Three changes in law, starting in June 2008, increased the amount of income protection provided to the unemployed.
- *(c)* The federal government increased monthly nutrition assistance grants (formerly called "food stamps") for needy families, and it provided generous subsidies to encourage state governments to provide better benefits to laid-off parents eligible for means-tested social assistance payments.
- *(d)* The federal government increased the subsidy rate that it provided to state governments so that they can pay for public health insurance benefits (Medicaid and State Child Health Insurance plans) for indigent populations.
- *(e)* The federal government has established a variety of programs to help home buyers obtain loans to buy a new home and to aid home owners who find it difficult to make timely payments on their home mortgages.

IV. *Evaluation of the U.S. government's social protection program for the financial crisis.* This section of the article will offer an assessment of the components of U.S. social protection and their likely success in the recession. Two aspects of the social safety net deserve comment: How well would the U.S. safety net work in a deep recession under the assumption that *no* special measures were enacted during the recession? How well is it likely to work in light of the fact that the Congress and President enacted special measures to deal with the problems arising in this recession?

V. *Are there lessons from the U.S. experience for other developed and developing countries?*

3. China's Social Policy Choices in Times of the World Financial Crisis

Zheng Gongcheng, Renmin University of China, China

Since the world financial crisis erupted in 2008, it has not only influenced world economics to a great extent, but also impacts on the social welfare of every country. For China, whose economy is rapidly developing, the effects in the areas of economic development models and social welfare are even more profound. There is necessity to pursue sustainable development. In designing social welfare reform and a new social welfare system, much attention should be paid to the burden sharing mechanism. The optimal level of social welfare should be placed as basic protection. In the pursuit of the goal of covering the entire citizen, a rational and prudent policy direction for the standardization of social welfare should be taken. Of course, China's mission on reform in social welfare system has not been accomplished yet, and is still facing a lot of challenges and difficulties. But in recent years the Chinese government has made great efforts to improve social welfare and recently to ease the pressure from the world financial crisis, which will enable the mission of establishing the new social welfare system to move forward a single step.

4. Weathering the Storm: Consociational Democracy and Crisis Management in the Netherlands

Karen Anderson, Department of Political Science, Institute for Management Research, Radboud University Nijmegen

The Dutch response to the economic crisis emphasizes stabilizing the domestic financial system and mobilizing the labour market so that Dutch firms and workers are well-prepared to take advantage of the expanding economy when the current recession ends. This approach has been heavily conditioned by two central elements of the Dutch political economy. First, the existence of a mature, comprehensive welfare state provides 'automatic stabilizers' during economic downturns; even if governments 'do nothing', social policies (particularly unemployment insurance) are an important source of demand stimulus. Second, the norms of political and economic decision-making in a consociational democracy like the Netherlands dictate that any response to the economic crisis requires time-consuming, detailed compromises that include the social partners. The government, backed by the social partners, announced a stimulus package in late March 2009 that provides €6 billion in additional spending in 2009 and 2010 for environmentally sustainable investments, including subsidies for energy-efficient cars and houses. The deal also includes extra funds (€220 million) for fighting youth unemployment. The government's approach to fight the crisis is not limited to short-term goals. The crisis package announced in March 2009 relies on stimulating consumption in the short term, restoring budget balance and reducing public debt in the medium term, and working towards the sustainability of public finances in the long term. The latter specifically includes dealing with the health care and public pension costs associated with population ageing.

5. Social Policy Stability in Times of Economic Crisis: The Case of Germany

Martin Seeleib-Kaiser, Green Templeton College, University of Oxford

The German economy was one of the hardest hit economies in 2009. Nonetheless, the government has stayed rather relaxed about fiscal stimulus measures and had not proposed any major expansion of social policy programmes. To some extent this can be explained by two facts: 1) the unemployment rate has been falling until very recently; and 2) despite cut-backs in the early 2000s, Germany still provides relatively generous welfare provisions for the short-term unemployed. As private or occupational pension coverage has not been very important in achieving adequate pension incomes, the decline in equity markets will have only a comparatively small impact on the income of future pensioners. The big question for Germany is not whether the welfare state is sustainable, but whether Germany can sustain its export-led economic model. The latter obviously will have a huge impact on the sustainability of the welfare state.

6. Crisis Governance in Denmark: Is Flexicurity Delivering?

Peter Abrahamson, Seoul National University

Denmark was in a very particular situation when the international economic crisis hit with the lowest unemployment and the highest employment rate ever. Hence, despite increasing unemployment the concern has been about increasing available man power. The advice given to the government on crisis governance has been rather uniform and has suggested taking initiatives that will increase work incentives by rolling back social rights and continuing the active turn in welfare policy. The Danish model can be characterized by the concept of *flexicurity*, which means that there is a combination of a very flexible labour market coupled with rather generous welfare benefits facilitated by active labour market policies. In such an environment employers are expected to easily hire in good times, since they can easily fire in bad times. Furthermore, most welfare benefits are universal and tax financed, and most Danes are in formal employment; women have a labour market participation rate of 85 per cent. Recent changes in welfare state organization in Denmark contributed to a high degree of preparedness for the crisis, and the many years of developing welfare provisions contributed to the robustness of the Danish model. The most important element of crisis governance has been a tax reduction package which is expected to increase private consumption by DKK 28 billion (US$ 5 billion) or one and a half per cent of GDP, but other measures have also been introduced mainly directed toward boosting activity within the construction, building and renovation sectors where unemployment has increased the most. Even if the government's major initiative will increase inequality further, it is not expected to threaten social cohesion since the increase started from a very low level. Denmark is still, and in the foreseeable future will continue to be one of the most egalitarian societies in the world with very few poor people.

7. Policy Tasks for Social Integration in Times of the Economic Crisis: the Case of South Korea

Yong Chan Byun, The Korea Institute for Health and Social Affairs (KIHASA), Seoul

The global financial crisis triggered by the subprime mortgage loans in the U.S. has spilled over to other businesses. The UN World Economic Situation and Prospects 2009 showed negative projections for high-income countries such as the U.S. (-1.9%), Japan -0.6%, and the Euro zone (-1.5%) as well as the global economy (-0.4%) (UN 2009). Export-driven South Korea is also expected to decrease at -2% in 2009 due to the spread of the global economic crisis. Moreover, South Korea needs to push ahead with such social policies designed to bring Koreans from all income brackets together in order to overcome economic woes and enhancing social values. For establishing a systematic social integration action plan for both addressing economic problems and social integration similar to that of the EU, Korea needs to learn from the experiences of the leading countries in the world.

8. The Relationship between the Economic Crisis, Non-regular Labourers and Social Security in Present-day Japan

Takanobu Kyogoku, The National Institute of Population and Social Security Research, Tokyo

Aiming at the construction of a new social security system for overcoming the unprecedented economic crisis. At present, in the midst of the worldwide financial crisis, Japan is also confronted with an unprecedented economic crisis. The breaking down of the conventional social security system which is centred on regular labourers is becoming increasingly noticeable, and the creation of a new safety net for non-regular labourers has an important meaning in the short term. Also, upgrading of long-term care services to cope with the advance of the super-aged society will perform a major role in the medium-to-long term. In any event, these two social security measures also have an extremely large economic effect for increasing domestic demand in the Japanese economy. This article covers (1) the actual situation and emergency measures for the economic crisis in Japan, (2) the relationship between social security and the increase in domestic demand, (3) the relationship among, economic growth, social security and employment, (4) the creation of a new safety net for non-regular labourers, and (5) the expansion of long-term care insurance. Considering these issues by making use of empirical evidence, we can realize that the construction of a second safety net and also the enhancement of social security through the expansion of long-term care services perform an important role in Japan's economic crisis measures. This situation leads to re-evaluation of the concept of a 'social market', as a cluster of social exchanges. In this context, social security should not be regarded as an existing economic market, but as the core of a new social market based on taxes, social insurance and user charge. Hence, a large mixed incorporated market is formed as a result of the mixing of the social with the economic market. This situation will strongly impact the economic market, and cause the domestic market to become stronger and to expand.

9. The Current Status of Health Insurance and Tasks Ahead

Jinsoo Kim, Rah-Il Hwang and Kyungha Kim, National Health Insurance Policy Research Institute, National Health Insurance Corporation, Seoul

Health insurance is a system under which economic burden of all community members would be resolved collectively by all people. As such, it constitutes an integral part of the overall social welfare system of the country and strives for promoting social justice and solidarity. Though most countries with a health insurance system have their own unique systems which incorporate unique historical, economic and social characteristics of their countries, medical insurance systems can be classified into four broad categories depending on the resource financing methods (contribution versus tax) and the mode of service provision (private provider versus public sector provider). In the case of South Korea, our health insurance system adopted the so-called 'social insurance method' under which resources are financed through contributions, and medical services are provided mainly by private providers (Cho 2001). The health insurance in Korea has contributed very much for promoting health and medical development by continuously expanding medical manpower, hospital beds and by improving benefit coverage. And yet, the health insurance has many inherent problems such as the existence of blind zones, unfair contribution burden sharing among regions, low benefit coverage and low public hospital bed ratios as well as other internal problems. As expectations of a better health service are rising to reflect globalization and aspirations of better quality of life, an ageing population and the introduction of new medical equipment and technologies will create quite a formidable demand for the health insurance system, and will push health costs upward. Moreover, a declining economically active population will aggravate the financial position of health insurance. Consequently, in order to ensure a sound financial position of the health insurance, it is desirable to enhance the benefit coverage of certain groups of patients (such as high costs, severe diseases and low income patients), reduce coverage for light patients (common cold for example), raise contribution rates, diversify revenue sources, rationalize the expense payment and drug management systems. These recommendations have been made several times in the past, but no action could be taken so far, due to the conflict of interests and difficulties of reaching consensus. Armed with thirty years history of achieving impossible tasks and know-how, and supported by the consensus that health insurance in Korea must be sustained at any cost; we should explore ways to resolve all these problems.

10. Efficient Management of Medical Treatment Costs of the Health Insurance for the Elderly

Chong Yon Park, Min Jung Ko, Jun Tae Han and Jin-Hee Kwon, Health Insurance Research Centre, The National Health Insurance Corporation, Seoul

Many countries throughout the world are feeling the strain of rising medical expenses triggered by their ageing population. In major OECD nations the ratio of medical expenditure incurred for senior citizens to total medical expenditure stands at around 40%. According to the OECD Health Data, as of 2005 Japan spent approximately US$ 300 billion for national health care, 47% of which was medical spending for senior citizens. In the United States, the biggest spender of medical expenses in the world, the medical expenses paid for elderly citizens accounted for 38% of the national medical spending of almost US$ 2 trillion. In most industrialized nations, medical expenses paid for the elderly are becoming an issue of grave concern. Most of all, the level of ageing serves as one of the main reasons behind the increase in national medical spending, and it is shown in the relationship between the ratio of the aged population to the total population and the ratio of medical spending for seniors to total national medical expenses. In the United States, elderly people accounting for 9.4% of the total population spent 19.7% of total medical expenses in 1963, and 9.9% spent 27.5% in 1970, highlighting the fact that the increase in medical spending for the elderly was much greater than the increase in the aged population. In 2000, senior citizens accounting for 12.6% of the total population spent 39.2% of total medical spending of the nation. It is necessary to pay attention to the increase in hospitalization fees at nursing hospitals as one of the reasons of medical expenses for the elderly. In particular, after the introduction of the long-term care insurance programme, due to regionally unbalanced distribution of senior nursing facilities and system glitches, some of the demand for senior nursing facilities is transferred to nursing hospitals, materializing the potential demand for medical services and eventually giving rise to the medical expenses for the elderly. In this context, review of the roles and functions of nursing hospitals and senior nursing facilities is urgent. To this aim, it is needed to define the function of nursing beds by adjusting the supply quality of nursing beds for long-term hospitalization based on an appropriate supply plan for nursing hospitals and senior nursing facilities, devised in consideration of the demographic and sociological characteristics of each region. In addition, in order to help enable appropriate judgement on the demand for medical and long-term care, a comprehensive screening tool for health conditions of elderly people should be developed to establish the gatekeeper function for comprehensive care, and the foundation to characterize the roles and functions of nursing institutions and senior nursing facilities should be prepared.

11. The Financial Crisis and its Impact on the Pension and Retirement Income System

Jhinyoung Shin, School of Business, Yonsei University, Seoul

The Current financial crisis was started by the collapse of the sub-prime mortgage market in the U.S.A. in 2007, and the financial markets and economies are still in severe turbulence, being unable to recover from the aftermath of the crisis. Pension and retirement income systems cannot avoid the fallout of the crisis. It is estimated that the plunge in prices of stocks and other financial securities wipes out $5 trillion from pension funds, as worldwide pension assets were reduced from $25 trillion to $20 trillion, a decrease of 19%. Many people are not only concerned about the security of their retirement pension, but also they are left with substantially decreased personal wealth, mostly invested in housing and financial securities. Their prices have plunged due to the financial crisis. A bit comforting fact is that the effect of the crisis on the pension and retirement income system is not as severe as on the financial markets and economies, although the impact of the financial crisis is diverse, depending on the differences in the pension systems and the individual characteristics of the members. The current crisis might provide a right incentive and opportunity for governments to reexamine the framework and implementation of policies to best achieve the objectives of the pension and retirement income system. It is imperative not to have any expedient responses under political pressure, which might threaten the long-term stability, financial health and sustainability of the whole pension and retirement income systems.

12. Korean National Pensions: Facts and Functions in 2009

Joonho Bae, College of Social Science, Hanshin University

The number of people above 65 years increased by about 190,000 persons every year in Korea, but the decrease of their labour participation rate according to the recent worldwide recession results in the reduction of labour income in the aged population, especially in the low income class. On the other hand pensioners of public pension including national pension increased by over 200,000 persons every year, so the stability of the retirement income may be become higher. But the decrease of labour income in the low income aged class may enlarge the inequality in income distribution within the old generation. Lee (2009) shows that inequality in consumption expenditure in the old generation has decreased steadily between 1998 and 2005 – using KLI panel data. This result may be concerned with the increase of benefactors in the public pension and public assistance systems during this period. This article arranges the composition of Korean retirement incomes, including public pension and the trend of the number of pensioners' and the amount of total benefits of the national pension, and also shows the voice of covered persons and the response of concerned authorities to these voices. And we review three studies that analyse the cases of Korea, Japan and Russia – respectively focusing on consumption smoothing. The cases of Japan and Russia comprise an analysis, searching for the impact on consumption of regular and large scale income variations that may be expected by the public pension system. This recession may enlarge inequality in the income distribution of the aged because of the reduction in labour income, especially in the low income class. However, this outlook should be clarified in the near future. And we also have to clarify, whether the increase of the pensioner's ratio within the old generation increases or decreases the inequality in the income distribution and consumption expenditure within the same generation.

Part I

1 How are Social Policies in the EU Responding to the Financial Crisis?

David Stanton

Introduction

In this article, I describe the social policy response of Governments within the European Union to the financial crisis. This raises the question of whether the response is financially sustainable, and I examine the problem in the context of other pressures on social protection budgets, particularly the start of the ageing process and its impact on social expenditure both pensions but also health and long-term care. The arguments are set in the context of recent trends in social expenditure; and I also draw on recent work showing how inequality has increased in most countries over the past 30 years. I examine whether the social response to the current crisis is best seen as part of longer term trends or a one off response to financial crisis.

Social Policy Responses to the Financial Crisis

This section draws on the monitoring process that has been set up by the EU Commission working through the Social Protection Committee (SPC) and its Indicators Sub group.

The financial crisis and social cohesion

Although no Member State in the EU is insulated from the effects of the world-wide financial crisis the timing and extent of the impact varies considerably across the 27 countries. The origins of the financial crisis were rooted in real economic trade imbalances that led many OECD countries running large current account deficits reflecting equally large trade surpluses experienced by China and other major manufacturing countries. These trade imbalances in turn were matched by financial flows, where excess liquidity searched for high returns and often this was linked to housing markets, not only the U.S. sub-prime mortgage market. Within the EU some Member States experienced rapid house price rises and large building booms: the U.K., Spain and Ireland are examples; others such as France and Germany experienced less buoyant markets in houses. This means that there have been some countries where the financial crisis has had social consequences that have been especially marked in housing.

The Labour Market

Labour market statistics throughout the EU are timelier than data used to monitor social cohesion and income inequality. At this stage of the recession in the EU, it is the labour market that is showing the most recent effects of the crisis. The first report from the SPC notes:

"Employment growth has come to a standstill. Unemployment rates have started to rise from a recent low at 6.8% in April 2008 to reach 7.6% in January 2009 and could go up to 10% in 2010 if policies and labour market behaviour remain unchanged. At the same time, demand for new workers has clearly started to fall in reaction to the slowdown in economic activity, and announced job losses now far outweigh those relating to job creation."

But there is great variation across the 27 Member States. The SPC report also says:

"At national level, employment remained unchanged in the third quarter of 2008 in France and Italy, fell in the U.K. (after remaining unchanged in the previous quarter), and contracted considerably in Spain (down 0.8% on the previous quarter), but continued to expand in Germany, Estonia and Poland.
In some Member States, the recent rise in unemployment has been especially stark (see annex 1). In Spain it reached 14.4% in December 2008, against 8.7% the year before. During the same period, it also nearly doubled in Ireland (8.2% against 4.7%), in Estonia (9.1% against 4.1%), Lithuania (8.0% against 4.3%) and Latvia (10.4% against 5.7%)."

Many Member States have expressed concerns about the potential impact on long term unemployment. The work force across the EU has aged and there is a large cohort of people approaching the end of their working lives. They are the generation that will retire and put upward pressure in pension transfers, public and private, in the coming decade. Older workers are less likely to lose their jobs but once unemployed they are at higher risk of becoming long-term unemployed. Many countries are entering the recession with levels of long-term unemployment that are already high:

"The long-term unemployment share (percentage of unemployed people who have been unemployed for more than 12 months) is especially high, at 55% for older workers, and has stopped decreasing in 2008. The long term unemployment share for older workers started rising significantly last year in Belgium (from 72% in Q3 07 to 75% in Q3 08), Italy (from 50% to 57%), Hungary (from 54% to 62%), Portugal (from 54% to 62%) and Slovenia (from 54% to 60%)."

Housing

The consequences of the financial crisis for housing would on their own be of concern in terms of social policy but the nature of the financial crisis puts housing in a special position. Many Member States saw house prices increasing to levels inconsistent with average earnings growth, often fuelled by mortgages equal to or greater than the purchase price of the houses. In these housing markets, there have already been sizeable effects from the financial crisis. House prices have fallen sharply in some countries for example Ireland, Denmark, Spain and the U.K., and repossessions of houses where mortgages have defaulted are increasing: in Denmark by 100% in 2008, in the U.K. by 70% in the same period and by 300% in Estonia.

Policy responses to the Financial Crisis

For most EU Member States the prime response is through the existing social protection systems. In Member States, where these are well established and where there is a comprehensive safety net, there are support systems responding to the growing numbers without work. The increases in social expenditures are themselves a countercyclical force in addition to the extra-policy responses introduced or announced. Some of these extra policy responses are described below.

- In Belgium, the plan adopted in December 2008 concentrates on supporting enterprises and employees, on strengthening the purchasing power of households and on investing in growth and sustainability.
- In Bulgaria, a wide range of measures include investment in public social infrastructure, measures to support employment, to strengthen social protection and better support people's income.
- In Germany, the package of measures focuses on safeguarding both jobs and businesses' capacity to invest. The measures will markedly increase public investments in future-oriented sectors with educational infrastructure at the forefront, but also in the social and health services and hospital infrastructure. The package will ensure the supply of credit to healthy, competitive companies, support the qualifications of the workforce and financial relief of households including an adequate income support for the most vulnerable.
- In Spain, all measures planned or taken in response to the crisis have been integrated in *Plan E* providing financial and budgetary support to the business sector and families alike, support to employment and modernising the economy. Recently adopted measures aimed at reducing current public expenditure by € 1,500 Mio in 2009 will not affect social benefits spending.
- In France, the *Plan de relance* adopted in December 2008 focussed on financial support to businesses and on public investment. It also includes a one-off payment (*solidarité active*) to low-income households. Additional measures adopted on 18 February 2009 concerned the improvement of unemployment insurance for the young unemployed and in case of temporary adjustment of working hours. They also included income support for the lower middle class (tax rebates, support to low-income families with children, and personal services vouchers for dependant elderly and for households with children).

- In Luxembourg, a package of new measures covers income support measures to individuals and families, and measures to support employment especially in the vulnerable sectors of the economy. Moreover, the social dimension is an integral part of the steel plan 'Lux 2010', finalised in December 2008.
- In Austria, the first recovery plan of October 2008 focused on supporting SMEs. The second recovery plan adopted in December 2008 foresees public investments in infrastructures, support to energy saving renovations by private households, regional programmes for employment, investments in R&D and provision of free child care services.
- Poland adopted a comprehensive plan for 2009-2010 covering financial stability, economic development, and protection of vulnerable groups. It also set up a 'Social Solidarity Fund'.
- In Portugal, the Government supplemented measures already taken in 2008 with a new package: the 'Investment and Employment Initiative (IEI)', which foresees investments in infrastructures in the fields of education, energy efficiency, modern information and communication technologies; special support to economic activity, exports and SMEs, and measures to protect employment and strengthen social protection.
- In the U.K., a National Economic Council was set up in October 2008 to give coherence and add momentum to the work of all Government departments in support of individuals, families and businesses. New measures include: 1) Increased support for working age mortgage holders, 2) a 'Find Your Way Back to Work' initiative, and 3) a 'Real Help' campaign, detailing the help available across Government in response to the downturn.

Labour Market responses

Most countries are relying on existing labour market policies to ensure those out of work actively seek work and are supported in doing so. Some countries are introducing special measures designed to support employment and reduce job losses. The countries doing so are summarized below.

- In Belgium, the economic recovery plan foresees measures in the field of tax and finances, social affairs, employment and energy. In parallel, the interprofessional agreement 2009-2010 was agreed between the social partners. It foresees measures aiming at supporting the purchasing power of people in paid employment, and that of benefit recipients, lowering the occupational costs of companies, supporting time-credit.
- The German plan provides a good example of such combination of measures: the public training programme me (WeGebAU), originally aimed at low-skilled and older employees, has now been extended to cover all workers in current need of training; job placement agencies will receive an

additional 6,000 headcount for intensive coaching of those made redundant; the period of receipt of short-work allowance has been extended to 18 months until 31st December 2009; in case of short-time work in 2009 and 2010, 50% (or 100% if the period is used for qualification) of social security contributions paid by employers will be returned to them. Reduced contribution to the unemployment insurance (2.8% instead of 3% in 2009 and 2010), and to the health insurance (by 0.6 %) will lift the burden on labour costs and stimulate both labour demand and supply. In addition, the budget available for education and training will be increased.

- Spain has established two specific State Funds to foster local investment and stimulate economy and employment, as well as measures for specific sectors, including the automotive industry (€ 11,000 million). Non-labour costs have also been reduced, by lowering employers' contribution for the recruitment of unemployed workers with family responsibilities (non-fixed term contracts); improvements of the Public Employment Service, and the active involvement of private employment agencies are also under consideration in the social dialogue process. Moreover, the Spanish Special Plan of Measures for Guidance, Vocational Training and Job Placement aims at reinforcing support provided to the unemployed in the search for a new employment, through new additional 1,500 orientation workers, and facilitating support in promotion of geographical mobility.
- The Portuguese IEI plan already referred to above encompasses measures in support of SMEs, e.g. mechanisms to permit the advance payment of EU funds granted to businesses, creation of PME *Investe* credit lines fostering corporate investment, reduced corporate income tax brackets. It also includes measures targeting employment such as a qualification programme, supporting young people in accessing employment, supporting labour market re-entry.
- In Slovenia, the Parliament was discussing a number of Government proposals to stimulate the economy such as decreasing the corporate income tax, and increasing tax rebates for independent entrepreneurs. The Government also approved supporting short-time work, and intends to promote social entrepreneurship, and self-employment for workers made redundant.
- In Finland, a Government stimulus package is designed to promote employment, by investing in public works, lowering social insurance contribution, increasing opportunities for vocational training, and investing in R&D.
- In the U.K., an extra £ 1.3 billion is being invested in Job Centre Plus and other services over the next two years as a response to the increase in the number of people claiming benefits, so as to not only maintain, but increase, the support offered. £ 158 Mio will come from the European Social Fund to help people who lose their jobs. The extra cash will help unemployed people and those facing redundancy retrain and develop their skills so they can

quickly move back into sustainable employment. The extra funding will help the Learning and Skill Council, with local colleges and training providers, to work closely with JobCentre Plus.

A key consideration in assessing the impact of the crisis on social policies is the age structure of the workforce. In all countries the workforce is much older than in the recession of the 1980s, when the main concern was the large cohort of young people entering the labour market. Heralding the start of the ageing of the population and the growth in the number of pensioners all countries have an unusually large cohort of older workers.

Maintaining Income

Many countries have implemented measures to increase the income of people affected by the crisis either through one-off payments or extensions in periods of eligibility or through higher benefit levels or minimum wages.

Housing, Over-indebtedness and Pensions

The financial crisis has had a big impact on housing in many countries. A long period of rapidly rising house prices engendered a willingness to give mortgages close to and even above 100% of the purchase price of the house. A belief in a never-ending house price rise lulled lenders and borrowers in a false belief that house values would soon mean mortgages were less than the price of the house. Many countries are seeing house prices fall as people lose their jobs. Many Governments have introduced schemes to reduce repossessions where mortgage defaults are likely.

In countries with larger pre-funded schemes in their pension systems authorities are seeking ways to help pension funds recover from the sharp deterioration in their ability to meet their long term liabilities resulting from the radical fall in the book value of their investments. In Denmark, regulators and the insurance and pension industry have agreed to temporary changes in the standards, by which the solvency of funds is calculated to avoid that funds lock in their losses by being forced to sell assets in the presently depressed markets. Thereby they have avoided both destabilisation of the mortgage market and substantial losses for pension savers.

Sustainability

There will always be concerns about the fiscal sustainability of public social expenditure. The automatic rises in social expenditure driven by the financial crisis will put heavy demands on fiscal policy and even more so given the other fiscal pressures that have emerged from policies to support banks and other financial institutions. The rest of this article looks first at the longer-term projections of age related social expenditure produced by the EU's Ageing Working Group.[1] These projections were carried out without reference to the current crisis and its impact on social expenditure. Long term sustainability then involves a judgement about whether the short-term increases are just that: cyclical and reversible, the start of a long term structural upward shift in social expenditure. This question is considered using the OECD's analysis of social expenditure trends over the last 25 years together with their recent report on growing inequalities in OECD countries.

Long term Trends in Age Related Social Expenditure

These projections have been produced on a set of assumptions about the effects of ageing on social expenditure covering pensions, health care, long-term care, education and unemployment. There is great variability across the 27 Member States in the projected increases. The total projected increases are shown in the figure below. The total effect of ageing on social expenditure is summarised on the chart below and is driven by:

- the population ageing effect, which is a measure of change in dependency ratio (number of people aged 65 and more to the working age population),
- the employment effect, which depends on the change in the share of population of working age relative to the number of employed,
- the coverage effect of pensions, which captures changes in the number of pensioners relative to the population aged 65 and more, This includes any reductions in early retirement assumed to follow from extrapolating higher employment rates for older workers and a reduction in structural unemployment, and
- the benefit effect, which reflects changes in the average pension relative to income.

Figure 1: The cost of ageing, EU27 (change in percentage points)

Total Cost of Ageing, 2007-60 (% of GDP)

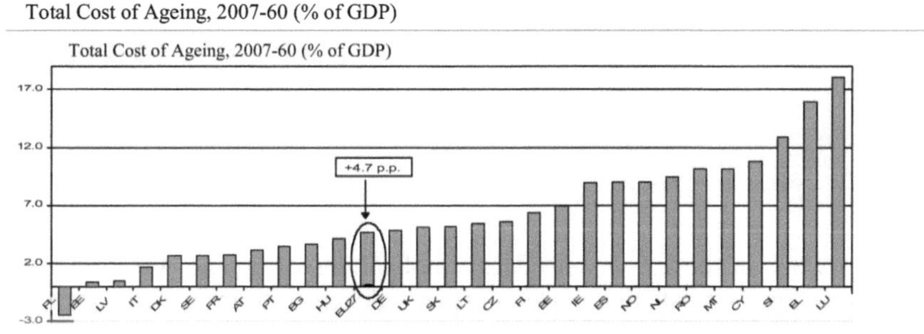

1 http://ec.europa.eu/economy_finance/publications/publication13782_en.pdf.

Figure 2: Factors contributing to changes in pension expenditure (% of GDP)

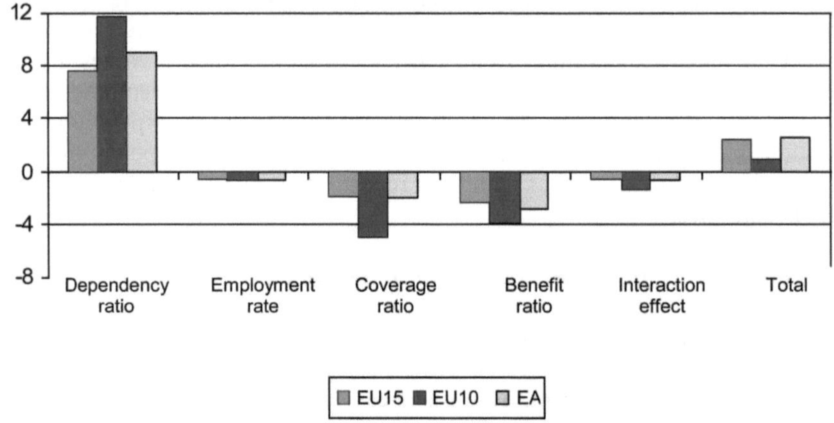

There has been considerable attention paid both in the EU and in most other countries round the world to the ageing of the world's population. The population pyramids that used to be familiar are being replaced by population columns. Longer life expectancy and low fertility are shaping populations where the size of cohorts of older people is similar to those of the working population. The figure 3 below shows this.

Figure 3: The population in the EU27 grows older

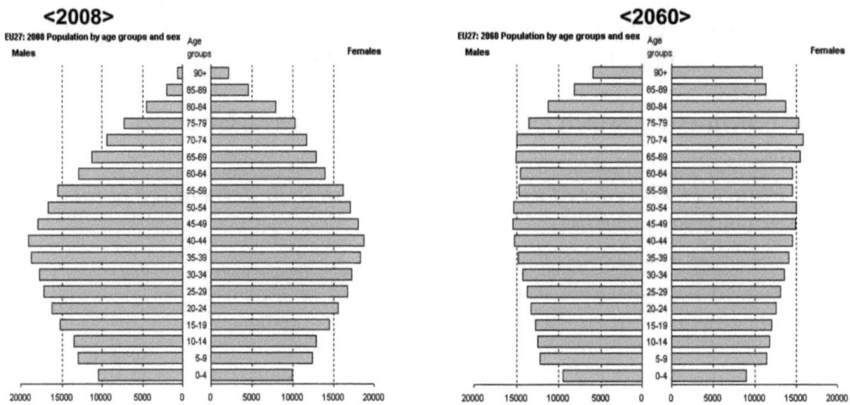

Earlier work in the EU on the fiscal implications of ageing was one important force leading to substantial pension reforms designed to make future pension expenditure fiscally sustainable. The projections just published are the first post pension reform projections to systematically show how important pension reform has been. A key has been the reduction in many Member States in the generosity of pension benefits. Figure 4 below shows how extensive this has been in many countries. In the EU10 countries – those joining the EU most recently apart from Romania and Bulgaria – the reductions in generosity will reduce age related social expenditure by 4 percentage points over the projection period. In the EU15 countries the effect is smaller – nearly 3 percentage points – but it is still one of the most important factors reducing age related expenditure in the future.

Figure 4: Substantial reductions in the benefit ratio in several Member States
(% change)

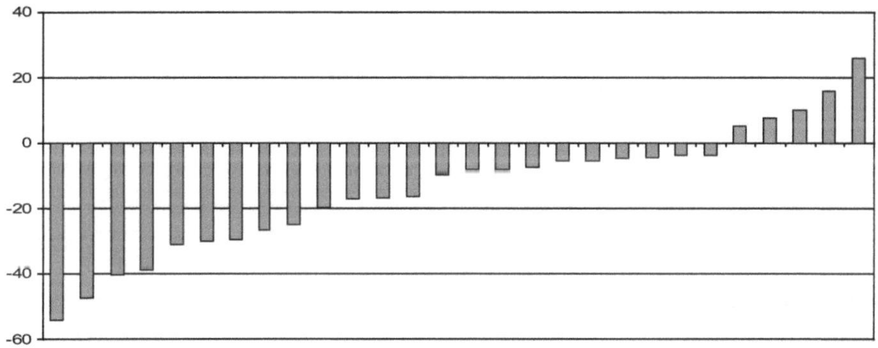

The other factors that determine the projections of age related expenditure are in one way or another related to assumptions about the labour market. The projections assume that countries with high levels of structural unemployment will reduce these towards lower NAIRU levels and the gain in employment will last throughout the projection period. Countries with low levels of long term unemployment but much higher numbers on incapacity benefits are not assumed to achieve reductions in these rates and corresponding higher employment rates. Associated with the assumed reductions in structural unemployment, higher employment levels and higher female employment the projections also assume the recent improvement in the employment rates of older workers as structural. One associated effect of these assumptions is that early retirement schemes that have been available in the past are assumed no longer to be available, and this reduces the number of people eligible for pensions as do the many pension reforms that will raise the age of retirement especially for women. The combined effect of these assumptions (see figure 5 for an illustration of the total effect) makes a substantial contribution to reducing the impact of ageing on the projected growth in social expenditure.

Figure 5: Employment rates rise due to reforms and cohort effects

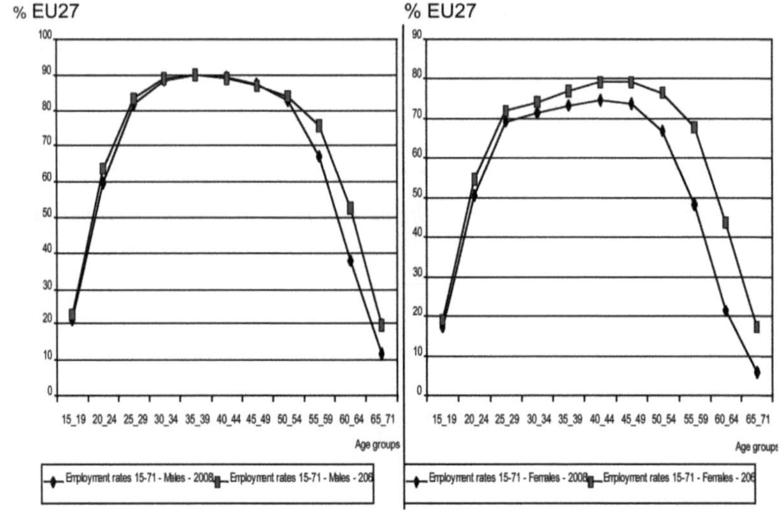

The Financial Crisis and its impact on longer term trends in social expenditure

The section above sets the background necessary to assess the possible impact of the current financial crisis on the longer term trends in social expenditure. Potentially unsustainable growth in age related expenditure is dampened in the EU projections by four key assumptions:

- Reductions in current high levels of structural unemployment, higher levels of employment,
- reduced eligibility for early retirement,
- increases in the official retirement rate being reflected in higher employment among older workers, and
- cuts in pension benefits being carried through.

One outcome would be for the impact of the current recession to be purely cyclical. The very high forecast levels of unemployment would decline as the EU economy bounces back. A very optimistic scenario would be for a complete bounce-back with the loss in output during the recession being compensated by an off trend recovery in output.

The history of previous large downturns in the labour market gives some help in assessing the likely impact of this financial crisis. The large increases in unemployment in the early 1980s and to a lesser extent in the early 1990s had lasting effects on most countries in the EU and more widely in the EU.

Figure 6: Income inequality, 1985-2005

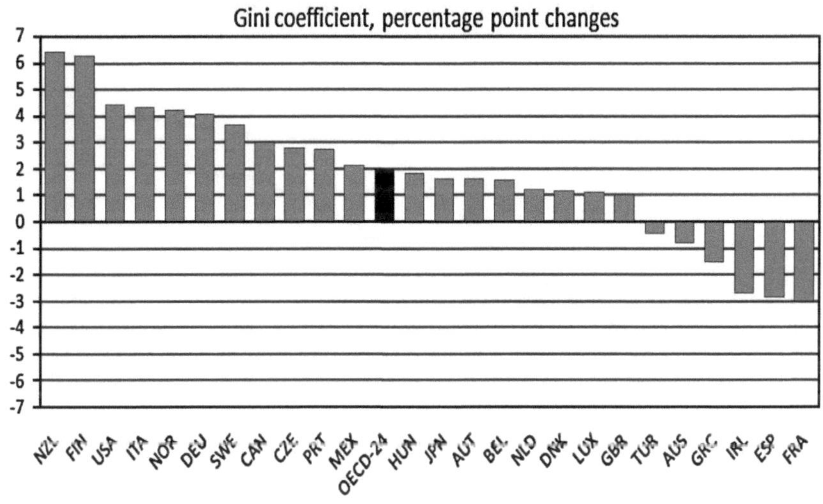

Source: Growing Unequal? OECD 2008.

An important source for analysing the issues faced by social integration policies is the recently released study of inequality and poverty in the OECD 'Growing Unequal? Income Distribution and Poverty in OECD Countries'.[2] The study reports that

- in the past 20 years income inequality has increased in three quarters of OECD countries,
- income poverty has increased in two thirds of the countries, and
- more recently the strongest increases happened in Norway, Germany and the United States.

The increases in inequality measured by changes in the Gini-coefficient are shown in the OECD's chart below. The OECD's study shows that the increases are the result of the increasing dispersion of market incomes, gross incomes from labour as well as incomes from capital. In addition there has been an associated widening of savings, partly reflecting the ageing of the work force in all countries. This is shown in figure 7. Redistribution through taxes has dampened the underlying market income dispersion but not offset it.

A further factor in the widening of income dispersion has been the way in which employment growth has been distributed. Alongside growing employment rates especially of women there has been a rise in the number of jobless households and a corresponding growth in two-earner households. This is also

2 www.oecd.org/els/social/inequality.

Figure 7: Market income inequality increased faster than disposable income inequality, except in the late 1990s

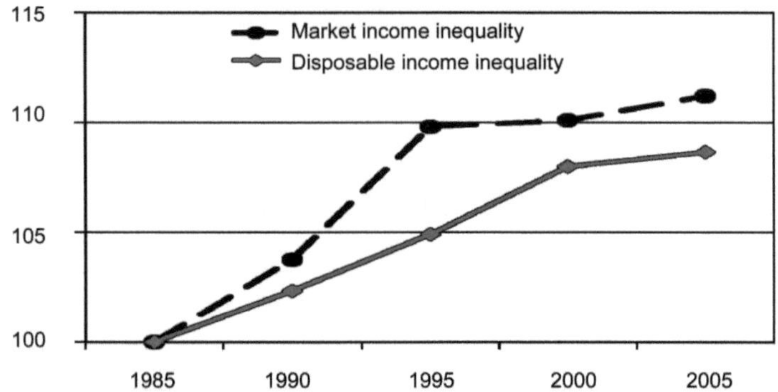

Source: Growing Unequal? (OECD 2008).

reflected in the pattern of household formation with growing numbers of single households and especially a growth in lone parent households. Job losses have been felt mainly among those with no qualifications and poor education.

The result of these changes has been a long term structural increase in social expenditure as policies designed to foster social integration have tried to offset the underlying increases in poverty and inequality. The chart below using OECD data on social expenditure shows that the consequences of growing inequality and poverty has been an increase of about five percentage points in social expenditure. This increase seems to be structural and permanent.

Figure 8: OECD Social Expenditure (percentage of GDP)

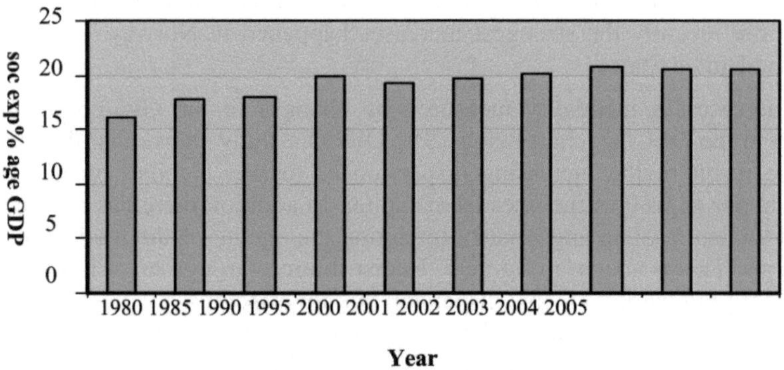

The key question facing social policies in the face of the current financial crisis is whether the pressures that are increasing social expenditure will be permanent or cyclical. The background is that the EU and most of the OECD countries are entering the period, when populations will age rapidly and bring added pressures on social expenditure. Projections of ageing expenditure in the EU suggest that provided optimistic assumptions are made about the labour market over the coming half century the increases in projected expenditure will be sustainable on average although some countries will be faced with particular challenges.

The assumptions necessary to achieve social expenditure growth are looking less plausible in the light of the consequences of the financial crisis. Recent forecasts of GDP growth are suggesting much larger falls in GDP in 2009 than previously projected and for many EU countries these falls will be greater than those experienced in the 1980s. The summary forecast taken from the spring forecast is shown below.

This will lead to increases in social expenditure at a time when the effects of ageing are starting to become apparent. If the financial crisis is a financial symptom of the need to make substantial real economy adjustments it is likely that these pressures will have long term consequences for social expenditure in the EU. The upward shift of five percentage points in total social expenditure seen since the 1980s could easily be repeated. Structural increases of this magnitude would wipe out the hoped for savings from improved labour market conditions in the EU's long term expenditure projections. In addition the fiscal consequences of sorting out the financial banking crisis will lead to public sector deficits unprecedented in peace time. All these factors will mean social protection expenditure will be under increasing scrutiny as Governments seek ways of reducing fiscal deficits.

Figure 9: Short-term EU economic forecasts
(GDP growth and unemployment rate)

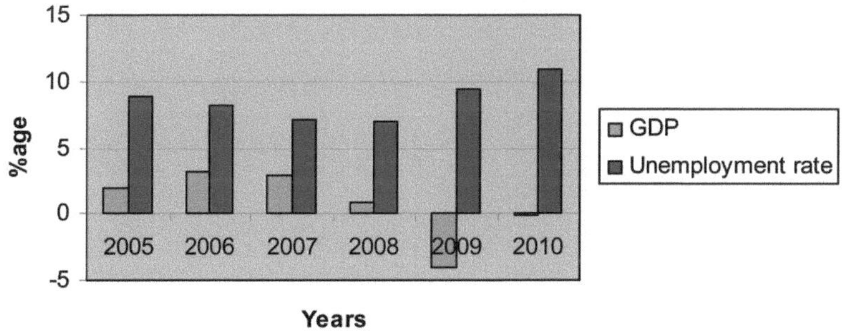

on social expenditure. Projections of ageing expenditure in the EU suggest that [illegible]

[illegible]

2 Social Protection for the Economic Crisis: The U.S. Experience

Gary Burtless [1]

Introduction

Since February 2008 the U.S. Government has taken a number of steps aimed at dealing with the most severe financial crisis experienced by the United States in nearly eight decades. The crisis originated in America's real estate and banking industries and has now spread to the rest of the economy and to much of the world. Emergency legislation passed by the U.S. Congress in 2008 and early 2009 attempted to (1) prevent the failure of major U.S. financial institutions; (2) minimize the impact of financial institutions' weakness on ordinary business and consumer borrowing; (3) provide immediate stimulus to consumer spending by raising after-tax household income through temporary tax reductions and increases in Government transfers; (4) provide temporary funds to state and local Governments in order to reduce their need to boost taxes or reduce spending during the recession; (5) protect the incomes and health insurance of newly laid off workers and members of other economically vulnerable populations; and (6) provide direct federal support for infrastructure investments and research and development projects in health, science, and efficient energy production.

In this article I focus on the measures Congress has taken to protect household incomes and improve the American social safety net. None of the emergency measures adopted by Congress will result in permanent changes to the U.S. system of social protection, but a couple of temporary programmes represent dramatic departures from the past. For the first time, Congress authorized generous subsidies so that laid-off workers can continue to receive employer-sponsored health insurance. Most working-age Americans and their families rely on an employer-provided health plan to provide their insurance. When they are laid off from their jobs they generally lose the employer subsidy for this insurance, and for many workers the loss of the employer subsidy makes continued health insurance coverage unaffordable. By offering to pay 65% of the cost of the first nine months of post-layoff health insurance premiums, the U.S. Government will make health insurance affordable for many of the newly unemployed. In another departure from past economic stimulus policy the Congress appropriated substantial funds for the nation's education system. State Governments were given large temporary grants to support primary, secondary, and

1 The opinions expressed in this article are the author's alone and do not reflect the views of the Korea Institute for Health and Social Affairs or the Brookings Institution.

post-secondary schooling, thus reducing the need for state and local Governments to make cuts in educational services. In addition, the federal Government appropriated special funds for a large increase in means-tested financial assistance so that low-income students can pay for post-secondary education. Stimulus funds will also provide major increases in grants for post-secondary institutions so they can invest in new buildings and research in innovative health and energy technologies. It is unusual for the federal Government to focus so much of its counter-cyclical stimulus policy on the education system and on research and development. Finally, state Governments were provided generous but temporary general fiscal relief, linked to the local unemployment rate, so they do not have to cut spending or increase taxes as much as would be necessary without the emergency federal aid.

This article considers the current financial crisis and the American Government's response to the crisis in the area of social protection. The remainder of the article is organized as follows. The next section considers recent trends in the U.S. economy, particularly those trends that make the current recession different from earlier ones. The following section discusses the U.S. Government response to the recession, with special reference to Congressional actions affecting the social safety net. Aside from the extraordinary measures taken by the Administration, Congress, and U.S. Federal Reserve to shore up the nation's ailing financial system, the Government's main instruments for addressing the crisis are designed to provide direct income assistance and public services to households, to offer fiscal relief to state Governments, and to encourage new investments in public infrastructure and research and development. The conclusion of the article offers a brief assessment of the U.S. social safety net response to economic crisis. The response has two main components. The first is the automatic stabilization system already in place, even before Congress and the Administration took special steps to address the crisis. The second is the extraordinary measures that Congress has authorized since February 2008. How likely is it that these two kinds of measures will assure social protection to Americans in the current economic crisis?

The Financial Crisis and the U.S. Economy

Since the end of World War II the United States has experienced 11 recessions. According to the National Bureau of Economic Research the current and eleventh post-war recession began after December 2007 when payroll employment reached a cyclical peak. Payroll employment has fallen in every month since then. At first the decline in employment and the accompanying rise in unemployment were slow (see figure 1). Between the fourth quarter of 2007 and the second quarter of 2008 the unemployment rate of Americans between 25 and 54 years old rose only 0.5 percentage points to 4.4%, indicating only a modest deterioration in the job market. In the next three quarters the unemployment rate jumped an additional 2.8 percentage points. In the first three months of 2009 the average unemployment rate of 25-54 year-olds was 7.2%, the second highest unemployment rate of any post-war recession. The only recession with a higher unemployment rate using this measure was the 1981-82 recession, when the peak unemployment rate reached 8.9%. As of May 2009 the U.S. unemployment rate is still rising rapidly, so it is conceivable that unemployment will reach a higher peak in this recession than in any other post-war recession.

Figure 1: Unemployment rate among Americans aged 25-54

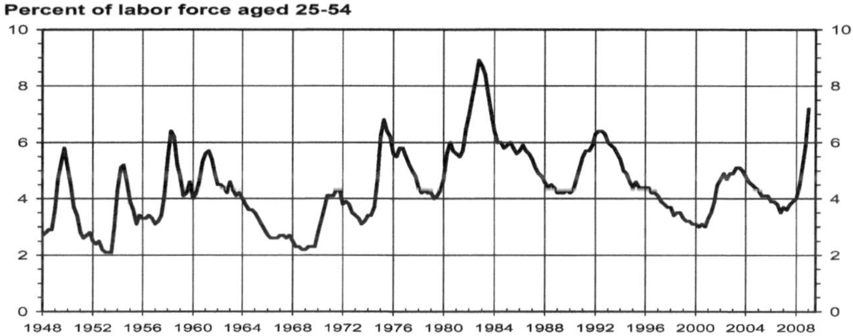

Source: U.S. Bureau of Labor Statistics.

Most economists agree that the origins of the current recession can be found in the troubled U.S. housing market. New kinds of home loans and a rapid expansion in new forms of securitized mortgages encouraged Americans to buy homes with very small down payments. Home buyers with questionable credit records were able to obtain mortgages with little money down and generous repayment terms. In spite of the weaknesses in many borrowers' credit histories, the U.S. and world financial markets had an apparently unquenchable appetite for financial securities backed by U.S. mortgages. One result of these developments was a steep rise in U.S. home prices. Figure 2 shows quarterly estimates of the real price of U.S. homes for the period 1975-2008.

House prices as estimated by the Federal Housing Finance Agency are deflated using the GDP deflator, a broad gauge of prices in the U.S. economy. After a long period of relative stability between the late 1970s and 1995, the real price of homes increased at an accelerating pace before reaching an all-time peak in the last quarter of 2006. Since then house prices have declined. In some parts of the United States prices have fallen by almost half compared with their peak values. Home buyers who purchased houses with small down payments now have little incentive to repay their loans, because their houses are worth substantially less than their remaining mortgages. A rising percentage of home owners have defaulted on their mortgages or are no longer making payments on their home loans.

Figure 2: Index of real U.S. house prices, 1975-2008

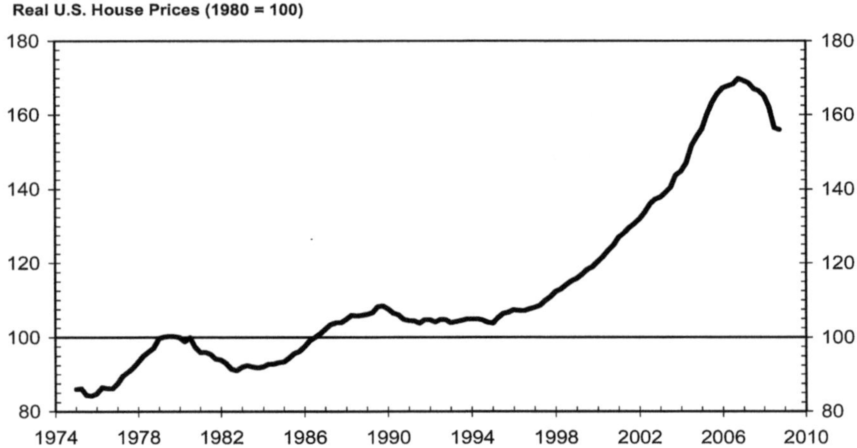

Source: Federal Housing Finance Agency and U.S. Department of Commerce, Bureau of Economic Analysis.

The continuing fall in home prices has made potential home buyers reluctant to invest in a house, because homes may be much cheaper six months or two years from now. As the inventory of foreclosed and unsold homes has risen, the rationale for building new homes has disappeared in many parts of the United States. The construction industry experienced massive job losses after home prices began to decline. Since reaching a cyclical peak in the third quarter of 2006, payroll employment in construction has fallen by more than a million workers, or about 14%.[2]

The cascading number of home foreclosures has sharply reduced the market value of many home mortgages as well as the financial market valuation of securities that are backed by those loans. Banks and other financial institutions that hold home loans or mortgage-backed securities have seen their balance sheets imperilled. In a number of cases, the institutions have failed causing large losses to investors who owned equity or bonds of the failing institutions. In many other cases, the unknown size of the institution's losses has meant that investors are uncertain about the creditworthiness of the institution, causing them to avoid lending to or investing in the institution. The inability of many banks to obtain financing, either from other banks or from investors, has reduced

2 This is the decline in seasonally adjusted average quarterly employment in construction up through the first quarter of 2009.

their willingness to lend. The Federal Reserve and U.S. Treasury have established an extraordinary set of programmes to restore credit markets. As of June 2009 these efforts have helped rescue major financial institutions and keep credits flowing, but they have been only partially successful. Many potential borrowers who would have had little trouble obtaining credit in 2006 found it impossible or very costly to obtain credit in late 2008 and the first half of 2009. The decline in home prices and the perceived credit problems of large financial institutions were eventually reflected in U.S. stock market prices (see figure 3).

Figure 3: U.S. stock market prices, 1950-2009

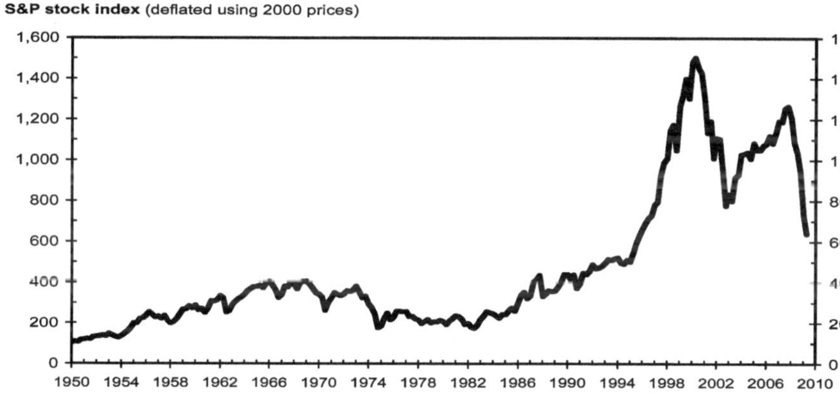

Source: Standard and Poor's composite stock index.

Like home prices, U.S. equity prices rose steeply after the mid-1990s. Unlike house prices, equity prices experienced a sizeable correction between 2000 and 2002. Stock market prices partially recovered after 2002 and continued rising until the fourth quarter of 2007. After achieving a peak in October 2007, stock market prices declined by about 50%. Plunging stock prices and falling house prices sharply reduced the net wealth of U.S. households (see figure 4).

The ratio of household net worth to household disposable income fell from 6.4 in the second quarter of 2007 to 4.8 in the last quarter of 2008. Although the current wealth-income ratio is not low by historical standards, the large losses in household wealth will probably restrain U.S. consumer spending for a number of years as households find it harder to borrow or as they attempt to add to their wealth holdings.

A drop in consumption is already evident in the national income and product account statistics. Commerce Department data show that U.S. personal consumption expenditures fell 1.5 percentage points between the fourth quarter of 2007 and the fourth quarter of 2008. This is the largest one-year drop in personal consumption since the 1974-75 recession (see the top panel of figure 5).

Figure 4: Ratio of net household wealth to household disposable income, 1952-2008

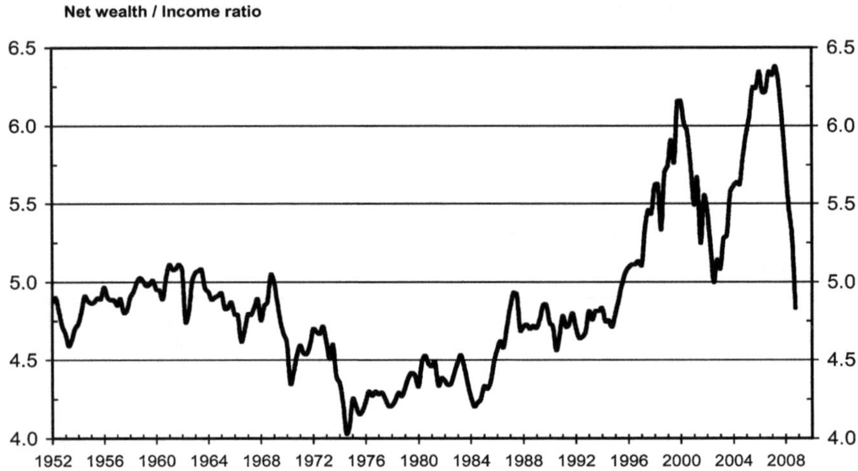

Sources: Board of Governors of the Federal Reserve System, Flow of Funds.

The slump in consumer demand has had a spill over effect on the wider economy, because consumer expenditures typically account for a little more than 70% of the total economy. According to Department of Commerce estimates published in May 2009, U.S. GDP fell 2.5 percentage points between the first quarter of 2008 and the first quarter of 2009, one of the steepest one-year declines in the post-war period (see lower panel of figure 5). Although the drop in U.S. GDP is large in relation to the post-war U.S. experience, especially in the years after 1984, it is not especially severe in comparison with the recent experience of other large industrial economies. The major economies in the European Union and Japan have posted even larger GDP declines than the one experienced by the United States (see figure 6). Among the G-7 countries, only Canada has experienced a slower rate of decline.

Figure 5: Year-over-year changes in U.S. consumption and GDP, 1948-2009

Per cent change from previous year: Personal consumption expenditures

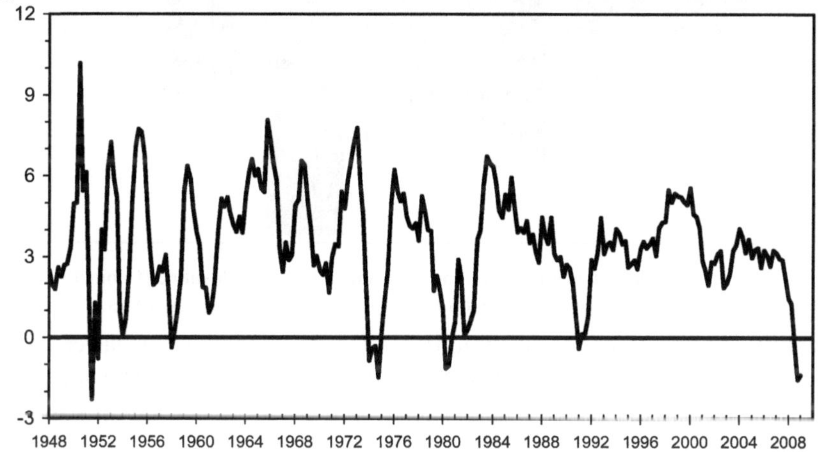

Per cent change from previous year: Real GDP

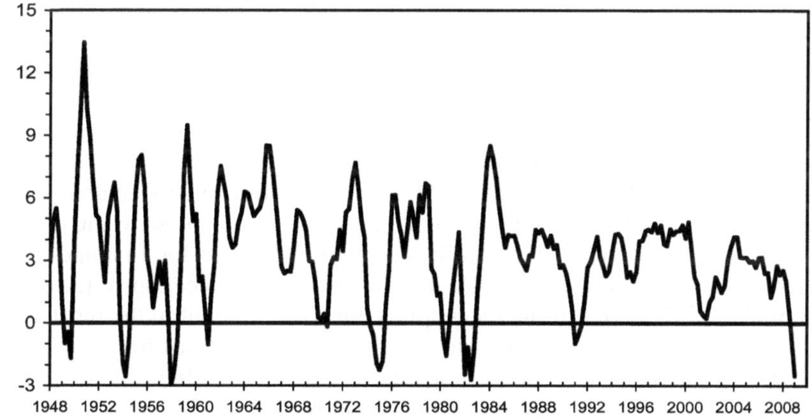

Sources: U.S. Department of Commerce, Bureau of Economic Analysis.

Figure 6: Annual change in GDP through first quarter of 2009, G-7 countries

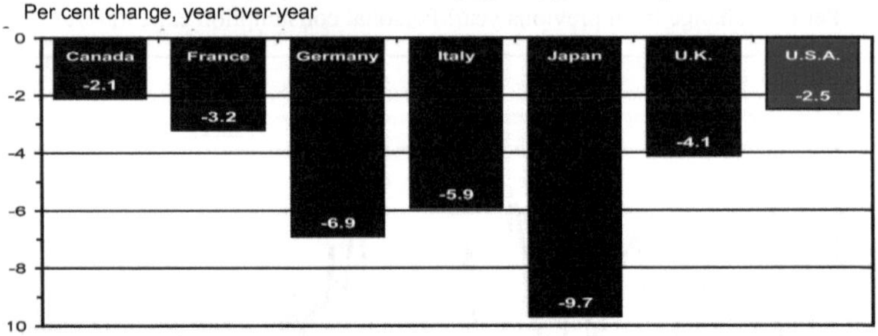

Sources: Eurostat, Statistics Canada, Economic and Social Research Institute (Cabinet Office, Japan), and U.S. Department of Commerce, Bureau of Economic Analysis.

How severe is the recession likely to be? Although economic forecasters do not have a good record of successfully predicting the onset of recessions, past historical experience offers some guidance to thinking about the possible duration and severity of the recession already underway. According to the business cycle dating scheme proposed by the National Bureau of Economic Research, the average completed post-war recession has lasted almost eleven months or about 3.5 calendar quarters, when the length of the recession is defined as the interval from the business cycle peak to the business cycle trough. Using a somewhat different method, we can trace out the trend of real economic output in quarters immediately after the peak quarter of GDP.

Figure 7 shows the trend of real U.S. GDP during selected post-war recessions. Included in the sample of recessions are the particularly severe or long-lasting recessions of 1981-82 and 1974-75. Using Commerce Department estimates available in May 2009, the present recession is equivalent to the most serious post-war recessions. Although the drop in real GDP in the first and second quarters of the recession was smaller than in some earlier recessions, the drop in GDP by the third quarter of the recession is equivalent to that in the most severe post-war recessions. The drop in total payroll employment has been 2.5% since U.S. GDP reached a peak in the second quarter of 2008 (see figure 8).

That is bigger than the drop in other recent recessions, but it is smaller than the decline that occurred in the 1957 recession. In the 1974-75 recession payroll employment actually rose in the first three quarters after GDP reached a peak (in the fourth quarter of 1973). It began to decline in the fourth calendar quarter after the quarter when peak GDP was attained.[3] The chart also shows how many quarters elapsed before payroll employment reached the level attained at the

3 Because the baby boom generation and many U.S. women were entering the labour force in the mid-1970s, labour force growth was very rapid at that time. The 1974-75 recession also saw a sharp fall in worker productivity, which accounts for the combination of rising payroll employment and shrinking real output.

previous GDP peak. In three of the recessions, this did not occur until 10 quarters after the previous peak level of GDP.

Figure 7: Trend of U.S. GDP during post-World-War-II recessions

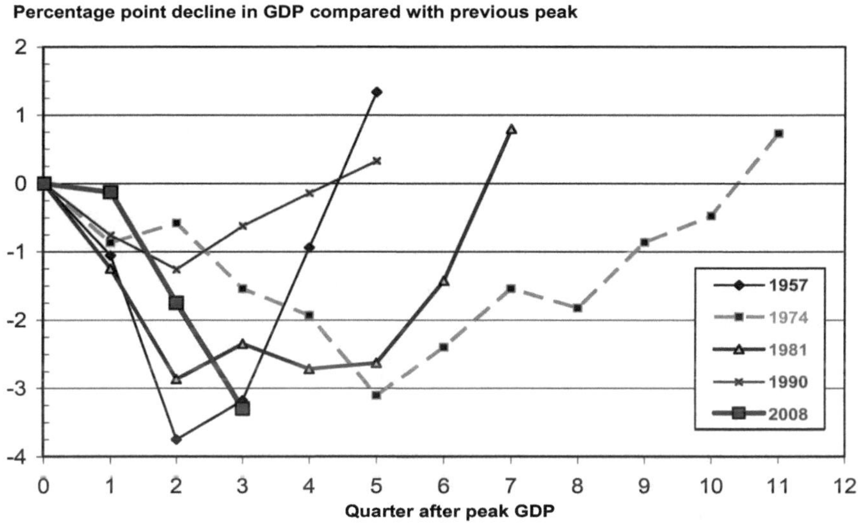

Source: U.S. Department of Commerce, Bureau of Economic Analysis.

Figure 8: Payroll employment trends in selected post-war recessions

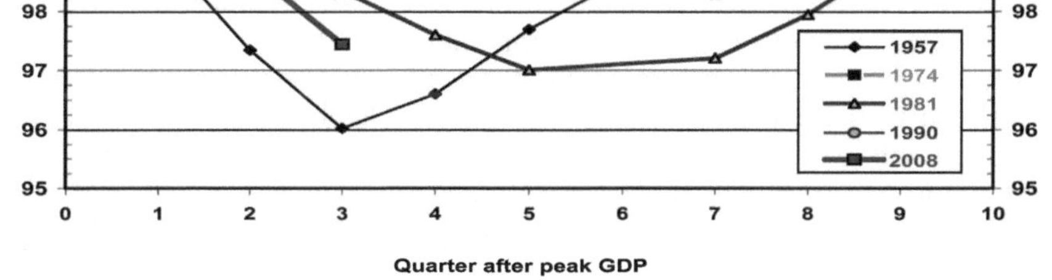

Source: U.S. Bureau of Labor Statistics.

A common way to measure the depth of a recession is to estimate the gap between actual national output and potential output if employment were equal to the maximum level that is consistent with nonaccelerating inflation. The U.S.

Congressional Budget Office (CBO) estimates that the lowest level of unemployment consistent with nonaccelerating inflation in 2008-2009 was 4.8% of the labour force age 16 and older. In May 2009 the unemployment rate of Americans older than 16 was 9.4% or 4.6 percentage points above the 'full-employment' unemployment rate estimated by the CBO. Figure 9 shows the CBO's estimates of the gap between potential and actual GDP over most of the post-World-War-II period. A positive number indicates that potential GDP is higher than actual GDP; a negative number reflects the fact that actual GDP is growing too fast to be consistent with nonaccelerating inflation. The estimated output gap in the first quarter of 2009 was about $ 960 billion, or 6.4% of potential U.S. GDP. Except for the GDP shortfall in the 1981-82 recession, this is the biggest gap between potential and actual output of the entire post-war period.

Figure 9: Gap between potential and actual U.S. GDP, 1949-2009

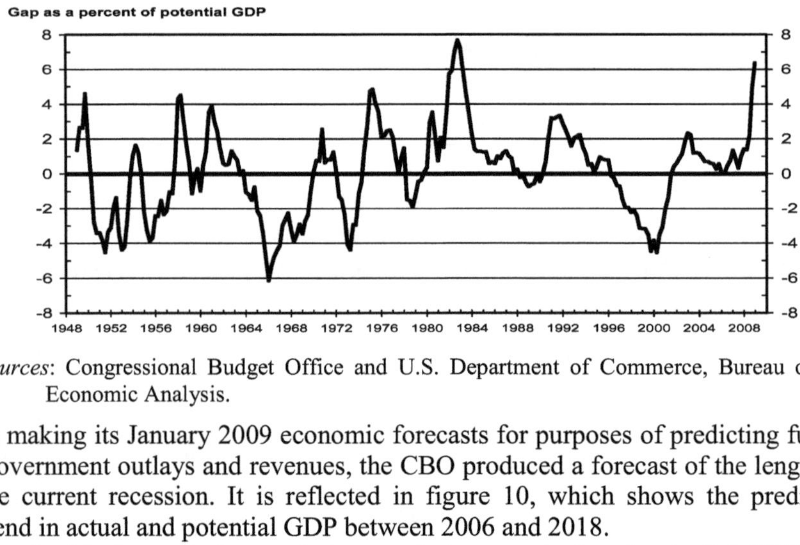

Sources: Congressional Budget Office and U.S. Department of Commerce, Bureau of Economic Analysis.

In making its January 2009 economic forecasts for purposes of predicting future Government outlays and revenues, the CBO produced a forecast of the length of the current recession. It is reflected in figure 10, which shows the predicted trend in actual and potential GDP between 2006 and 2018.

In this forecast, the maximum gap between actual and potential GDP will be attained in fiscal year 2010, that is, between October 2009 and September 2010, and will gradually shrink until almost all the gap is eliminated by 2014. By definition, the unemployment rate will increase as long as actual GDP is either shrinking or expanding more slowly than potential GDP; the unemployment rate will begin to decline when the growth of actual output is faster than the growth in potential output. In its most recent forecast of future GDP and unemployment, which was made in March 2009 after the Congress passed a large stimulus package ('The American Recovery and Reinvestment Act of 2009'), the budget office's predictions became more pessimistic. Nonetheless, the annual unemployment rate at the trough of the recession was predicted to be only

9.0%, a rate that is nearly one-half percentage point lower than the 9.4% unemployment rate recorded in May 2009. Under this forecast the United States will suffer a recession that is very serious by post-World-War-II standards, but is not unprecedented in its severity. Even if the March 2009 CBO forecast is too optimistic, the nation does not now appear to face an economic or humanitarian crisis on the scale of the Great Depression. In the second quarter of 2009, as this article was written, some indicators of U.S. economic performance were beginning to improve or at least to decline more slowly. Consumer confidence, for example, has improved since the beginning of the year. Job losses declined slightly in April and May compared with job loss rates earlier in the year. After reaching a low point in early March, U.S. stock prices began to rise, and the creditworthiness of many of the nation's largest financial institutions appeared to improve.

Figure 10: Potential GDP and predicted GDP under Congressional Budget Office forecast, 2006-2018

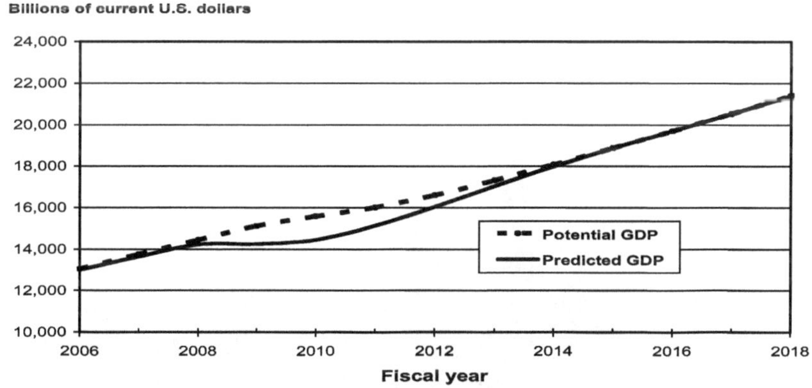

Sources: Congressional Budget Office January 2009 forecast and U.S. Department of Commerce, Bureau of Economic Analysis.

The U.S. Safety Net and the Stimulus Package

Even if neither the Congress nor the President took special actions in response to a recession, a number of Government programmes, including unemployment and disability insurance, social assistance programmes, and the income tax system, would provide automatic stimulus and protection of household income. The unemployment insurance programme me undoubtedly shows the biggest proportional change in spending whenever the economy falls into recession (see Figure 11). When the economy is growing strongly and unemployment is low, unemployment insurance benefits represent only about 0.3% of disposable personal income. In the midst of a recession, that percentage more than doubles primarily because the number of workers collecting benefits rises steeply. Part of the increase in the number of unemployment insurance recipients is often due to special measures passed by Congress. Typically, those measures permit laid-off workers to collect benefits for longer than the standard period (six months), but much of the increase in unemployment insurance beneficiaries would occur even if the Congress failed to act. Federal income taxes and social insurance tax payments also shrink when the economy contracts. Because the income tax system is strongly progressive, income tax collections decline proportionately much faster than personal and corporate income. Economists Alan Auerbach and Daniel Feenberg (2000) estimate that the consumption response to the decline in federal taxes offsets 8% of the initial impact of an adverse shock to U.S. GDP. Since income and payroll taxes represent a much bigger share of the U.S. economy than unemployment benefits, the tax system plays a much bigger quantitative role than unemployment insurance in stabilizing the economy.

Figure 11: Unemployment benefits as a per cent of U.S. personal disposable income, 1960-2007

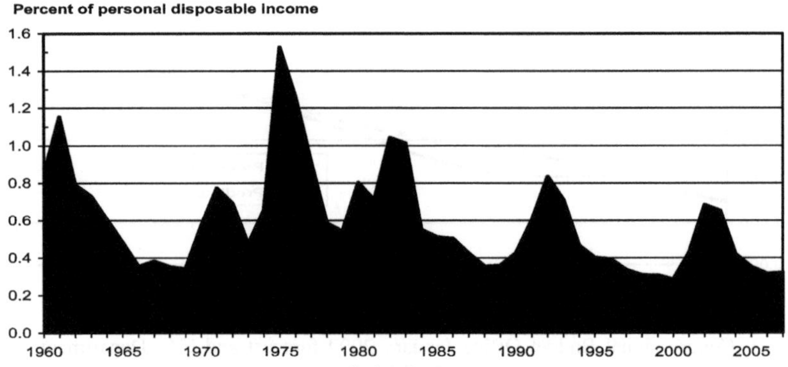

Source: U.S. Department of Commerce, Bureau of Economic Analysis.

The tax and benefit system also plays an important role in equalizing incomes and smoothing net income changes across U.S. states and regions. The U.S. is a very large and diverse country. In 2007 the poorest American state (Mississippi) had per capita personal income that was only about half of that of the richest state (Connecticut). The progressive tax system and the progressive formula for determining social insurance and social assistance benefits mean that the difference in net incomes between states is smaller than the difference in their before-tax, before-transfer incomes. States and regions that experience the biggest proportional losses in market income during a recession will generally receive proportionally bigger net gains from their financial transactions with the federal

Government. Thus, the automatic stabilization that is built into federal taxes and transfer benefits tends to spread the economic pain of a recession more equally across the country than would be the case in the absence of the federal tax and transfer system.

Unemployment insurance. For American workers the most important protection they receive when they are laid off is provided by unemployment insurance. Experienced U.S. workers who are dismissed from their jobs can claim unemployment benefits that replace about half of their lost earnings up to a maximum weekly benefit amount. In most American states this maximum amount is roughly half the wages earned by an average worker covered by the unemployment insurance system. This means laid-off workers who earn above-average wages collect benefits that replace less than half of their lost earnings. Benefits are taxed as ordinary income in the income tax system. Unemployment insurance benefits do not last indefinitely. Under ordinary circumstances, U.S. benefits are restricted to just 26 weeks. Laid-off workers who fail to find work within six months after losing a job will run out of unemployment benefits before they start earning another pay check. In recent years between 31% and 43% of workers who claim unemployment benefits exhaust their eligibility for benefits before finding a job. The percentage which exhausts benefits is higher when the nationwide unemployment rate is high. As in many OECD countries, there has been a long-term rise in the percentage of unemployed workers who suffer long spells of unemployment. This is reflected in the statistics on unemployment insurance benefit exhaustion. In the 1960s the percentage of claimants who exhausted unemployment compensation ranged between 20% and 25% of all the workers who filed a successful claim for benefits. In spite of the long-term growth in the percentage of workers who suffer lengthy spells of unemployment, long-term unemployment remains comparatively low in the U.S. compared with other industrialized countries. Figure 12 shows the percentage of labour force participants in various OECD countries who were unemployed for one year or more in 2004, a year of solid economic growth in most industrialized countries. The United States ranks fourth from the bottom in this list of 20 countries, indicating that long-term unemployment is a much smaller problem than it is in other OECD countries.

The OECD has made estimates of the generosity of member countries' programmes for replacing earned income after workers lose their jobs. The OECD calculates that in 2007 U.S. workers in single-earner households obtained a net replacement rate of about 52% to 61% in the case of unemployed workers who earn two-thirds of the average U.S. wage. Workers who earn the average wage typically received net unemployment benefits that replaced between 52% and 56% of their net wages, and workers earning 1.5 times the average wage obtained a replacement rate between 37% and 39% of their net wages (OECD 2009). These replacement rates are lower than rates available in most other rich countries, and the gap is particularly large in the case of unemployed workers who have dependents or who have above-average earnings.

Figure 12: Unemployed who have been jobless for one year or more as a per cent of the labour force, 2004

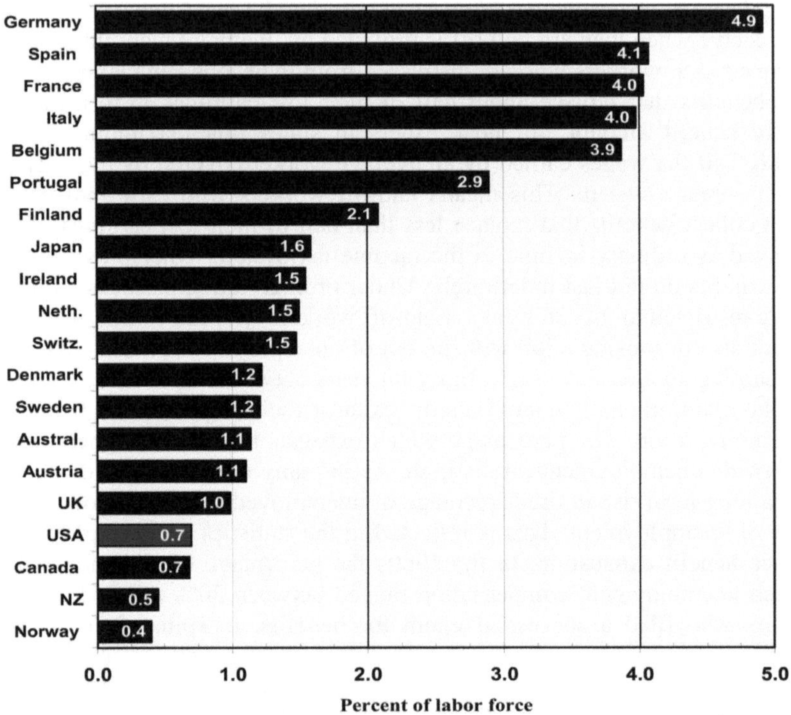

Source: Author's calculations based on *OECD Employment Outlook* (2004), pp. 237, 258.

Figure 13 shows the net replacement rate for a laid off married worker who has a nonworking spouse and two dependent children and who earned the average national wage before losing his or her job. OECD estimates are displayed for 22 rich countries ranked according to the replacement rate that unemployed workers received in 2007 during the first six months after losing a job. For this type of unemployed worker the United States ranks 19th out of 22 countries, though its rank varies depending on the exact wage and family circumstances of the laid off worker. For workers at other wage levels and in other family circumstances, the replacement rate in the United States can be slightly higher or well below the average replacement rate available to counterpart workers in the other 21 countries. Usually, however, benefits are lower in the U.S. than they are for comparable unemployed workers in other rich countries.

The U.S. unemployment insurance system only replaces the money wages that workers lose when they are laid off. It does not insure workers against the loss of health insurance or other fringe benefits that were provided by their former employers. For a private-sector employee, the employer's contribution for health, retirement, and insurance benefits, excluding mandatory social insurance, averages about 16% of the worker's money wage (U.S. BLS 2005). The loss of fringe benefits is particularly important for workers who depend on their employers for health insurance. Insurance purchased outside an employer's health plan is so costly that few unemployed workers can afford it.

Figure 13: Indicator of unemployment benefit generosity in 22 OECD countries, 2007 (*Source:* OECD 2008)

(Per cent of net earnings, initially replaced by after-tax value of unemployment benefits)

(Married single earner with two children who is paid the average wage)

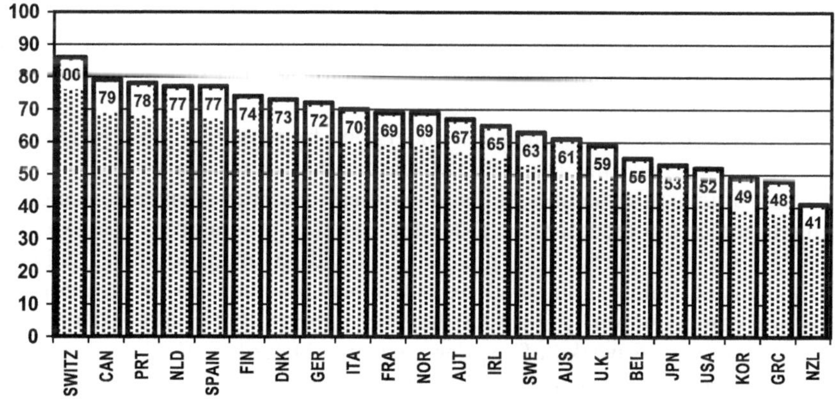

When the state or national unemployment rate is high, laid off workers often qualify for unemployment compensation in addition to the standard 26 weeks of benefits. For the past 50 years the Extended Benefits programme me has provided an additional 13 or 20 weeks of compensation payments for workers in states where the unemployment rate is higher than a threshold or 'trigger' rate.[4] Half the cost of this programme me is paid with funds from the federal Government and the other half is paid by states where the programme me triggers on. (All of the cost of the regular, 26-week package of benefits is paid with payroll taxes raised by state Governments.) The Extended Benefits programme does not work as well in recent years as it did in the 1970s and early 1980s. During the past 25 years the programme has rarely if ever triggered on in most states, even when the local unemployment rate was high. For example, in June 2003 when the U.S. civilian unemployment reached a peak after the 2001 recession, Extended Bene-

4 Details of the trigger mechanism can be found in U.S. House of Representatives, Committee on Ways and Means (2000), section 4.

fits were available in only three out of the 50 states. While the local unemployment rate was exceptionally high in those states, it was also higher than 6.5% in six other states, including California, Michigan, and Texas. Before the current recession, the Extended Benefits programme had failed to 'trigger on' in 33 states during any month after the 1981-83 recession (Vroman 2009).

On both humanitarian and economic grounds it makes sense to provide longer duration benefits to laid-off workers when the unemployment rate is high. Because unemployed workers usually need more time to find work in a weak job market, there is a compelling equity argument for offering insurance over longer spells of job search. In addition, the counter-cyclical effectiveness of unemployment compensation is reduced when a large percentage of laid-off workers is dropped from the rolls as a result of exhausting their benefits entitlement. For obvious reasons, workers are more likely to exhaust their regular unemployment benefits when the unemployment rate is high. If no extensions of regular unemployment compensation are available, the percentage of all unemployed workers who collect benefits will decline when the length of a recession extends beyond the maximum eligibility period.

The logic of these arguments is understood by most U.S. policymakers. In every recession since the late 1950s Congress has enacted a federally funded extension of unemployment benefits in addition to whatever extension might be available under the federal-state Extended Benefits programme. The extension in 1975-1977 was particularly generous, providing unemployment claimants who exhausted both regular and extended benefits with up to 26 additional weeks of compensation (for a total benefit duration that could last up to 65 weeks, including 26 weeks of regular insurance benefits and 13 weeks of Extended Benefits). The special benefit extensions in 1982-1985, 1991-1994, and 2002-2004 were less generous but still provided extra federally-financed benefits that could extend a worker's total eligibility period by up to six months. Special programmes to extend the duration of unemployment benefits have been in effect during all or parts of 15 out of the 35 years since 1975. Depending on a worker's state of residence and the details of the federal supplemental programme in effect in a particular year, a worker might qualify for 6 to 39 weeks of additional unemployment compensation beyond the 26 weeks available under the regular state insurance programme.

In most years, however, unemployment compensation is limited to the first 26 weeks after a worker is laid off. This eligibility period is one of the shortest in the industrialized world. Workers who experience very long unemployment spells receive considerably less income protection in the U.S. than they would obtain in most other industrial countries. Average-wage workers who are unemployed for five successive years would typically receive unemployment and social assistance benefits that replace 40% to 50% of their lost net earnings in the other 19 countries. In the United States unemployment benefits replace just 5%

or 6% of lost earnings over that five-year span. Even if we add the social assistance benefits available to jobless workers in a long unemployment spell, the replacement rate in the United States falls substantially below the average rate in the other 19 countries (OECD 2004, table 3.3b).

The U.S. stimulus package for laid-off workers. The Congress has taken a number of steps to expand the protection ordinarily available to laid-off workers. As in earlier post-World-War-II recessions, it provided federally funded extensions to standard unemployment insurance. As noted above, the Extended Benefits programme does not usually trigger on in many American states, unless the local unemployment rate reaches an exceptionally high level. This experience was repeated in the current recession. In the middle of March 2009, when the national unemployment rate among adults 16 and older was 8.5%, the Extended Benefits programme had 'triggered on' in only 15 of the 50 American states (Vroman 2009). Recognizing the shortcomings of the Extended Benefits programme, the Congress established a temporary Extended Unemployment Compensation (or EUC) programme in July 2008. Depending on the state-level unemployment rate, a laid-off worker who exhausts the standard 26 weeks of regular benefits can collect EUC benefits for between 20 and 33 extra weeks, giving workers an entitlement of both regular and EUC benefits that may range between 46 and 59 weeks. By the middle of June 2009, 33 weeks of EUC benefits were available in 42 of the 50 states, and 26 weeks of EUC benefits were available in the other 8 states. The full cost of EUC benefits will be paid by the federal Government. Under the law in effect in May 2009, Congress has authorized EUC benefit payments through the first five months of 2010, although the programme is likely to be extended if the U.S. unemployment rate remains high.

In addition to creating the temporary EUC programme the Congress also created major incentives for state Governments to change the 'trigger' rules for the state-federal Extended Benefits programme. Under previous law, one-half the cost of Extended Benefits was financed by states. Under temporary rules established in the February 2009 stimulus package, Congress authorized the federal Government to pay for 100% of the cost of Extended Benefits for benefits paid in 2009 and the first few months of 2010. Because states do not have to pay for any of the benefit costs, they have an incentive to adopt a lower unemployment rate threshold for triggering Extended Benefits. States that follow this strategy can make an additional 13 to 20 weeks of unemployment compensation benefits available to laid-off workers at no extra cost to employers in the state. (In nearly all U.S. states, the unemployment insurance payroll tax is imposed solely on private employers in the state. Workers do not directly pay the tax.) Thus, in some states with exceptionally high unemployment rates, workers may be eligible to receive unemployment compensation for a total of up to 79 weeks, or one and a half years. This is the longest duration of unemployment insurance that has ever been offered to laid-off U.S. workers. Workers who lose their jobs in states with lower unemployment rates may be eligible for up to 46 weeks of benefits.

In addition to temporarily extending the maximum period that workers can collect unemployment benefits, Congress also took two other steps to improve the protection provided by unemployment insurance. First, it temporarily increased weekly benefit payments by $ 25, or about 8% of the previous average benefit amount. All of the cost of the benefit increase will be financed by the federal Government. Second, it temporarily eliminated the federal income tax on the first $ 2,400 per year of unemployment benefits. This step will increase the after-tax value of unemployment compensation payments by roughly $ 240 to $ 360 per year, because unemployed workers typically face a marginal tax of 10 or 15%. In no previous recession has Congress increased the value of weekly benefits in this way.

Congress also gave incentives for states to change some of the qualifying conditions for unemployment benefits. The goal was to make benefits available to some unemployed or laid-off workers who had previously been excluded from receiving benefits by state laws. For example, one change in the rules would make it possible for laid-off workers to count wages earned in a more recent qualifying period than the standard period that is used under most states' rules. Another rule change would permit workers who are laid off from part-time jobs to obtain unemployment benefits. (Roughly half of states do not permit part-time job seekers to claim benefits.) Under the terms of the 2009 stimulus package, the federal Government would assume the full cost of the more generous qualifying provisions for the first couple of years after they are adopted. If states take full advantage of these provisions, the cost to the federal Government would represent about one-seventh of the full package of federal unemployment insurance stimulus. These provisions have proven controversial, however, because some state Governments are unwilling to make permanent changes in their qualifying requirements in exchange for a temporary payment from the federal Government. Of course, most Members of Congress want the states to permanently change their rules to allow more of the unemployed to collect benefits. They are using the funding formula in the stimulus package to achieve this objective. In the end, a majority of states will adopt two or more of the rule changes that Congress wants, and there will be a permanent change in the qualifying rules in those states.

The most surprising feature of the stimulus package for laid-off workers was the provision of generous federal subsidies to help unemployed workers pay for health insurance premiums. The subsidy, which is limited to 9 months per worker, covers 65% of the cost to laid-off workers of continuing their coverage under their former employer's health insurance plan. Most working Americans who are not poor receive health insurance through their employer or the employer of another wage earner in the family. Employers typically pay for most of the premium costs of this insurance. Most workers who are laid off lose the employer subsidy. The total, unsubsidized cost of health insurance is typically quite high, around $ 4,700 a year for single workers and $ 12,700 for workers with a spouse and child dependents (Vroman 2009). These amounts are 10 and 32%, respectively, of the average year-round wage of American workers. Not surprisingly, relatively few workers can afford to pay the full cost of these premiums after they are laid off. The result is that many laid-off workers lose their health insurance until they find another job where health insurance is offered as a fringe benefit. (Unemployed workers, especially those with child dependents, may become eligible for means-tested public health insurance under the Medicaid and State Child Health Insurance, or SCHIP, programmes, but families must usually have low incomes and few assets to qualify for this insurance.)

Citizens of other rich countries are often shocked to learn that U.S. workers can lose their health insurance coverage when they lose their jobs. In most wealthy countries, health insurance is provided to nearly all the resident population, including the unemployed and their dependents. In the United States, free or low-cost public health insurance is provided to the elderly population, to most of the disabled, and to the non-elderly and non-disabled population which is poor (that is, to the population which has an income below a low-income threshold). For non-elderly, non-disabled Americans with incomes above the low-income threshold, inexpensive group health insurance is available only to employees who work for employers that provide health insurance and to the dependents of those employees. Some companies do not provide health insurance to their employees, so their employees do not lose health benefits when they lose their jobs. But for the workers who are provided health insurance through their jobs, the loss of employment typically causes a much bigger loss than the loss of wage income. It also causes the worker and his or her dependents to lose health protection. By providing generous subsidies so these workers can continue their health insurance after they are laid off, Congress dramatically expanded the protection available to laid-off workers who lost good jobs.

Temporary tax reductions. A substantial percentage of the 2008 and 2009 federal stimulus packages were devoted to providing one-time or short-term income tax reductions to households and, on a smaller scale, to businesses. The first Congressional response to the financial crisis occurred in February 2008, almost six months before U.S. GDP started to decline, when Congress passed a law which gave income tax rebates to households and more generous tax treatment of investments to businesses. The 2008 stimulus package also raised the maximum value of a home mortgage that could be purchased by the Federal National Mortgage Association (Fannie Mae) and the Federal Home Loan Mortgage Corporation (Freddie Mac). Of these measures the most important was the income tax rebate given to taxpayers. Individual taxpayers received a rebate of $ 600; married couples received $ 1,200; and taxpayers with child dependents received

$ 300 for each child. Even Americans who had no tax liabilities could receive partial rebates if their earned incomes were at least $ 3,000. Social Security beneficiaries also received rebates under the 2008 stimulus law. Rebate checks were scaled back for households with gross incomes above a certain limit. Single taxpayers with incomes above $ 75,000 and married taxpayers with incomes above $ 150,000 saw their rebates reduced by $ 0.05 for every $ 1.00 by which their incomes exceeded these limits. Thus, rebates of roughly equal size were received by most Americans in the bottom 90% of the income distribution. Only people with virtually no income or with incomes near the top of the distribution received no tax benefits under the plan. The estimated one-year cost of the rebates was about $ 126 billion, or about 1% of potential U.S. GDP. The miscellaneous tax concessions for business provided estimated tax relief equal to about one-seventh the amount provided to households through the income tax rebates.

The 2009 stimulus package was about 5.4 times more expensive to the U.S. Treasury than the 2008 package, and it contained a much wider variety of tax and spending provisions. The most costly tax provision, accounting for more than 40% of the tax concessions in the stimulus bill, was the temporary 'making work pay' tax credit. This credit was modelled closely on a proposal made by President Barack Obama during the 2008 presidential campaign. He pledged to increase the reward for work by giving low-income workers an income tax rebate for part of the payroll taxes they pay. The credit provides workers with a credit equal to 6.2% of their earnings, capped at $ 400 for single taxpayers and $ 800 for a married couple. The credit rate is equal to the worker's portion of the Social Security payroll tax. The credit is phased out for taxpayers with high incomes, in particular, for single taxpayers with incomes above $ 75,000 a year and married couples with incomes above $ 150,000 a year. The credit unquestionably reduces the marginal tax rate on earnings received by Americans in the bottom 90% of the income distribution, and thus it should boost the available supply of labour. The Congress and Administration decided to pay the credit through lower tax withholding rates in 2009 and 2010. Thus, most workers started receiving bigger pay checks in March or April 2009. The tax credit is temporary, however. It ends after 2010. In the 2008 campaign, candidate Barack Obama pledged to make the tax credit permanent. Of course, this would greatly increase its cost. The cost of the credit as enacted is predicted to be $ 116 billion between 2009 and 2011. If the credit instead became a permanent part of the tax code, the cost of the credit over the next 10 years would be $ 640 billion.

The second most expensive tax provision in the 2009 stimulus package, at a cost of nearly $ 70 billion, raised the income level at which the 'alternative minimum tax' begins to apply. This is a technical change in the tax code, but it has important practical effects for people with high incomes or large deductions from their countable incomes. The original purpose of the 'alternative minimum tax' was to prevent high-income taxpayers from escaping all taxes as a result of claiming many deductions and exemptions on their income tax returns. How effectively it achieves this goal is a matter of debate. In any case, a growing percentage of taxpayers is at risk of paying income taxes under the alternative minimum tax rules, and in many cases these taxpayers do not have particularly high incomes. To prevent middle-income families from paying the alternative tax, the Congress has taken steps every one or two years to 'temporarily' increase the income levels at which the alternative minimum tax begins to apply. Whether or not the alternative minimum tax rules were suspended in the 2009 stimulus bill, they almost certainly would have been suspended by Congress sometime in 2009. Few taxpayers expected to pay the alternative minimum tax in 2009. According to estimates of the Brookings-Urban Institute Tax Policy Center, almost 80% of the net benefits from suspending the alternative minimum tax rules flow to the richest 20% of U.S. households (Altshuler et al. 2009). Viewed as an economic stimulus measure, this was a poor way to target tax concessions, since high income households have a lower propensity to immediately spend their tax savings than do lower income households.

The stimulus package contained two important provisions to liberalize tax credits that are particularly important for low-income households containing the children. One increased the value of the Earned Income Tax Credit (EITC) for households containing three or more children. This credit was originally introduced to encourage low-income parents to enter the workforce and increase their annual work effort. For workers with very low earnings it gives families a refundable tax credit equal to either $ 0.34 or 0.40 for every dollar they earn. There is a maximum annual credit – it is about $ 3,000 a year for parents with a single child and $ 5,000 a year for parents with two or more children – and when family income rises above some threshold the credit is phased out. The EITC is widely considered successful, partly because the tax benefits are heavily concentrated on a deserving population – working poor parents – and partly because of abundant evidence the credit achieves its goal of encouraging low-wage parents to join the paid workforce. The temporary reforms included in the 2009 stimulus bill provided increased tax credits to parents with three or more children and increased the income levels at which the credit begins to be phased out for married couple families. These are worthy changes, though it is unclear why they are only temporary. Given the population that will receive tax concession under this provision, it is likely that a large percentage of the tax reductions will be spent soon after they are received.

A second provision of the stimulus bill alters the child tax credit. This credit provides permanent tax concessions to families that contain children. Under the terms of the stimulus bill, some features of the child tax credit will be temporarily changed so that low income households receive bigger tax benefits under the credit. Like the change in the EITC, the temporary change in the child tax credit is narrowly targeted on low-income working families containing children.

In both cases it is likely that a high fraction of the tax benefits will be spent soon after they are received by families. Since this population includes a high proportion of families with working but poor breadwinners, it is more vulnerable to the effects of a recession than other low-income populations, which may include few working breadwinners. (Pensioners and the disabled are often poor, but they only rarely depend on wage earnings for their support. Therefore, most of them are largely unaffected by weakness in the job market.)

In addition to the temporary tax concession offered to people collecting unemployment insurance, mentioned earlier, the 2009 stimulus package also contains a provision that assists students who are enrolled in post-secondary education. U.S. tax law already contains a permanent 'Hope tax credit' that provides students with a tax credit equal to 100% of the first $ 1,200 per year spent on tuition and fees plus 50% of the second $ 1,200 spent on such fees. However, the credit is only provided to students in their first two years of post-secondary schooling. The temporary replacement for the Hope tax credit is called the 'American Opportunity credit'. It provides a credit equal to 100% of the first $ 2,000 spent on tuition, fees, and other expenses plus 25% of the next $ 2,000 spent on those items. Thus, the maximum annual credit will be $ 2,500 versus only $ 1,800 under the Hope tax credit. In addition, the American Opportunity credit will cover educational expenses in four years of post-secondary education rather than only the first two. However, like other items in the stimulus package, this is only a temporary tax credit. Unless the credit is extended by a later Congress, it will only provide tax benefits for educational expenses incurred in 2009 and 2010. When the credit expires, it will be replaced by the old Hope tax credit.

The notable feature of the American Opportunity credit is that it targets temporary tax concessions on Americans investing in higher education. It is one of several provisions in the stimulus package aimed at maintaining or increasing Americans' investments in education. In the spending portion of the stimulus package, Congress funded a major expansion of Government grants to low-income students so they can pay for post-secondary schooling. These provisions make good sense. Between December 2008 and April 2009 the number of wage and salary jobs in the U.S. dropped by more than 5.7 million. In the same period the number of unemployed job seekers increased by 6.2 million. Because it is hard for jobless workers to find employment, it makes sense for some of them to stop looking for work and start investing in their own skills so they are better equipped to find work when the job market improves. By providing tax assistance and direct grants to post-secondary students, the Government encourages more of the unemployed to adopt this strategy. It is a good strategy for many workers, especially for younger unemployed workers. At the same time, the increased incentive for jobless workers to attend college or participate in training programmes may reduce the number of unemployed who are seeking immediate employment.

The 2009 stimulus package also contains a number of other miscellaneous tax provisions, some of them aimed at providing tax incentives for businesses to make energy-saving investments. Some business tax incentives, including time-limited tax concessions for capital investments undertaken in a specified period, can spur business spending in the short run. Many others, however, will probably encourage spending over such a lengthy period that much of the increased spending will occur when the recession is long past. Some of these tax concessions may have a sound justification, quite apart from their success or failure in spurring business investment in the recession. However, to the extent that they cause investment to increase long after the recession is over, these tax concessions will do nothing to speed the recovery or to improve the well-being of workers or families during the recession.

Other direct income assistance and provision of services. From the perspective of social protection, the most important component of the 2009 stimulus package is direct provision of income assistance and social services to households. I have already described some of the most important measures to offer additional income assistance: temporary extensions in unemployment benefits, a temporary increase in the weekly benefit payment for unemployment compensation, temporary health insurance subsidies for workers who lose their health insurance when they are laid off, tax rebates for most American taxpayers and pensioners, targeted tax concessions to working parents who have children, more generous tax credits and means-tested educational grants so that students can afford college. In addition to these measures, Congress took other steps to protect vulnerable populations. It increased for two years the amount of money available in federally funded training programmes to pay for retraining unemployed workers and improving the skills of hard-to-employ young people and adults. It provided substantial extra assistance so that states could pay for larger caseloads in the Temporary Assistance to Needy Families (TANF) programme, a social assistance programme that provides cash transfers to indigent children and their parents. The 2009 stimulus package temporarily increased the generosity of food stamp benefits (now known as Supplemental Nutritional Assistance). This programme is essentially a negative income tax programme that offers benefits payable in the form of food coupons. As a family's income rises, the value of food coupons provided to the family falls. Families in the top 60% of the income distribution are not eligible to receive food coupons. All of the measures just mentioned target assistance benefits on populations that are directly affected by a weaker job market, namely, populations containing working-age adults who can lose jobs or wages.

Fiscal relief for state Governments. By my estimate a little more than one-fifth of the 2009 stimulus package, or about $ 175 billion, was devoted to providing fiscal relief to state Governments. This relief was provided in a variety of forms.

A little less than $ 3 billion in federal grants were authorized to help pay for local law enforcement, for example. Nearly $ 30 billion was authorized to pay for aid for particular aspects of state and local education. Most of this was targeted on education for the economically disadvantaged and for children who have learning or other disabilities. Since most educational spending is fungible, however, it is likely that the extra federal funds earmarked for one educational purpose can be reallocated to other educational functions at the discretion of state and local policymakers.

Congress created two temporary programmes to provide general fiscal relief to the states. One gives almost $ 50 billion to be divided among the states "in order to minimize and avoid reductions in education and other essential services". In exchange for the generous grants, state Governments must show they are making progress in "(1) making improvements in teacher effectiveness and in the equitable distribution of qualified teachers for all students, particularly students who are most in need; (2) establishing pre-K-to-college-and-career data systems that track progress and foster continuous improvement; (3) making progress toward rigorous college- and career-ready standards and high-quality assessments that are valid and reliable for all students, including limited English proficient students and students with disabilities; and (4) providing targeted, intensive support and effective interventions for the lowest-performing schools". (U.S. Department of Education 2009, p. 1) All 50 states will submit applications for these funds, and the applications will be duly considered by federal officials. However, there can be little doubt that nearly all of the funds will be disbursed according to the formula specified by Congress. For most states, no changes in their education policies will be needed to obtain the generous but temporary federal assistance.

The second important form of fiscal relief was provided through a temporary change in the funding formula for Medicaid, the federal-state public health insurance programme for low-income Americans. The Medicaid programme is administered by state Governments, but most of its costs are financed with large federal grants to state Governments. If a state maintains a qualifying public insurance programme for its indigent population, the federal Government pays for a percentage of the state's programme costs. The fraction of costs paid by the federal Government, known as the Federal Medical Assistance Percentage (or FMAP), is determined by a formula that links the state's federal reimbursement rate to its per capita income. States with high average incomes get 50% of their Medicaid programme costs reimbursed, while states with low average incomes receive a higher federal subsidy rate. Medicaid is one of the most costly Government programmes. In 2007 benefit payments under the programme represented 2.8% of GDP. This means that the federal Government's Medicaid grants to state Governments are a major source of state revenues. By changing the FMAP formula, the federal Government can dramatically raise or lower total state revenues. The 2009 stimulus package temporarily changed the FMAP formula to make it more favourable to states. All states were guaranteed that the percentage of Medicaid costs borne by the federal Government would rise by at least 6.2 percentage points (reducing the percentage of programme costs borne by the state by an equivalent percentage). In addition, the Congress authorized even bigger increases in the federal match rate for states experiencing large increases in their unemployment rates. These changes in the FMAP formula are effective for the period from October 2008 through December 2010. The cost of this temporary formula change to the U.S. Treasury is estimated to be $ 90 billion spread over three years.

Both the temporary measures just described provide immediate relief to state Governments. Nearly all state Governments in the United States operate under balanced budget rules. Although these rules differ across states, they generally mean that the planned operating budget of the state, excluding the budget for capital investment, must be fully financed with current revenues. These rules, which are usually included in state constitutions, mean that a shortfall in expected revenues must be matched within a few months by an equivalent reduction in planned state spending. Unlike the federal Government, which can borrow unlimited funds to pay for its operations, state Governments must generally plan to cover the cost of their programmes with current tax revenues, fees, or grants from the federal Government. The provision of generous fiscal relief in the current recession means that state Governments will not have to cut spending or increase taxes as much as they would have to do in the absence of the federal aid.

Federal fiscal relief to the states is particularly important for education and for maintaining social protection to the poor. In the United States, education is primarily the responsibility of state and local Governments. The federal Government typically pays for only about 10% to 12% of the total cost of public primary and secondary schools. State and local Governments pay for the rest. Since balanced budget rules make state and local budgets pro-cyclical, state legislatures face pressure to reduce school budgets during recessions. The federal Government pays for most of the cost of social safety net programmes for the poor, but state Governments still pay for a substantial share of their costs. Equally important, state Governments are responsible for administering some of the biggest means-tested programmes, including Medicaid and Temporary Assistance for Needy Families. State Governments make the rules that help determine who is eligible for benefits and the amount of benefits. Even though they do not pay for the full cost of the programmes, when a recession occurs many states are tempted to curtail eligibility or cut benefits. This is the opposite policy from the one urged by most economists, who think it is important for benefits to be maintained or even improved during a recession.

On the whole, Congress provided states with fiscal relief in a sensible way. The funds were guaranteed to states within a few months of the jump in U.S. unemployment rates, allowing states to maintain educational and social spending they otherwise would have cut. Although a number of state Governments will be forced to raise taxes and cut spending, the number is smaller than it would have been if Congress did not provide fiscal relief. The state tax increases and spending cuts will also be smaller. By providing much of the fiscal relief through its matching grants for the Medicaid programme, the federal Government improved the likelihood that Medicaid insurance protection for indigent Americans will be maintained during the recession. While it is true that the cost savings to states are fungible, many state legislators will be unwilling to cut state Medicaid spending when a Medicaid budget cut would bring with it an even bigger cut in federal matching funds.

Investments in infrastructure and research and development. When the extent of the financial crisis became clear, the Bush Administration and Congress acted quickly to prevent the collapse of major banks and insurance companies. Almost immediately critics of the financial institution rescue package demanded that actions be taken to protect the broader economy. A great deal of the early discussion focused on alternative investments the Government could make to improve the transportation system, reduce greenhouse gas emissions, and improve the energy efficiency of the economy. This kind of discussion dominated the early phase of the public debate about desirable components of a good countercyclical stimulus plan. In the end the 2008 and 2009 stimulus packages contained relatively small budget allocations for these kinds of investments, especially in the first two or three years after the onset of the recession.

I have divided the various individual components in the 2009 stimulus package into three broad categories: (1) fiscal relief for state Governments; (2) direct income assistance and social services; and (3) investments in infrastructure and technology development. Figure 14 shows the allocation of resources in the 2009 stimulus package across these three broad categories, and it further divides the budget totals between two periods, 2009-2010 and 2011-2019. In much of the discussion up to now I have emphasized the time-limited nature of many of Congress's actions. Most tax concessions are limited to the 2009 and 2010 tax years. Nearly all the transfer programme benefit increases are scheduled to end by 2011. Nonetheless, a surprisingly large percentage of the total costs to the federal Government occur after 2010. An overwhelming fraction of the late-period costs are for the infrastructure and technology investment projects. In the case of tax concessions, benefit increases, and state fiscal relief packages, it is relatively easy for the federal Government to start spending and to stop it. It is much more difficult to obtain useful results from an investment in infrastructure or a research and development project if the Government is committed to obtain results within a very short period. It takes time to plan a well-designed project and even more time to assemble and carefully manage the resources needed to complete it.

Figure 14: Expected stimulus spending under the American Recovery and Reinvestment Act of 2009, 2009-2015

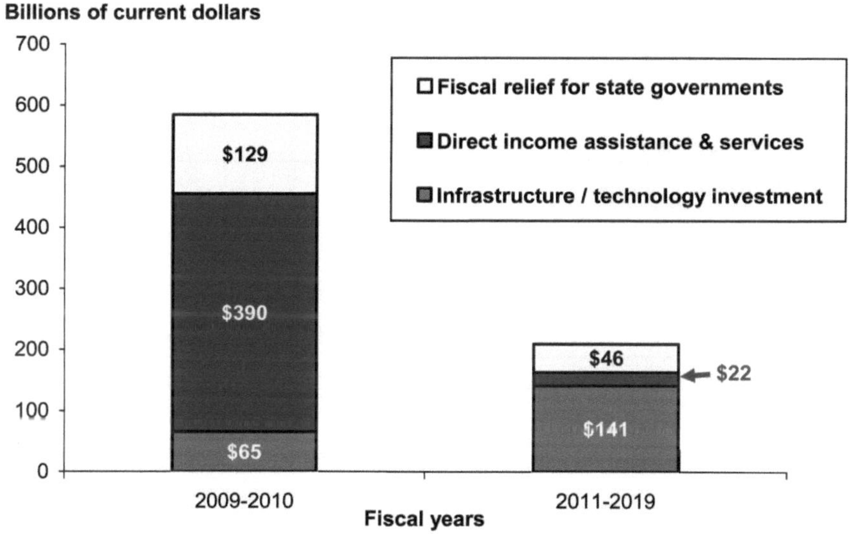

Sources: Congressional Budget Office and Joint Committee on Taxation.

The different time horizons of the three kinds of stimulus activities is plain in figure 15. It shows predicted stimulus spending in years between 2009 and 2015 measured as a percentage of the potential GDP in those years. At the peak of the stimulus programme, in fiscal year 2010, total spending will be slightly more than 2.5% of potential GDP. Only a small portion of the funds will be spent on infrastructure or R&D projects. An overwhelming share will be devoted to direct income assistance and to state fiscal relief. The funding for infrastructure and R&D projects will be spread fairly evenly over most of the next six years. Even if the projects ultimately prove to have high value, their value as counter-cyclical stimulus is questionable. Only a small percentage of funds devoted to the projects will be spent in the next two years, when the gap between potential and actual U.S. GDP is expected to be greatest.

Figure 15: Expected stimulus spending under the American Recovery and Reinvestment Act of 2009, fiscal Years 2009-2015

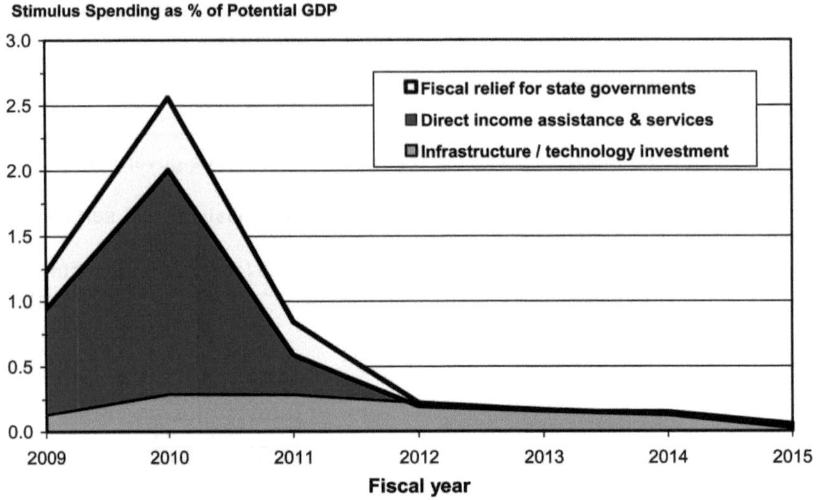

Sources: Congressional Budget Office and Joint Committee on Taxation.

Conclusion

American social protection in a recession consists of two main elements, the regular system of social protection that is available in good times and bad and special measures enacted by Congress to provide counter-cyclical stimulus and deal with the humanitarian fallout from labour market weakness. Even without any special measures the U.S. system of social protection provides automatic counter-cyclical stimulus that helps offset the impact of a fall in demand. Millions of additional workers apply for and receive unemployment compensation benefits. These benefits help laid off workers maintain their consumption in spite of the sharp fall or complete loss of their wages. At the same time, the existence of a progressive income tax causes personal and business income taxes to fall proportionately faster than taxable income. Government revenue from the income tax falls much faster than the after-tax incomes of households and businesses. A number of other Government transfer programmes also provide extra assistance to many of the households hurt by a recession. For example, with a lag of 12 to 24 months the number of workers collecting disability insurance benefits also tends to increase. Jobless workers who are in fragile health are more inclined to apply for disability benefits when it is difficult for them to find a job. Those who qualify for benefits will eventually begin to collect Government-financed disability and health insurance benefits. Food stamp and cash social assistance payments also increase after the onset of a recession, when laid-off workers with little income and few assets exhaust their unemployment benefits.

The shortcomings of American social protection are widely recognized in the United States. Average benefits under many transfer programmes are lower than those provided by comparable programmes in other rich countries. Except for food stamp benefits and Social Security Disability Insurance, most U.S. Government transfers available to working-age households are provided by state Governments. Benefit amounts and eligibility conditions are determined by state legislatures rather than under a uniform, nationwide standard set by Congress. Because the federal Government provides funding to pay for part of the cost of these programmes, the Congress usually establishes minimum standards to guide state legislatures in setting benefit levels and eligibility conditions. Nonetheless, there are wide variations across states in the generosity of weekly benefit amounts and in eligibility conditions. In January 2009 the maximum weekly unemployment insurance benefit was $ 584 in the state of New Jersey but only 230 in Mississippi. Although the cost of living is higher in New Jersey than in Mississippi, the cost difference is much smaller than the proportional difference between weekly benefits in the two states. Many states impose tough qualifying requirements for unemployment insurance, for Temporary Assistance to Needy Families, and for Medicaid health insurance benefits, making it hard for workers and families to obtain benefits under these programmes, both in recessions and in prosperity. This means that unemployed workers who are entitled to benefits in some states would be ineligible for benefits in other states. Despite these cross-state differences, when a recession occurs a greater number of workers and families begins to receive benefits in all of the 50 states, regardless of whether the state imposes lenient or tough qualifying requirements for benefits.

The most serious shortcoming of U.S. social protection for working-age Americans is the high cost of health insurance for people who are not employed by companies providing subsidized insurance to their workers. Obtaining unsubsidized insurance is very costly for most of the unemployed as well as for workers who are employed in firms that do not offer group health insurance. In 2007 about 47 million Americans, or slightly more than 15% of the U.S. population, lacked health insurance. Nearly all of the uninsured are working-age adults and their children. Obviously, the loss of jobs during recessions increases the number of unemployed and the percentage of the population that is at risk of losing health insurance. Until 2009 the U.S. Government did not provide affordable health insurance to most of the unemployed or to their dependents. A notable exception was the low-income population, which has long been entitled to receive free Medicaid health insurance. However, few middle- and high-wage workers are entitled to receive Medicaid when they become unemployed.

The stimulus package passed by Congress in February 2009 filled some major holes in the standard U.S. social safety net. Most importantly, the Congress established a temporary programme to provide health insurance subsidies to workers laid off from jobs that provided health insurance coverage. Even though this programme is currently scheduled to expire in 2010, it will provide crucial protection of a kind that has never before been available to laid-off American workers. Many of the other temporary improvements in social protection provided by the 2008 and 2009 stimulus packages will be familiar from stimulus packages enacted in past recessions. For example, Congress has temporarily extended the potential duration of unemployment insurance benefits beyond the 26 weeks of benefits that are ordinarily available, and it has offered to pay for the full cost of the benefit extension out of federal funds. This kind of measure has been adopted by Congress in every recession dating back to the late 1950s. Most economists approve of this kind of temporary benefit extension because it is an effective way to improve the spending capacity of people who are likely to spend immediately a large percentage of the extra benefits. On the other hand, the benefit extension will also encourage unemployed workers to delay accepting a job offer, increasing the average duration of their unemployment spells.

The variation in state benefit levels and eligibility conditions also creates a problem of benefit equity. Laid-off workers who live in states with generous eligibility conditions and high benefit levels can expect to derive much greater benefits under the federal benefit extensions than workers who live in states with more restrictive qualifying requirements and lower weekly benefit amounts. As a result, federal taxpayers will pay for much larger additions to standard benefits for residents in high-benefit states compared with residents in low-benefit states. It is hard to justify this benefit discrepancy on equity grounds. Since the extra benefit payments are financed solely out of federal funds, it is unfair to give higher benefits to laid-off workers in some states than in others. The benefit disparity seems particularly unfair because many of the low-benefit states are in the American south and southwest, where poverty rates are high and income levels are below the national average. Nonetheless, unemployment insurance benefit extensions are straightforward to implement and are more effective than most other measures in spurring higher consumer spending.

Two features of the 2009 stimulus package are notable. First is the emphasis on providing generous fiscal relief to state Governments. Second is the provision of large, though temporary, incentives for states and young adults to invest in education and training. It is not clear how effective these two measures will be in encouraging higher state and household consumption. In past recessions, federal stimulus plans have emphasized extra spending on unemployment benefits, increases in infrastructure investment, and temporary tax cuts to boost consumer spending and encourage business investment. State fiscal relief and temporary incentives for human capital investment have seldom played a large role in stimulus packages. As a result, we have little evidence to assess their short-term impact on Government and household consumption. In my view, both kinds of stimulus deserve serious tests. Based on evidence on state spending patterns and post-secondary educational investments in the current recession we will learn more about the counter-cyclical effectiveness of these two policies.

A fundamental question about the stimulus package is whether it is the correct size in view of the severity of the recession. At this stage it is hard to make a clear judgment on this question. No Government agency or forecasting organization can offer a credible prediction of the drop in GDP we should expect. It is clear, however, that the United States adopted an earlier and bigger counter-cyclical stimulus package than other countries. Table 1 shows estimates by the International Monetary Fund (IMF) of the size of stimulus packages in nine large economies (2009).

Table 1: Fiscal stimulus packages in nine large countries, 2008-2010

(per cent of GDP)

	Calendar years			*2008-2010*
	2008	*2009*	*2010*	*Total*
Canada	0.0	1.5	1.3	2.7
China	0.4	2.0	2.0	4.4
France	0.0	0.7	0.7	1.3
Germany	0.0	1.5	2.0	3.4
India	0.0	0.5	...	0.5
Italy	0.0	0.2	0.1	0.3
Japan	0.4	1.4	0.4	2.2
United Kingdom	0.2	1.4	-0.1	1.5
United States	1.1	2.0	1.8	4.8
Average [1]	0.5	1.6	1.3	3.4

Note: [1] PPP GDP-weighted average.

Source: International Monetary Fund (February 2009).

The size of each fiscal package is measured in relation to the size of the country's GDP. According to the IMF's February 2009 calculations, the United States has enacted the largest stimulus package of the nine countries on the list. The next largest stimulus package was adopted by China. The size of stimulus packages bears little if any relation to the drop in GDP these countries have experienced since the beginning of 2008 (see figure 6). Through the first quarter of 2009, the drop in U.S. GDP was smaller than average, but the size of its stimulus package was considerably larger than average. Similarly, Chinese GDP has continued to grow over the past year, though at a slower pace than in the previous four years, but China is implementing a large stimulus programme.

One reason that countries may have adopted a small stimulus package is that they expect a modest economic downturn. Another is that their operating deficit or public debt were large at the start of the recession, giving them little room for additional fiscal stimulus. Finally, some countries may be confident their existing automatic stabilization policies are robust enough to deal with the current economic crisis. Special counter-cyclical measures are less necessary in these countries. The IMF analysts note, for example, that the United States "has less extensive social benefits (unemployment insurance, training), particularly compared with Europe" (IMF 2009, p. 2). Even though this is true, it does not follow that the United States fiscal system provides less automatic stabilization than is available in Europe or elsewhere. As noted above, the automatic stabilization provided by the progressive U.S. tax system is quantitatively much more important than the counter-cyclical stimulus provided by unemployment insurance and other benefits targeted on the unemployed. What matters for stabilization is the combined response of taxes, transfers, and other Government spending to the overall state of the economy. The IMF analysis sheds no light on this question. If tax systems in other countries are less progressive and more proportional than the U.S. system, then the United States may have more automatic stabilization built into its standard fiscal policy. At least in the short run, the United States probably faces a less binding public borrowing constraint compared with the other countries listed in table 1.

The most questionable items in the U.S. stimulus package are the appropriations for public infrastructure investment and incentives for investments in energy-saving or health related research and development. These programmes may encourage worthwhile investments in socially desirable activities, but it is not clear how much of the extra spending will occur when the economy is shrinking and when other sources of demand are weak. Because much of the additional public spending will not occur for several years in the future, it is conceivable the economy will already be near full employment when the spending occurs. If the recession is severe and prolonged, the extra spending will of course be highly welcome. If the extra spending takes place when the economy is near full employment, the Congress and Federal Reserve Board can make other changes in fiscal or monetary policy to reduce the adverse side effects of the planned spending.

On the whole the 2008 and 2009 stimulus packages were enacted in a timely fashion. The main components of the packages seem defensible in view of knowledge available to lawmakers when the packages were adopted. More than half of the total fiscal effort is devoted to improving the social safety net and providing temporary tax relief to households and businesses. The temporary benefit improvements are appropriately targeted on households with modest incomes or on households whose incomes will shrink as a result of the recession. The temporary tax concessions are more widely distributed across households, but on the whole they will boost net incomes by a larger proportional amount at the bottom of the income distribution than at the top. A little more than one-fifth of the 2009 stimulus package is devoted to providing temporary fiscal relief to the states. The additional federal aid to states will indirectly help preserve social protection because it will reduce the need for state Governments to scale back Medicaid, social assistance, and other programmes during the recession. About one-quarter of the 2009 stimulus package will support or encourage investments in infrastructure and new technologies. This spending will have little impact on U.S. social protection, though it may serve other worthwhile goals and may turn out to be very useful if the U.S. recession is long and severe.

References

Altshuler, Rosanne et al. (2009), *Tax Stimulus Report Card: Conference Bill as of February 18, 2009.* Washington/D.C.: Urban Institute & Brookings Institution Tax Policy Center. http://www.urban.org/UploadedPDF/411839_conference_reportcard.pdf.

Auerbach, Alan J. & Daniel Feenberg (2000), 'The Significance of Federal Taxes as Automatic Stabilizers', *Journal of Economic Perspectives* 4 (3) (Summer), pp. 37-56.

International Monetary Fund (2009), *The Size of the Fiscal Expansion: An Analysis for the Largest Countries.* Working paper (February). Washington/D.C. http://www.imf.org/external/np/pp/eng/2009/020109.pdf.

OECD (2004), *Benefits and Wages: OECD Indicators 2004.* Paris.

OECD (2009), *Benefits and Wages: Statistics*. Paris. http://www.oecd.org/document/29/0,3343,en_2649_34637_39618653_1_1_1_1,00.html

U.S. Bureau of Labor Statistics (2005), *Employer Costs for Employee Compensation.* March. Washington/D.C. USDL 05-1056.

U.S. Department of Education (2009), *Guidance on the State Fiscal Stabilization Fund Programme.* Washington/D.C. http://www.ed.gov/programs/statestabilization/guidance.pdf.

U.S. House of Representatives, Committee on Ways and Means (2000), *The 2000 Green Book: Background Material and Data on Programmes within the Jurisdiction of the Committee on Ways and Means*. Washington/D.C.: U.S. GPO.

Vroman, Wayne (2009), *Unemployment Insurance in the American Recovery and Reinvestment Act (HR1).* Mimeo. Washington/D.C.: Urban Institute. http://www.urban.org/publications/411851.html.

3 China's Social Policy Choices in Times of the World Financial Crisis

Zheng Gong-Cheng

Since the world financial crisis erupted in 2008, it has not only influenced world economics to a great extent, but also impacts on the social welfare of every country. For China, whose economy is rapidly developing, the effects in the areas of economic development models and social welfare are even more profound.

The Influence of the World Financial Crisis on China's Economy

The influence of the world financial crisis on China's economy can mainly been seen in the following three areas:

China's Economic Growth is on a Downslide

Economic growth in China has been +10% on average for the last 30 years, however since being faced with the world financial crisis, China's economic growth has been slowing. China's GDP growth rate will probably go down to 8% and its revenue will slow to 8%. Compared to 2009's first quarter, China's GDP increased 6.1%, however, compared with the same period last year, it has drifted back towards 4.5%, the lowest record since 1992 (see figure 1).

Figure 1: GDP growth

Lack of Job Security

Firstly, foreign demand decreases and commercial export orders have been reduced, which led to bankruptcy or staff redundancy. Secondly, it influences the level of confidence in investment. Some enterprises originally planned to expand their investments and increasing the number of employers but have chosen to abandon such plans. Thirdly, it also influences public consumption as well as employment. With regard to employment, the number of university graduates in 2009 will reach 6,100,000, other labour forces accounting for around 8,000,000 people. At the same time, there are nearly 8,000,000 unemployed or laid-off workers. Thus, job protection has become an important policy goal for the Chinese Government.

Its Impact on Chinese Citizens

Economic depression leads to a reduction in income growth rate and financial assets, and also a lack of consumer confidence. The probationary salary of the newly employed has been greatly reduced. Rural-urban migrants have more difficulties in finding jobs and the incomes they can earn decrease. Furthermore all sorts of risks in life became more pervasive. Consumer confidence has been influenced to some extent.

Overall, the impact of the financial crisis on China's economy is great. The Chinese Government introduced policies to boost investment, stimulate domestic consumption. A number of social welfare polices has also been established in order to maintain economic growth, to protect employment and the living standard of Chinese people. The impact of these policies is huge and is producing very positive outcomes.

What can Social Welfare do in Times of the International Financial Crisis?

In the face of the world financial crisis, negative influence on China's economic growth and employment and the living standard of Chinese people, a number of people including Government officials, academia and the voluntary sector all think that the currently underdeveloped Chinese social welfare system, should be improved to promote a stable establishment of the social welfare system and to develop its vital role in society. What should social welfare do in times of international financial crisis? Some options on which most people agree are:

- The establishment of social welfare should be accelerated, which will protect the basic living standard of low-income individuals and families in times of financial crisis and to solve the problems of falling into poverty, and to play a greater role in maintaining a peaceful society and social order. This is the very fundamental social foundation to fight the world financial crisis.
- The establishment of social welfare should be accelerated to provide Chinese people with clear expectations on safety and improve peoples' confidence in life and consumption. That is to boost people's consumption, domestic consumption and to promote necessary conditions for economic growth. Also it

laid the foundation to create a transition from investment and foreign investment-based economic growth to a consumption-centred one possible in China.

- The establishment of social welfare should be accelerated in order for all people in China to realize the goal of obtaining their share from the national development and to finally realize the development goal of common prosperity. The difference in income distribution in China is too big, the gap between rich and poor, different areas, cities and the villages are significantly related to the underdevelopment of social welfare and the injustice of the current system. Thus, the stable establishment of the social welfare system could promote social justice, lighten social conflicts and realize harmonious social development.

As has been discussed above, China has accelerated the pace towards the establishment of social welfare system in recent years. In particular, in the face of the world financial crisis the rapid march towards the establishment of social welfare system is clearly identified. This has been shown in the following aspects:

First of all, investment in social welfare has increased on a regular basis. Regarding the index of economic development and national revenue in 2009, China is planning to reach its GDP growth target in the 8 percentile range and its financial budget in the 8 percentile range. But financial investment for social welfare has increased to the range of 17.1%. This is unprecedented.

Second, the standard of social welfare has greatly improved. The standard of social welfare including the Minimum Living Standard Guarantee System, old-age pension, medical insurance and welfare-related services have greatly improved.

Finally, launching of social welfare systems in rural areas is fully under way. This includes improvements in the Minimum Living Standard Guarantee System in rural areas, a new version of the cooperative medical service and possibly introduce a pilot scheme of old-age pensions in rural areas.

From what has been presented previously, social welfare has already developed comprehensive measures to deal with the world financial crisis, stimulating domestic demand, protecting people's lives and helping them realize the goal of obtaining their share from the national development. This is not only an important direction for China's social and economic development, but also an important means of promoting continuous economic development as well as helping to resolve the impact of the crisis.

Basic Direction for the Development of China's Social Welfare System

With the start of the 21st century, China clearly began to clarify the objectives and direction for reform in social welfare: to establish a stable social welfare system and its basic direction. This includes the following:

- to lay the foundation for an equal and universal-based social welfare system,
- to follow the principle of integration between urban and rural areas and the principle of gradual development. In establishing China's new social welfare system, the previous system of urban-rural division, the previous tradition of putting priority on urban rather than rural development has on the one hand been diminished for the establishment of social welfare systems in rural areas based on the principle of urban-rural equality. At the same time, a large amount of public resources from the Government has been invested in rural areas. On the other hand, the Chinese Government should make up for the deficiencies in the present system and cover all residents in China through multi-dimensional systems. At the same time, differences in welfare among different groups should be allowed, but this difference should be gradually reduced in order to realize an equal and universal type of social welfare.
- The key point here is to establish the basic social welfare system, which promotes "preventing two, getting rid of one". All residents in China can be relieved of the burden of medical fees through a comprehensive social assistance system. With the help of the establishment of universal medical service, all citizens in China can be exempted from medical costs. And the fear of trouble in old age can be relieved through the establishment of the systematic and multi-dimensional pension system and its workable system. These three basic protections are the key points in our current stage of establishing China's social welfare system.
- Legislative progress in social welfare law should be accelerated to quicken the legislative process for social welfare. The 'Social Welfare Law' has already gone through its second trial and it will prepare for the third trial. In October 2009, some basic parts of social welfare including 'Social Assistance Law' and 'Charity Law' will be drawn into a draft. The three years will be an important period of forming the framework for China's social welfare law. At the same time, a series of regulations, management and operation-related acts or laws in the field of social welfare are in the middle of being formulated. China's social welfare system is moving from the experimental stage to the standardization and stable development stage.
- There is necessity to pursue sustainable development. In designing social welfare reform and a new social welfare system, much attention should be paid to the burden sharing mechanism. The optimal level of social welfare should be placed as basic protection. In the pursuit of the goal of covering

the entire citizen, a rational and prudent policy direction for the standardization of social welfare should be taken.

Of course, China's mission on reform in social welfare system has not been accomplished yet, and is still facing a lot of challenges and difficulties. But in recent years the Chinese Government has made great efforts to improve social welfare and recently to ease the pressure from the world financial crisis, which will enable the mission of establishing the new social welfare system to move forward a single step.

Part II

4 Weathering the Storm: Consociational Democracy and Crisis Management in the Netherlands

Karen M. Anderson

Talk to any Dutch politician about the economic crisis and he/she will remind you that the extreme openness of the economy sets limits on what the Government can do in terms of crisis measures. To a large extent, the recovery of the Dutch economy depends on what happens in larger economies, especially Germany and the United States. This means that the Dutch response to the economic crisis emphasizes stabilizing the domestic financial system and mobilizing the labour market so that Dutch firms and workers are well-prepared to take advantage of economic recovery when it does eventually occur. These two elements of the Dutch Government's response to the economic crisis have been heavily conditioned by two central elements of the Dutch political economy. First, the existence of a mature, comprehensive welfare state provides 'automatic stabilizers' during economic downturns; even if Governments 'do nothing', social policies (particularly unemployment insurance) are an important source of demand stimulus. Second, the norms of political and economic decision-making in a consociational democracy like the Netherlands dictate that any response to the economic crisis requires time-consuming, detailed compromises that include the social partners.

Even after two decades of substantial reform, the Dutch welfare state is one of the most comprehensive and generous in Western Europe. The social insurance system, most prominently the unemployment insurance system, offers adequate compensation for those forced out of the labour market because of the crisis. Other schemes, such as re-training programmes and subsidized working time reductions offer employers temporary relief from short-term falls in production. In other words, the Dutch welfare state kicks in immediately and generously when the economy worsens, and it does so in ways that, for example, the US and British welfare states do not. These 'automatic stabilizers' were never meant to provide the sole remedy for severe economic downturns like the current one, however. In a consociational democracy like the Netherlands, political compromises rule the day, and compromises require detailed negotiations, even when an economic crisis is raging outside. This means that any response to the crisis beyond the scope of the 'automatic stabilizers' requires time and painstaking negotiations. It also requires the inclusion of the social partners in the Government's policy response. In the Netherlands, 90% of wage-earners are covered by collective agreements, and important areas of social policy belong to the wage-bargaining arena, including occupational pensions. This means that wage moderation and other economic policy goals require the cooperation of the social partners. Thus not only the governing parties have to extensively consult each other about how to fight the crisis, but they also have to try to get the social partners on board.

Briefly, the Government's approach to fighting the crisis relies on stimulating consumption in the short term, restoring budget balance and reducing public debt in the medium term, and working towards the sustainability of public finances in the long term. The latter specifically includes dealing with the health care and public pension costs associated with population ageing.

It is important to add that the world-wide financial crisis has led to severe problems for the Netherlands' extensive system of funded occupational schemes. Dutch pension funds have sustained substantial investment losses during the past year. Under the current regulatory rules, pension funds are required to restore full solvency within three years. In the current financial climate, this would require significant contribution increases and/or cuts in pension pay-outs. Such measures would obviously exacerbate the effects of the economic crisis on households and firms, so the Government and social partners are under intense pressure to find a politically viable solution to this challenge. In other words, the international financial crisis has caused an occupational pensions crisis in the Netherlands, and the solution to this crisis is part of the overall Dutch response to the world-wide recession.

This article analyses the Netherlands' response to the global economic crisis, highlighting the ways in which the welfare state and Dutch corporatism interact to shape the Government's response. The next section of this article discusses the detailed content of the crisis measures, including the negotiations that produced it. The second section of the article analyses the current crisis measures in light of two decades of welfare state reform and labour market reform. The last section of the article discusses the long-term goals included in the crisis package: preparing the country for population ageing by tackling health care costs and reforming the pension system. The article concludes with an analysis of the political and social sustainability of the Dutch Government's and social partners' plans for fighting the crisis and meeting the challenges of population ageing.

The Dutch Approach to Fighting the Economic Crisis

The Dutch Government announced a stimulus package on March 24, 2009 after nearly three weeks of laborious negotiations between the three coalition parties (Christian Democrats, CDA; The Labour Party, PvdA; and the Christian Union, CU). In separate negotiations with the Government, the social partners agreed to accept the deal (with some reservations). The central elements of the stimulus plan are (Prime Minister's Office, 2009):

- € 6 billion in additional spending in 2009 and 2010. These will be primarily environmentally sustainable investments, including subsidies for energy-efficient cars and houses. The deal also includes extra funds (€ 220 million) for fighting youth unemployment.
- Budget reduction measures totalling € 5 billion starting in 2011 if the Netherlands Bureau for Economic Forecasting (*Centraal Planbureau*, CPB) forecasts economic growth of at least 0.5% for 2011. These cuts would include € 3.2 billion savings from freezing public sector salaries and social insurance benefits linked to the statutory minimum wage. An additional € 1.8 billion in savings would come from sources to be discussed in next year's regular budget negotiations.
- Increase in the retirement age for the state pension (AOW) from 65 to 67.
- Other long-term measures include a reduction in the health insurance subsidy [1] (*zorgtoeslag)* and limits on mortgage interest deductions for homes worth more than € 1 million.
- In a separate decision in early 2009, the Minister of Social Affairs extended the deadline for occupational pension funds to restore full solvency after heavy losses in financial markets (see details below). Without the extension, many pension funds would have to raise contributions or cut pension payments, thereby dampening consumption.

Table 1 shows the breakdown in stimulus spending contained in the March 2009 crisis package as well as additional spending by local and provincial Government. The table does not include spending to stabilize Dutch banks.

Table 1: Stimulus measures 2009-2010 (millions of €)

	2009	*2010*
Labour market, education and innovation	709	1,049
Environmentally sustainable economic measures	621	606
Infrastructure and housing construction	724	1,087
Liquidity-enhancing measures for firms	677	464
Subtotal	*2,731*	*3,206*
Stimulus measures by municipalities and provinces	500	1,000
Higher unemployment insurance/assistance payments	1,000	3,900
Total [Source: www.minfin.nl]	*4,310*	*8,234*

1 All residents of the Netherlands are required to purchase basic health insurance on the private insurance market. Basic insurance is relatively inexpensive (about € 100 per month), and low-income households receive a subsidy to offset these costs. The subsidy is financed by earmarked contributions paid by employers and taxes paid by employees on these contributions.

Besides these concrete measures, the Government secured agreement from the social partners on wage moderation, occupational pensions and the state pension. The latter two issues have been high on the political agenda for several years and the subject of much conflict. The fate of the proposed increase in retirement age for the state pension is still in doubt. Unions bitterly oppose the measure, and the Government and social partners agreed to seek alternative solutions (see below).

After the crisis package was announced, the cabinet started negotiations with the social partners. The reaction of the largest union federation, the Dutch Federation of Trade Unions (FNV),[2] was lukewarm, largely because of the proposal to raise the state pension retirement age from 65 to 67. Union pressure resulted in a compromise: the tripartite Social Economic Council (SER)[3] will have six months to study the issue and propose alternatives that will result in similar savings for the state budget. In an internal referendum on the social pact, 94% of voting FNV members approved the agreement (turnout was about 20%; the vote was conducted by internet and postal mail; see www.fnv.nl).

The Details of the Crisis Measures

The first response of the Dutch Government to the crisis involved the largest financial institutions in the country. Since October 2008, the Government has pursued an active policy of supporting Dutch banks, most prominently ABN AMRO (the country's largest bank), with capital injections and stock purchases. ABN AMRO was effectively nationalized; on 3 October, the Dutch state assumed ownership of the Dutch division of Fortis Bank and the parts of ABN AMRO owned by Fortis Bank. The Government also increased its guarantee for individual savings accounts to € 100,000. In addition, the Government has made € 20 billion available for financial institutions facing liquidity shortages, and € 200 billion in guarantees for inter-bank loans and loans from institutional investors to banks (www.regering.nl). These initial measures are considerable: in total the Government has pumped € 80 billion into the financial sector with another € 200 billion in guarantees. The automatic stabilizers (discussed below)

2 The Dutch Federation of Trade Unions (FNV) has 17 member unions for a total membership of 1.4 million workers.

3 The tripartite Social Economic Council (SER), established in 1950, plays an important advisory role in the legislative process; in nearly all important matters, the Government asks the SER for an advisory opinion before initiating legislation. The SER has 33 members; 11 each from unions, employers and the Crown. The SER's influence has declined in recent years, but its advisory opinions are still important. According to van Waarden (2002, p. 56), the SER "forces the social partners to engage in scientific discourse to justify their demands".

add another € 50 billion in 2009 and 2010.[4] This includes € 1 billion in 2009 and € 4 billion in 2010 in higher spending for unemployment insurance payments (www.minfin.nl; see table 1 above).

In autumn 2008, the Government initiated its first crisis policies concerning the labour market. The 2009 budget (presented in September 2008) included measures aimed at maintaining employment (Prime Minister's Office 2009, p. 7). Tri-partite negotiations (the '*participatie-top*' or 'labour market participation summit') between the Government, unions and employers began in 2007 in the context of tight labour markets. The negotiators agreed to mobilize 'less active' groups, primarily immigrants, low-skilled women, and older workers to work more hours or, in the case of older workers, to work longer.[5] These policies are aimed at increasing labour supply, both in the short-term and long-term. As noted, pre-crisis labour markets were tight. But this supply-side strategy is also an important component in the Government and social partners' strategy for dealing with the labour market effects of ageing. As the baby boom generations retire, the number of pensioners will increase substantially, exacerbating labour market shortages.[6]

The autumn consultation with the social partners also provided an opportunity to devise an early response to the emerging crisis and to build on the reorientation in labour market policy initiated earlier. At the suggestion of the social partners, the Government agreed to delay a planned increase in the VAT (from 19% to 20%) and to reduce unemployment insurance contributions. The Government and social partners also agreed to increase financial resources for training and re-training and to speed up the introduction of new active labour market policies.

The Government also moved quickly to create some breathing room in the market sector by introducing subsidized working time reductions and speeding up the introduction of the already planned 'mobility centres'. The Minister of Social Affairs, Donner (CDA), made € 200 million available to firms facing a 30% of more decrease in volume (sales) in a two month period. This measure is intended to be temporary, and it is by nature conservative. Firms apply to the Ministry of Social Affairs for subsidies so that they can continue to pay full wages for reduced working time. The idea is to provide temporary financial

---

4 This number includes both increased spending and decreased tax revenues.

5 The Netherlands is Europe's largest part-time labour market, largely because women work part-time (Visser 2002).

6 The core elements of the Government and social partners' strategy for increasing participation is to improve active labour market policies and increase labour supply. In 2007 and 2008, Parliament adopted several amendments to existing legislation Government active labour market policies (the Dutch call these policies 're-integration' policies) in order to step up activation and improve the coordination between central and local Government as well as between public and private actors.

support to firms facing temporary dips in sales and production because of the recession. The Ministry of Social Affairs closed the scheme on 21 March 2009. The Ministry approved 849 applications for support, for a total of 761,678 subsidized working hours. The highest number of approved applications was in the metal-working sector (Ministry of Social Affairs 2009b). A part-time unemployment insurance benefit scheme has been introduced (in 2009) to replace the working-time reduction scheme. The cabinet negotiated the scheme in cooperation with the social partners. The Minister of Social Affairs has allocated € 375 million for the new scheme.

The mobility centres are an institutional innovation: They are regionally organized, and their central task is to manage the transition from one form of employment to another. The idea is to prevent unemployment by shifting workers from declining sectors/firms to expanding ones, and where necessary to provide re-training in order to facilitate this transition. The approach is innovative in that it tries to shift workers threatened with unemployment into new jobs *before* they become unemployed. The mobility centres provide job counselling, job search assistance, and other related services. They are also linked to the so-called 'LWI-plus facilities', which are regionally-organized 'Locations for Work and Income' whose task is to coordinate the activities of local Government and the UWV in facilitating clients' job searches.[7] There are thirty mobility centres are planned, and ten have already opened.[8] The centres cooperate closely with all stakeholders in a region, both public (usually local Government) and private (private employers). The Labour Foundation (STAR) assists the centres by providing detailed labour market analyses.[9]

The overall strategy of the stimulus package negotiated in March is to allow the 'automatic stabilizers' to do their work, which will result in increased Government spending in 2009 and 2010, primarily for employment-related measures. In addition, € 3 billion are allocated for both 2009 and 2010 in the areas of employment (especially fighting youth unemployment), education, and policies to enhance environmental sustainability, spending on infrastructure and housing, and measures to increase the liquidity of firms. The municipalities and provinces are estimated to add another € 1.5 billion in stimulus measures. The

7 The LWIs provide access to unemployment support and provide job-seekers with resources such as an individual coach.

8 The first mobility centres opened on 1 March 2009.

9 See Ministry of Social Affairs (2009a) for more details. The mobility centres complement the existing institutions for active labour market policy. In 2008, the old CWIs (Centre for Work and Income) were merged with the UWV (Uitvoeringsinstituut WerknemersVerzekeringen), the organ responsible for administering the unemployment benefit system (among other things). The new agency is called UWV Werkbedrijf, and its primary responsibility is to match job-seekers with potential employers, as well as to administer unemployment benefits and other work-related benefit schemes.

costs of increased unemployment insurance payments are estimated to be € 1 billion in 2009, € 4 billion in 2010 and € 4.5 billion in 2011 (see table 1). These extra expenditures will not be subject to the budget rules that require increased spending to be compensated by cuts in other parts of the (sectoral) budget.[10]

The investment projects are based on several motions presented to Parliament in early 2009. Three motions, all introduced by governing parties or governing parties in cooperation with opposition parties, focused on four areas:

- maintaining employment, especially among youths;
- investing in environmentally sustainable infrastructure (the goal is 20% renewable energy use by 2020). This includes investments in wind energy, energy-efficient housing, subsidies for switching to newer, more fuel-efficient cars, and sustainable agriculture;
- speeding up infrastructure investments in housing, roads/water transport, health care, and education; and
- expanding the liquidity of firms.

The package includes a hard promise to pursue budget consolidation measures starting in 2011 in order to compensate for the extra spending in 2009-2010. Under 'normal' circumstances, a projected budget deficit (according to the EMU definition) of 2% or more triggers budget consolidation rules. The public debt is forecast to increase by € 130 billion within a few years: € 80 billion in aid to the financial sector [11] and € 50 billion because of the increase in the deficit resulting from the automatic stabilizers and stimulus measures (Prime Minister's Office 2009, p. 12). The rescue plan thus envisions a speedy return to budget discipline as soon as economic circumstances permit.

Finally, the package includes measures aimed at pursuing the long-term goals of environmental sustainability, the promotion of innovation and the knowledge economy, and urban renewal. In addition, the package includes measures aimed at improving the long-term sustainability of collective social welfare arrangements. This is to be achieved by cost-containment in the health care sector, increasing the state pension retirement age to 67, and limiting the tax deductibility of mortgage interest for houses worth more than € 1 million.

---

10 The major parties agree that reducing the public debt is a priority, so they have introduced a budgeting rule that requires additional spending to be offset by reduced spending elsewhere when the projected budget deficit is 2% of GDP or higher.

11 One half of this amount consists of loans and the other half represents ownership in financial institutions.

The Crisis and the Dutch Economy

The Netherlands is often viewed as a model for successful economic and social reform. After the difficult decades of the 1970s and 1980s (skyrocketing unemployment, increasing budget deficits, etc.) Governments since the 1990s have adopted an impressive array of reforms aimed at making the welfare state more efficient, increasing employment, and reducing budget deficits and accumulated public debt. By the mid-1990s, the Netherlands could claim to have produced an 'employment miracle' (Visser & Hemerijck 1997). As recently as 2008 the OECD proclaimed the Dutch economy to be 'in good shape' (OECD 2009). All of the major parties agree on the goal of reducing the public debt and building budget surpluses that can offset the projected costs of ageing. When the baby boom generations retire starting in 2020, health care and pension costs are forecast to rise substantially.

Before the crisis hit, the Dutch economy was for many observers the envy of Europe. Dutch policy-makers had found a way to reverse the trend of 'welfare without work' (see Visser & Hemerijck 2007). In 2007 and 2008, economic growth was 3.5% and 2.0% respectively, and the budget showed a surplus of 0.3% in 2007 and 1.0% in 2008. In autumn 2008, the main economic institutes were forecasting respectable growth for 2009, but as the crisis deepened, the forecasts turned increasingly alarming. According to the latest Government statistics, the economy will shrink by 3.5 percentage points in 2009. Unemployment is forecasted to more than double, to 9% of the labour force in 2010. Government finances are showing similarly dismal numbers: the 1% surplus achieved in 2008 will be a 5.5% deficit by 2010, and the public debt will increase from 42% to 58% of GDP in one year (CPB 2009, p. 6).

Given that the recovery of the Dutch economy depends on international developments, the logic behind the crisis package is to maintain households' and firms' consumption in the short term and to use the crisis as an opportunity to step up efforts to promote the long-term sustainability of public finances in the long term. The latter goal is consistent with the central concerns of the main political parties, especially the Christian Democrats (CDA). A central theme in the addendum to the coalition agreement is intergenerational fairness: Younger generations should not be saddled with high levels of public debt caused by older generations.

Another key aspect of the stimulus package is the maintenance of social cohesion, expressed most clearly in the decision to suspend budget consolidation rules when the budget deficit exceeds 2% of GDP. Most of the extra money will finance increased unemployment insurance payments as well as measures to counter youth unemployment (training, apprenticeships, and other policies). The emphasis on social cohesion is clearly in line with the political priorities of the main political parties as well as the social partners. The contours of consociational politics and the consensual support for comprehensive social policies militate against policies that reduce the social safety net.

Negotiating the Stimulus Package

In the Netherlands, political power is centralized, but power-sharing is institutionalized in several practices: multiparty majority Governments and extensive consultation norms. A good example of this consultation are the Autumn and Spring negotiations on social and economic policy between the unions, employers and the Government in the Labour Foundation (STAR) These negotiations usually form the basis for Government legislation. Although there has been some decline in corporatist practices, consociationalism continues to characterize political decision-making. After a period of corporatist decline in the 1970s, the 1980s saw the re-emergence of Dutch consociationalism with the 1982 Wassenaar Accord. Unions promised wage restraint in return for increased emphasis on boosting employment. The Wassenaar Accord facilitated a period of sustained economic growth and welfare state reform that Visser and Hemerijck (1997) call the 'Dutch Miracle' (see also Hemerijck & van Kersbergen 1997; Cox 2001). It is fair to say that the spirit of Wassenaar continues to guide policy-making, even if negotiations are not always smooth.

Because of the specific workings of Dutch parliamentary democracy, the stimulus package required the three governing parties to re-negotiate their coalition agreement from February 2007 (negotiated following the parliamentary election on 22 November 2006). The three-party Government was led by Prime Minister Jan-Peter Balkenende (CDA). Labour Party leader Wouter Bos was Minister of Finance, and Christian Union leader André Rouvoet was Minister of Youth and Family.[12]

The negotiations resulting in the stimulus package were very difficult. Dutch parliamentary democracy is based on detailed compromises, such as the coalition agreements negotiated after national elections. Majority coalition Governments are the norm in the Netherlands, and the process of coalition formation is relatively long. It usually takes several months for the coalition parties to work out the details of their governing accord and to form a Government. According to Andeweg and Irwin (2002), Dutch coalition agreements are among the most detailed and lengthy for countries that usually have coalition Governments. Negotiating the stimulus package required revisiting the painstakingly agreed coalition agreement and hammering out amendments to it.

As soon as the coalition parties concluded their agreement, they met with the unions and the employers in the Labour Foundation (*Stichting van de Arbeid*, STAR) to seek their support for the deal, as well as commitments concern-

12 The three parties controlled 80 of the 150 seats in the Second Chamber (CDA = 41 seats, PvdA = 33, and CU = 6).

ing wage moderation. The negotiations were based on three relationships: solidarity between those in employment and those out of employment; solidarity between the collective and market sector; and solidarity between the generations. A key example of these goals is that financial resources are to be used for re-training and job security before they are used on income support. The cabinet called on the social partners to seek wage moderation in order to promote employment and secure competitiveness. The cabinet's contribution was the stimulus package, especially efforts to deal with rising unemployment. The cabinet called on the social partners to do their part by concluding moderate wage agreements so that Dutch firms could profit immediately when the world economy begins its recovery (STAR 2009).

As noted, the key line of conflict between the social partners (mainly the unions) and the Government concerns the proposal to increase the retirement age for the state pension from 65 to 67 years.[13] The FNV in particular has led the opposition to this measure, forcing the Government to delay the decision while the Social Economic Council investigates alternatives. The other union federation, the CNV (Christian Trade Union Federation) is more willing to accept the proposal, but its smaller membership means it wields much less weight in negotiations with the Government. The section below on pensions will discuss the reform of the state pension in more detail.

Before the Crisis: the 'Dutch Miracle', Welfare State Reform, and the Challenge of Pension Reform

By now the outlines of the 'Dutch miracle' are well-known. During the past two decades, the Netherlands has recovered from 'the Dutch disease' by increasing employment and implementing major reforms of the welfare state. The Dutch story has been told well by others (Visser & Hemerijck 1997; Green-Petersen 2001; Hemerijck & van Kersbergen 1997; Cox 2001) so this section will emphasize the aspects of welfare state reform that are relevant for the current crisis. The 'Dutch miracle' is often attributed to the revival of social partnership beginning with the Wassenaar accord on wage restraint in 1982. Reforming the social insurance schemes, especially pensions, has been more conflictous, with the Government often insisting on reforms that the unions (and employers) bitterly opposed. The central element of these reforms has been to increase activation and cut costs. To put it another way, the Netherlands used to be everyone's favourite example of a 'passive' welfare state in which labour-shedding was often the preferred approach to economic recession. After two decades of far-reaching reforms, the Netherlands is now held up as a model of 'active' welfare policy.

13 The proposal stipulates that workers with physically demanding jobs should be subject to less stringent rules.

Despite these reform successes, the Dutch have not been able to fundamentally reform the state pension, and it is not because they have not tried. This section discusses the challenges of population ageing and pension reform as they relate to the Dutch response to the current economic crisis.

As noted, the most contentious aspect of the crisis package is the proposal to raise the retirement age for the state pension, so it is worth discussing the specifics of this programme and why it is so difficult to change. I begin with the basic structure of the state pension and its relationship to the Dutch welfare state as a whole. The Dutch welfare regime is a mix of universalism and Bismarckian programme structure, and the pension system is the classic example of this: universal, flat-rate public pensions (the AOW) provide relatively generous benefits to the aged population, whereas (nearly universal) pre-funded earnings-related pensions are organized by the social partners as part of collective wage agreements. The AOW is intended as a basic level of retirement provision sufficient to keep pensioners out of poverty, while occupational pensions top up the AOW so that the combined AOW-occupational pension benefit mirrors previous earnings from employment.[14]

Today, the AOW (*Algemene ouderdomswet*) pension pays a fairly generous benefit to all residents over 65 who have lived in the Netherlands for 50 years between the ages of 15 and 65.[15] In comparative terms, AOW benefits are generous and in most cases sufficient for preventing old-age poverty (see appendix 1). In January 2007, the pension benefit for a single person was 70% of the net minimum wage, or (gross) € 1,038.54 per month including vacation supplements. This is about 55% of average wages. For married pensioners the net pension is 50% of the net minimum wage, or (gross) € 712.19 including vacation payment for each spouse. The pension amount is indexed to 'net minimum wages'.[16] In 2007, AOW expenditures totalled about 5% of GDP.

Wage-earner contributions levied as part of the first two income tax brackets finance the AOW (17.9% of income in 2008 up to a ceiling of € 31,122).[17] AOW is constructed as a pay-as-you-go system (PAYG), and until recently (see below) financing was designed to be self-regulating in that the level of pension contribution is set every year so that revenues cover expenditures. Since the late 1990s there is an upper limit on contributions (18.25%) and financing shortfalls are financed from general revenues. The recently established AOW Reserve Fund will help to finance benefits starting in 2020 out of its forecast € 126 billion reserves. Reserves are financed by annual Government deposits.

14 Until the 1980s, Dutch welfare institutions were based on the breadwinner principle. Most benefit programmes are not based on individual entitlement. See Anderson (2007).

15 2% is deducted for every year of missing residence.

16 Parliament sets the level of the net minimum wage twice per year.

17 See notes on taxation at the end of this article.

The AOW serves both as a basic minimum during retirement and as the floor above which supplementary pensions are paid. Occupational pensions negotiated as parts of collective wage agreements currently cover about 90% of wage earners. At the end of 2006 there were 784 pension schemes: 669 company pension schemes, 81 compulsory sectorial pension schemes, 22 non-compulsory pension schemes and 12 professional pension schemes.[18] Until recently, the typical occupational benefit was 70% of the final wage, including the AOW. Occupational pensions are fully funded (for funds legally classified as pension funds and not life insurance schemes) and in late 2005 had a combined coverage ratio of 134%. This means that the nearly € 500 billion in 'technical provisions' or pension liabilities were backed up by € 620 billion in financial assets.[19] The professional pension funds are small in comparison, with about 3% of total assets in the second pillar, or about € 18 billion. In 2005 pension schemes paid nearly € 18 billion in benefits; € 11.5 billion for old-age pensions, € 3.6 billion for survivor pensions; and the rest for early retirement and other types of benefits (all data from www.dnb.nl). This is about 3.5% of GDP (2005). As I discuss below, this rosy picture of funded occupational pensions is deceptive. By 2009, most pension funds had lost 20% of more of their value, prompting widespread concern about the ability of the system to deliver on its promises.

In 2005, the AOW made up slightly more than one half of retirement income for individuals, with supplementary pensions accounting for 40% (figure 1). The aggregate size of the first and second pillar are approximately equal in terms of the value of benefit pay-outs, but as the accumulated pension rights in the second pillar grow, this proportion will change in favour of the second pillar (table 2; figure 1).

Figure 1: Retirement income by source 2001-2005

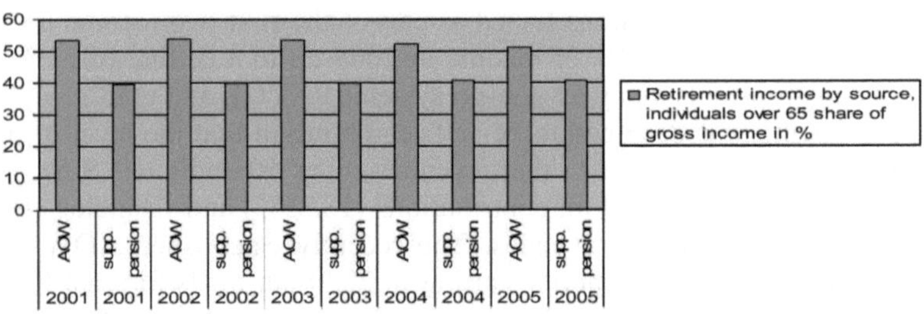

Source: CBS 2008.

18 For professions such as doctors, dentists, accountants etc.

19 About one third of pension fund assets are held in company pension funds and two thirds in sectoral pension funds.

Table 2: Pension benefits as per cent of GDP

	2001	*2020*	*2040*	*2060*
AOW	4.7	6.8	9.0	8.3
supplementary pensions	4.1	7.3	12.9	13.4

Source: Westerhout et al. 2004, p. 31.

Figure 2: Size of pension pillars in the Netherlands

Benefits per annum (€ billion)

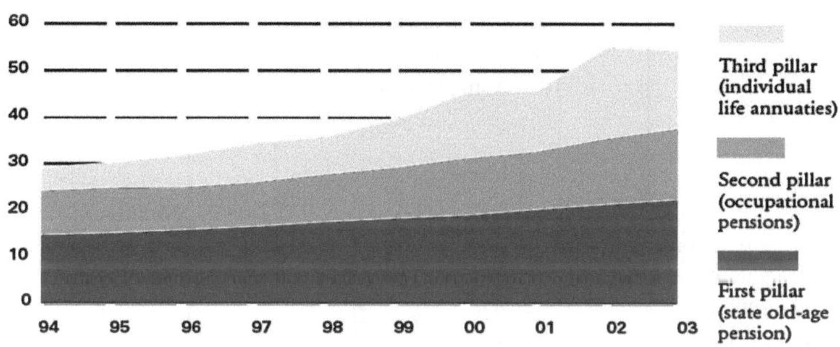

Source: Statistics Netherlands, DNB.

Table 3: Second pillar pension assets 2005 and 2006 (billions of €)

	2005	*2006*	*pension funds*	*group insurance*	*book reserves*
Austria	21.92	23.32	12.56	1.30	9.46
Belgium	45.80	47.17	14.21	32.96	
Denmark	149.60	165.70	59.70	106.00	
Finland	9.91	10.33	5.53	4.80	
France	140.00	150.00			
Germany	401.50	413.55	93.32	46.76	273.47
Hungary	2.60	2.70	2.70		
Ireland	77.83	87.70	78.93	8.77	
Italy	50.05	51.48	43.29	3.64	4.55
Netherlands	722.38	780.00	690.00	90.00	
Portugal	7.78	8.69	8.69		
Spain	95.14	98.34	55.80	31.02	11.50
Sweden	155.80	160.47	12.46	133.08	14.94
U.K.	1496.00	1557.00	1423.00	134.00	
EU TOTAL	3376.32	3551.32	2500.19	592.33	313.90
Iceland	1.42	1.62	1.62		
Norway	93.19	98.00	23.00	75.00	
Switzerland	533.73	549.74	355.85	193.89	
Europe Total	4004.65	4200.68	2880.66	861.22	313.90

Source: European Foundation for Retirement Provision 2008.

Figure 3 below summarizes the main features of the Dutch multi-pillar pension system.

Figure 3: The Dutch pension system

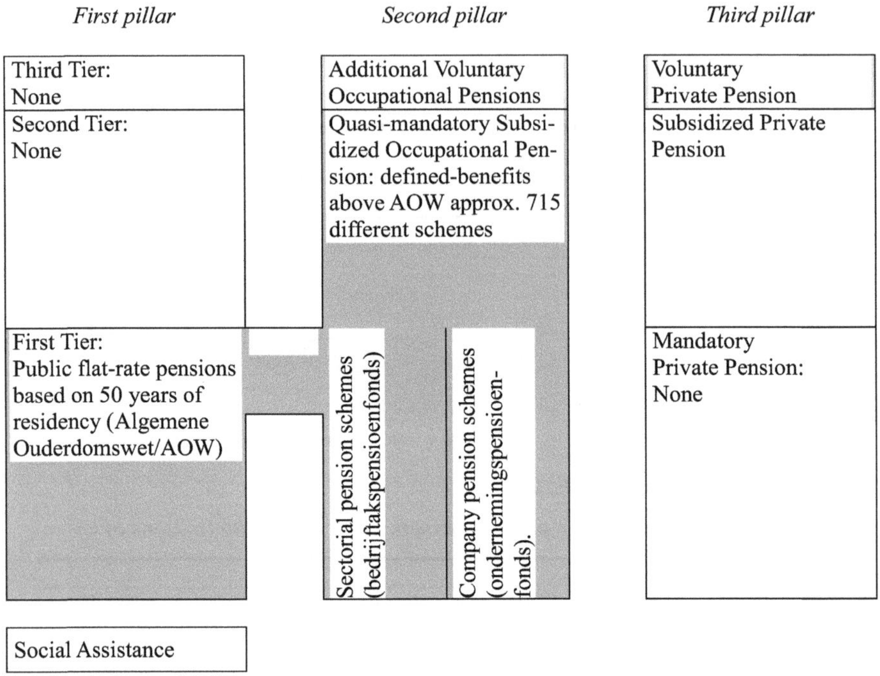

Source: Anderson 2007.

Pensions Reforms: The State Pension

AOW costs and the premiums that finance them have increased steadily since 1957. The contribution rate has increased from 6.75% of income (up to a ceiling) in 1957 to 17.9% in 2001. Since the 1980s, a series of Government commissions has been charged with analysing the financing of the AOW and proposing policy changes. In 1986 the 'Drees Commission' concluded that the current system was financially sustainable if appropriate measures were taken and predicted increases in premiums to 15-17.5% of qualifying income by 2030 (Commissiee Financiering Oudedagsvoorziening 1987). The Drees Commission report was the first step in a long debate about how to deal with the demographic and financial challenges faced by the AOW. In the 1980s, growing AOW costs prompted ad hoc measures even if politicians could not agree on more comprehensive reform. In the context of central Government budget constraints, Governments began to suspend the indexation of the AOW to wage increases. Nominal benefits stayed the same, but lost some of their real value and their value in relation to wage growth. What began in 1980 as an ad hoc measure to control costs and to prevent rapidly rising wages from causing substantial social insurance benefit increases gradually turned into a more or less permanent feature of the annual budget negotiations.

The 1990s saw another round of expert reports about the future financial sustainability of the AOW system, as well as the adoption of several important changes. In 1991 there were 18.7 persons over the age of 65 for every 100 persons between the ages 15 and 64. In 2035 the number of persons over 65 (per 100 of working age) was forecast to rise to between 32.6 and 42.9% (WRR 1992, p. 25). The by now common practice of freezing AOW pension benefits had substantial repercussions on national politics, and the Christian Democrats' (CDA) promise to continue the practice led to its worst election defeat ever in 1994.

In 1989 the Centre-Left Government made AOW indexation conditional on moderate wage increases and increased labour market participation. This informal rule was later transformed into legislation with the Law on Conditional Indexation in 1992 (WKA). The WKA stipulates that if there are more than 82 inactive for every 100 active, there will be no indexation. Indexing was suspended in 1993, 1994, and 1995 (Alber 1998, p. 28; Visser & Hemerijck 1997).

The cancellation of indexing also had repercussions for occupational pensions. Since occupational pensions are linked to AOW benefits, the pension schemes have to compensate for the decline in the AOW. This was generally not a problem for the pension funds since the 1980s were advantageous: the real rate of return was higher than real wage increases and the growing number of participants meant that pension funds had extra cash that could be used to improve benefits and make up for lower AOW benefits. However, the pension funds and their spokespeople began to join the elderly in calling for a return to full AOW indexing.

The 'Purple Coalition' (Labour, Social Liberals, and Liberals) in power from 1994-2002, failed to introduce fundamental cost-saving measures in the AOW, largely because of the electoral risks associated with such a strategy. Instead, the Government settled on improving the financing of the AOW by introducing a special AOW Savings Fund. The Reserve Fund would be invested in Government bonds, and would start to help finance AOW pensions in 2020. Indeed, the number of AOW pensioners was projected to double by 2035, increasing from 13% of the population in 1995 to 24% in 2045. The state contribution was calculated at NLG 350 million in 1997 and a one-time deposit of NLG 2.1 billion. In 2007 there was € 4.2 billion in the AOW Spaarfonds.

To summarize, Dutch policy-makers have struggled for three decades to improve the financial sustainability of the basic pension, without much success. Reform of the AOW has been a controversial issue in nearly every election campaign since the early 1980s, and the only substantial change that Governments could muster support for was the introduction of the AOW Savings Fund. As the number of AOW beneficiaries increases, however, the cost of the AOW will start to strain public finances. Unless policy-makers find a way out of this financing dilemma, a return to the benefit freezes of the 1980s and 1990s seems inevitable.

Occupational Pensions

As noted, occupational pensions are negotiated as part of collective agreements, so legislation only provides the legal framework governing access to schemes, benefit accrual, and rules concerning the investment of assets. If the Government wants to influence occupational pension policy, the typical route is to avoid legislation and to try to negotiate directly with the social partners in order to get them to move policy in a particular direction. For more far-reaching reforms, the Government may try to change the regulatory framework.

The development of occupational pensions since the early 1990s has been marked by tri-partite attempts to adjust supplementary pensions to changing demographic and labour market trends. Corporatist bargaining 'in the shadow of hierarchy' (van Riel et al. 2003) has marked this process. Government-initiated efforts to improve the coverage and portability of occupational pensions are a good example. The Government took the initiative in 1987 by asking the SER to produce an evaluation and recommendations. The SER issued its advisory report in 1990 (SER 1990); the cabinet responded with a green paper (TK 22 167) on supplementary pensions in 1991, outlining its view of how the supplementary pension scheme should develop in the following decades. Although the cabinet confirmed the central role and responsibility of the social partners in the area of supplementary pensions, the cabinet expressed its preference for a switch from final salary benefit formulae to average salary formulae, both for reasons of cost containment and in order to accommodate atypical employment biographies.[20] Negotiations with the social partners began in 1991. The social partners agreed on most issues, except the switch to average earnings schemes. This line of conflict would turn out to be the main source of conflict between the Government and social partners, and it would not be settled until the stock market downturn in 2001/2002 (see below). In 1994 Parliament passed legislation amending the regulatory framework (rules on the mandatory inclusion of part-time workers and the transfer of pension rights; TK 23 123).

In 1997 the Social and Economic Council (SER) facilitated the negotiation of a 'Pension Covenant' between the social partners and the Government. The Government and social partners were particularly concerned about controlling

20 In 1987 72% of participants were in final salary schemes.

pension costs because of their share in total labour costs; increasing the coverage of supplementary pensions; and modernizing benefit rules in order to increase flexibility and individual choice (Stichting van de Arbeid 1997). In particular, the social partners agreed to reduce reliance on final pay benefit schemes and to expand coverage of part time and flexible workers.

The Financial Crisis and Occupational Pensions

The 2000-2002 stock market downturn prompted substantial cuts in occupational pension benefits, sharp premium increases, and led to a tense renegotiation about the regulations governing the coverage rate of occupational pensions. Since the early 1990s, most Dutch pension funds had been investing significantly in equities (30-40% of assets), so when stock prices fell, the pension funds sustained heavy losses. The reserves of many pension funds fell below the required 105% coverage rate for the first time in 2002. The drastic deterioration of the financial position of many funds prompted the pensions' regulator, PVK, to introduce tougher rules governing pension fund solvency. For most funds, restoring solvency meant increasing premiums, suspending pension indexation, or both.

In 2001, pension funds lost an average of -2.8% after averaging gains of 10% per year for a decade. In 2002 in the wake of substantial stock market losses, the social partners and pension funds joined to pressure Government to relax rules about the coverage ratio (the ratio between assets and liabilities). The average coverage ratio was 118% at the end of 2001, down from 139% in 1999 (table 4).

Table 4: Average coverage ratios for occupational pension funds 1996-2004 (%)

1996	*1997*	*1998*	*1999*	*2000*	*2001*	*2002*	*2003*
	126	133	139	132	118	101	104

Source: DNB.

Two factors exacerbated the effects of the stock market downturn. First, the method for calculating pension fund liabilities (until 2002) yielded optimistic estimates of the coverage ratio. In the 1990s, pension funds were probably also underfunded, but the method for calculating liabilities was based on a discount rate (4%) that underestimated liabilities. In the context of good investment returns, this meant that funds could lower premiums or even cancel them altogether, and the social partners could use the extra capital to finance benefit improvements. In other words, pension funds underestimated their liabilities at a time when stock markets were booming. This created the illusion of overfunding. A CPB report estimated that the underfunding rate was about 30% in the early 2000s (Westerhout et al. 2004, p. 14). When interest rates began to fall in the late 1990s, the 4% discount rate for estimating liabilities was out of line with the market. Since 2002 the discount rate has been replaced by a fair market rate (see below). Moreover, funds had increased their investments in shares to about 50% so when share prices fell, pension funds were much more exposed to investment risks than in the past.

Most schemes adopted a mix of measures to restore solvency: suspended benefit indexation; non-indexation of accrual; contribution increases; and switching to average earnings benefit formulas. There has been a massive shift from final benefit schemes to average salary schemes. Only 10% of active participants are in final salary plans in 2004, down from 50% in 2003 and 66% in 1998. About 75% now participate in average salary schemes and indexation is overwhelmingly conditional on fund solvency (DNB 2005). As Ponds and van Riel (2007, p. 6) document, occupational pension premiums (for all pension funds, not just ABP) have increased by 83% in the period 2000-2005.

To sum up, the stock market downturn of 2001-2002 forced rapid changes in occupational pensions. Pension funds increased premiums drastically, suspended or reduced the indexation of accrued pension rights, and froze or partially indexed pension pay-outs. Most pension funds followed a strategy of spreading the pain across current workers and current retirees, but it is clear that for many groups of current workers, the shift to average salary schemes is a substantial deterioration in pension provision. This adjustment pattern breaks with previous practices. In the past, pension funds adjusted the contribution rate to fluctuations in liabilities, so current pensioners were largely spared from cost-cutting measures. The 2001-2002 stock market down-turn was the first time that pensioners had to share some of the costs of adjustment.

Reforming the Occupational Pensions Regulatory Framework

Even before the 2001-2002 stock market down-turn, revision of the regulatory framework (PSF) had been lingering for several years on the political back burner. The stock market downturn exposed the weakness of the existing regulatory framework and pushed PSF to the top of the political agenda. Policy-makers focused on two issues: updating rules for calculating the coverage ratio and clarifying the "ownership" of both pension fund deficits and surpluses. The PSF gave the PVK considerable latitude to determine the rules for solvency, and the PVK quickly made use of this by issuing tough rules for restoring full funding (see previous section). At the same time, reform of the PSF was considered incomplete, and with the change of Government in 2002, the initiative rested with the centre-right coalition led by the Christian Democrats. What the social partners and pension fund organizations could not get from the pensions regulator (more flexibility for restoring the coverage rate), they now tried to achieve within the reform of the PSF.

The new legislation took effect in 2007 and has three goals: to increase transparency; clarify the roles of the social partners, pension fund/insurance company, and pensioners; and to modernize the rules governing pension fund solvency. Pension funds will be required to inform participants about their pension accrual, and issues like what to do in cases of under or overfunding will be clarified. The law also changes, how the present value of pension liabilities are calculated. Rather than discounting the liabilities at a fixed rate of 4%, funds will use a market rate. If interest rates go up, the present value of liabilities decreases.[21] The proposal also introduces a 'minimum test' and a solvency test in order to get pension funds to increase their buffer funds. The minimum is essentially the coverage rate (the ratio of assets to liabilities plus a minimum capital requirement; 105%) while the solvency test is a complicated buffer arrangement.[22] These two provisions mean that pension funds should aim for a funding level of 125%. If the coverage ratio drops below 125% (the solvency level), pension funds have 15 years to restore balance; if the coverage ratio drops below 105%, pension funds have three years to restore balance.

The 2008/2009 financial crisis provided the first tough test of the new supervisory framework. By the end of October, the average coverage ratio for pension funds had fallen to 109%, prompting most pension funds to announce that they would probably have to suspend or decrease the indexation of pension rights and pension pay-outs. ABP, the largest Dutch pension fund, saw its assets decrease by 9.8% in value between January and September 2008, pulling its coverage rate down from 140% to 118% (Henderson 2008). The pensions' regulator, the Dutch Central Bank, extended the deadline for pension funds to submit both short-term and long-term recovery plans by six months in order to wait for markets to calm and to give pension funds more flexibility in meeting funding requirements (DNB 2008).

By early 2009, it was clear that the pension funds had sustained massive losses, and it would be difficult to maintain the current level of pension pay-outs without contribution increases. 350 of the 650 pension funds had coverage ratios below the legally required 105% level. According to the Central Bank's statistics, pension funds' assets totalled € 697 billion at the end of 2008, a decrease of € 66 billion compared to the previous year. The experience of the largest Dutch pension fund, ABP (for civil servants) is a good example of the difficulties faced by the funds. ABP's coverage rate had plummeted to 89.5% by the end of 2008,

21 The solvency test and minimum funding test are part of the 'Financial Assessment Framework' (*Financiële Toetsingkader*/FTK) that is embedded in the new pension legislation.

22 The solvency test is a way of assessing whether pension funds can withstand financial shocks and remain at 105% coverage after one year of market movements. There should be more than 97.5% probability that a fund can meet all its obligations in one year (using a standard risk model).

well below the required 105% level, in less than one year. As a result, ABP will raise contributions by 1 percentage point in 2009 and 2 additional percentage points in 2010 if necessary. This brings the total pension contribution (shared by employers and employees) to 23.3% of income above the AOW offset.

Given these difficulties, the social partners pressed the Government to extend the deadline for restoring solvency (105% coverage of liabilities) from three to five years. After a fierce lobbying campaign, the Minister of Social Affairs relented, but the damage is done. Many current retirees receiving occupational pensions will see their pension pay-outs frozen or nearly-frozen for several years, and many current workers will see their pension accrual frozen. To sum up, the world financial crisis has caused a crisis in the Dutch occupational pension sector. The Dutch are justifiably proud of their extensive system of funded occupational pensions, but the losses sustained in the current crisis threaten to permanently damage the legitimacy of the system. Moreover, the contribution hikes and pension pay-out freezes required to restore solvency are pro-cyclical in that they exacerbate the effects of the recession. The Minister of Social Affairs has responded to the crisis by granting pension funds more flexibility in restoring solvency, but the damage will be difficult to repair quickly.

The problems facing the state pension are potentially more serious, partly because politics and not markets determine the trajectory of change. As the discussion of attempts to reform the AOW shows, it is exceedingly difficult to change the basic features of the AOW, despite increasing costs. The electoral costs are extremely high. The unions, led by the FNV, vigorously oppose raising the retirement age. It is not surprising, then, that the current Government is trying to use the economic crisis to gain support for AOW reform.

Outlook and Conclusion

It should be clear from the analysis in this article that social integration is a central goal guiding the Dutch Government's response to the economic crisis. Social integration and the promotion of social cohesion are time-honoured features of consociational politics in the Netherlands. The central roles played in the current Government by two socially-oriented parties – the Christian Democrats and Labour Party – increase the emphasis on social integration, even if the two parties differ in terms of what social integration looks like.

A striking feature of the current Dutch approach to social integration – and to fighting the economic crisis – is the emphasis on 'work before welfare'. Reforms of the labour market and welfare state since the 1990s have dramatically increased the activating potential of the welfare state. The current Government's strategy, supported by the social partners, of promoting training, re-training, and mobility clearly demonstrate this policy orientation. The contrast with the 1970s and 1980s could not be greater; during earlier recessions, the Dutch policy response relied heavily on labour-shedding, whereas today the emphasis is clearly on labour retention. Keeping people in paid employment or training is seen as the key to surviving the current crisis and meeting the long-term challenges of population ageing.

To what extent are the current crisis measures sustainable? Indications are that the Netherlands will weather the current crisis, largely because most of the hard work of reforming the welfare state and labour market has already been completed. Most of the Government's policies for fighting the crisis are based on policies already in place or policies already decided but not yet implemented. This means that the crisis package rests on widespread support, not only among the political parties but also among the social partners. This does not mean that the crisis package has been without controversy or criticism. Indeed, there was widespread criticism of the slow pace of decision-making. Moreover, the stimulus package is notable for what it did *not* contain: significant limits on the home mortgage tax deduction and a liberalization of dismissal laws. The CDA is the chief defender of the mortgage interest tax break, while the Labour Party is the chief opponent of relaxing current dismissal law. Despite the severity of the crisis, neither party was willing to budge on these core issues. To be sure, neither policy would have much impact on short-term demand, but given the crisis agreement's emphasis on the medium and long-term sustainability of public finances, it is surprising that both issues quickly disappeared from the bargaining table.

There is one dark spot in this cautiously optimistic picture, and it is the pension system. The occupational pension system is currently experiencing its worst crisis ever, which is not surprising given that these are funded schemes that invested significantly in equities. It will take several years, or perhaps a decade, for many pension schemes to fully recover from their losses, and this will have major repercussions on future collective bargaining rounds and retirement incomes. The Government has shown some flexibility in allowing the pension schemes extra time to restore solvency but has stopped short of promising any sort of bailout.

The fate of the state pension is even more uncertain. The AOW is hugely popular, and the unions intensely oppose raising the retirement age. The Government has already signalled its malleability on the issue by agreeing to give the Social Economic Council six months to come up with an alternative proposal that would produce equivalent savings for the state budget. Barring a serious deterioration of the Dutch economy (beyond what is already forecast), I think that the proposal, at least in its current form, will be shelved. The Government needs the cooperation of the unions for wage moderation and other goals, and the unions are already claiming victory on the issue.

References

Alber, Jens (1998), *Recent developments in continental European welfare states: Do Austria, Germany, and the Netherlands prove to be birds of a feather?* Paper presented at the 14th World Congress of Sociology, Montreal, 29 July.

Anderson, Karen M. (2007), 'The Netherlands: Political Competition in a Proportional System', in Ellen M. Immergut; Karen M. Anderson & Isabelle Schulze (eds.), *The Handbook of Pension Politics in Western Europe*, Oxford: Oxford University Press, pp. 713-757.

Andeweg, Rudy B. & Galen A. Irwin (2002), *Governance and Politics of the Netherlands*. Houndsmills, Basingstoke: Palgrave Macmillan.

Cox, Robert H. (2001), 'The Social Construction of an Imperative: Why Welfare Reformed Happened in Denmark and The Netherlands, but Not in Germany', *World Politics*, vol. 53 (3), pp. 463-498.

Centraal Planbureau/CPB (2009), *CPB Nieuwsbrief*. March/April.

Dutch National Bank/DNB, < www.dnb.nl>.

Hemerijck, Anton & Kees van Kersbergen (1997), 'A miraculous model? Explaining the new politics of the welfare state in the Netherlands', *Acta Politica,* vol. 32 (3), pp. 258-301.

Ministry of Social Affairs (2009a), *Letter to the Second Chamber of Parliament 'Mobilisatie arbeidsmarkt met oog op economische neergang'*. January. Den Haag.

Ministry of Social Affairs (2009b), *Letter to the Second Chamber of Parliament, 'Overzicht maatregelen arbeidsmarkt'*. 25 March. Den Haag.

Ministry of Social Affairs (2009c), *Letter to the Second Chamber of Parliament, 'Werktijdverkorting'*. 6 April. Den Haag.

OECD (2008), *Netherlands. Economic Survey*. Paris.

Prime Minister's Office (2009), *Werken aan toekomst, een aanvullend beleidsakkoord bij 'samen werken, samen leven'*. Addendum to the Coalition Agreement. Den Haag.

Stichting van de Arbeid (2008), *'Samen doen wat mogelijk is'. Tripartiete Verklaring Najaarsoverleg 2008*. 7 October.

Stichting van de Arbeid (2009), *Akkoord Stichting van de Arbeid 25 maart 2009.*

van Riel, Bart; Hemerijck, Anton & Jelle Visser (2003), 'Is there a Dutch way to Pension Reform?', in Gordon L. Clark & Noel Whiteside (eds.), *Pension Security in the 21st Century. Redrawing the Public-Private Debate*. Oxford: Oxford University Press.

Van Waarden, Frans (2002), 'Dutch Consociationalism and Corporatism. A Case of Institutional Persistence', *Acta Politica,* vol. 37, pp. 44-67.

Visser, Jelle (2002), 'The first part-time economy in the world: a model to be followed?', *Journal of European Social Policy*, vol. 12 (1), pp. 23-42.

Visser, Jelle & Anton Hemerijck (1997), *A Dutch miracle: Job growth, welfare reform and corporatism in the Netherlands*. Amsterdam: Amsterdam University Press.

Westerhout, Ed; van de Ven, Martijn; van Ewijk, Casper & Nick Draper (2004), *Naar een schokbestending pensioenstelsel. Verkenning van enkele beleidsopties op pensioengebied.* CPB report no. 67.

APPENDIX 1: Characteristics of Basic Pension Schemes in the Netherlands, Switzerland and Denmark

	Gross benefit per month (2007)	*Pension in relation to average wages*	*Basic pension financing (2007)*	*Residence requirement*	*Extent of funding*
Netherlands (*Algemene ouderdoms-wet*/ AOW)	•single: € 1,010 •couple: € 1,384	31% of average gross wages	•employee contributions 17.9% of earnings be-tween € 13,160 and € 29,543 •Government subsidy if necessary	50 years of residence between age 15 and 65; 2% benefit reduction for each missing year	AOW savings fund € 31 billion (end 2007)
Switzerland *(AHV/AVS)*	CHF 1,105-2,210 (€ 670-1,340) per month in 2007	20-40% of average gross wages	•4.2% employer •4.2% employee •flat rate con-tributions for those not employed •no ceiling •Government subsidy 20%	contribu-tions every year from age 21; proportional reduction for missing years	reserve fund equal to one year of benefit pay-ments
Denmark (*folkepen-sion*)	•basic amount: DKK 4,952 * (€ 664) •supplement: DKK 4,985 ** (€ 670) for singles, DKK 2,328 (€ 312) each for couples	35% of average gross wages	general revenues	40 years of residence between 15 and 65	none

* reduced if non-pension income above DKK 252,400 (€ 33,889).

** reduced if income more than DKK 55,700 (€ 7,478);
no basic pension for those with incomes over DKK 450,400 (€ 60,473).

APPENDIX 2: Taxation Issues

The first two income tax brackets consist of both social contributions ('premies') and tax. At age 65 the taxpayer is no longer liable for the AOW contribution (17.9%) but continues to pay contributions to two other social programmes (Anw/Algemene nabestaandenwet and AWBZ/Algemene Wet Bijzondere Ziektekosten). The income tax rate for taxable income less than € 31,122 is thus 17.9 percentage points lower.

Tax rates for under and over 65s

Taxable income in box 1			
more than	not more than	tax rate for those under 65	tax rate for those over 65
€ 0	€ 17,319	33.65%	15.75%
€ 17,319	€ 31,122	41.40%	23.50%

The tax rate for income over € 31.122 is the same for all age groups.

Example: the gross annual income for a single AOW pensioner with no occupational pension income is: € 12,456.
Pensioners can deduct € 1,015 per year for health insurance costs, so the taxable income is:

€ 12,456
- € 1,015
€ 11,456

The tax rate is 15.75% so the tax due is € 11,456 x 0.1575 = € 1,804.

The pensioner is eligible for a general tax credit (*heffingskorting*) of € 957 and a pensioner tax credit of € 380 (for income below € 31,757). Thus the pensioner is eligible for € 1,337 in tax credits (€ 957+€ 380).

This amount is thus deducted from the pensioner's tax bill:
€ 1,804 - € 1,337 = a total tax bill of € 467 per year.

→ the AOW pensioner receives about net € 12,000 per year, and pays about € 90 per month in health insurance, for a 'real' net income of about € 910 per month.

5 Social Policy Stability in Times of Economic Crisis: The Case of Germany

Martin Seeleib-Kaiser

Introduction

The German economy will be one of the economies hardest hit by the global recession in 2009, due to its overreliance on exports. Some politicians and political observers fear 'social unrest' and 'dangers for democracy' (Niejahr 2009). Nonetheless, the Government has stayed rather relaxed about fiscal stimulus measures and has not proposed any major expansion of social policy programmes. To some extent this can be explained by two facts: 1) The unemployment rate has been falling until very recently; and 2) despite cut backs in the early 2000s, Germany still provides relatively generous welfare provisions for the short-term unemployed. As private or occupational pension coverage so far has not been very important in achieving adequate pension income, the decline in equity markets will have only a comparatively small impact on the income of future pensioners. The big question for Germany is not whether the welfare state is sustainable, but whether Germany can sustain its export-led economic model. The latter obviously will have a huge impact on the sustainability of the welfare state.

In part 1 of this article, I will first provide a rough overview of the socio-economic context. In part 2 of the article I discuss major welfare state reforms enacted in the late 1990s and early 2000s, before dealing with the very few changes enacted in social protection as a consequence of the economic crisis in part 3.

The Socio-Economic Context

As indicated in the introduction, observers expect the German economy to be one of the economies hardest hit by the global recession in 2009. Although the German banking sector was not immune to the global crisis, Germany does not have a home-grown sub-prime mortgage market and consumer debt is much lower than in the Anglo-Saxon economies. Moreover, the German economy relies heavily on exports in certain manufacturing sectors, such as machine tools and cars. Historically, the export sector has been the Achilles' heel of the German model; achieving substantial trade surpluses year after year, even after the economic crises of the 1970s and early 1980s. For a short period the economy was more balanced after unification in 1990; but starting in the early 2000s economic growth was once again primarily reliant on achieving substantial export surpluses (see figure 1), as the German export engine had regained international competitiveness through limiting labour unit costs. As the world economy went into recession following the banking crisis in late 2008, German export orders have plunged. It seems very unlikely that the unbalanced German economic model, with its overreliance on trade and comparatively low domestic demand, will change as a result of adaptations driven by domestic economic and political actors in the near future. Thus, the severity and the duration of the recession in Germany will to a large extent depend on the economic development of her trading partners. Moreover, the future of the German model is dependent, on the one hand, on the ability to produce high quality products and sustain international competitiveness in certain manufacturing sectors, and on the other hand on the willingness of the international community to support free trade.

Figure 1: Exports and imports as a percentage of GDP

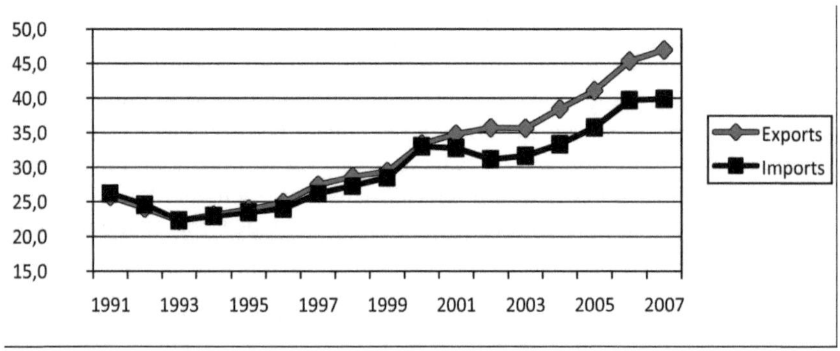

Source: BMAS 2008.

In assessing the current economic situation, we have to remember that for a number of years in the early 2000s German economic growth had been relatively low, hovering below the average of the Euro Area (see figure 2). So far the sharp economic decline witnessed since 2008 has not significantly impacted the labour market, due to various elements associated with the German model of social protection. Firstly, the rigidities of the German labour market, which in the past have often been highlighted as contributing to low employment growth, have protected core workers with standard employment contracts from dismissals. Secondly, German industry seems to make considerable use of short-time work allowances, which provide wage subsidies for companies operating on reduced hours (this element will be discussed in greater detail below). Thirdly, in many companies unions and works councils have agreed to wage reductions or to waive parts of the negotiated wage increases in return to secure employment (Niejahr 2009; Hamann & Jungbluth 2009).

Figure 2: Real GDP growth rate

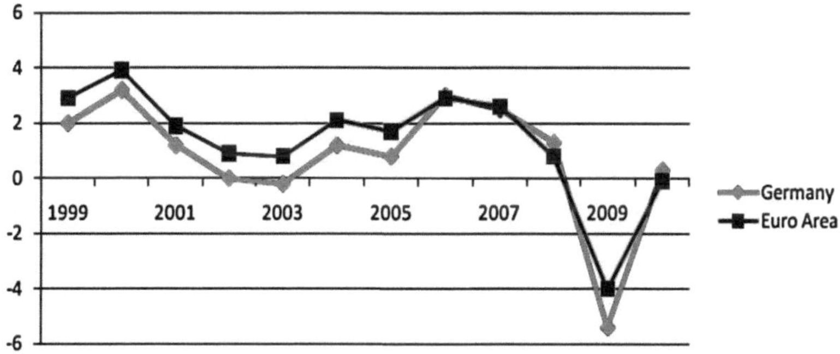

Source: Eurostat 2009, 2010.

When assessing employment and unemployment data over the last couple of years, it has to be emphasized strongly that at the beginning of the current recession, the German labour market had been quite buoyant. The employment ratio was almost five percentage points higher than in 1995, and the unemployment rate had declined to its lowest level in more than a decade (see figures 3 and 4).

Figure 3: Employment/population ratio (15-64 years)

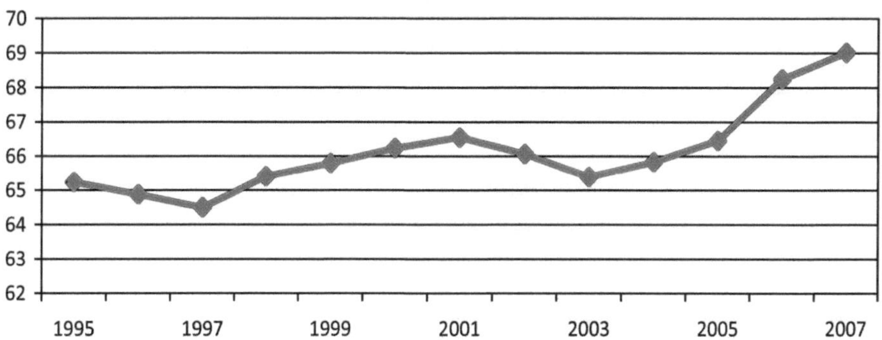

Source: OECD.

With regard to public finances the situation had also significantly improved since 2003. Whereas Germany continuously did not meet the criteria of the EU stability pact from 2002-2005, she has made significant progress since. In 2008, Germany almost achieved a balanced budget (see figure 5). Social expenditure as a percentage of GDP in 2007 reached its lowest level since 1991, largely as a result of increased economic growth and employment (see figure 6).

Figure 4: Unemployment rate

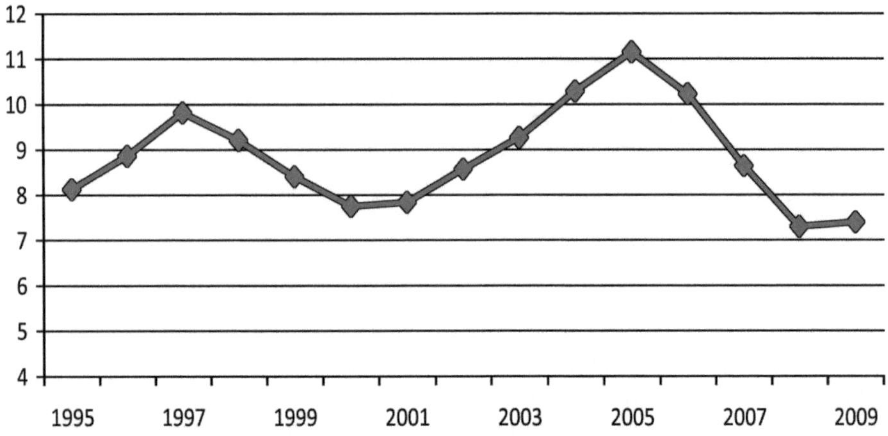

Source: OECD 2009, first quarter.

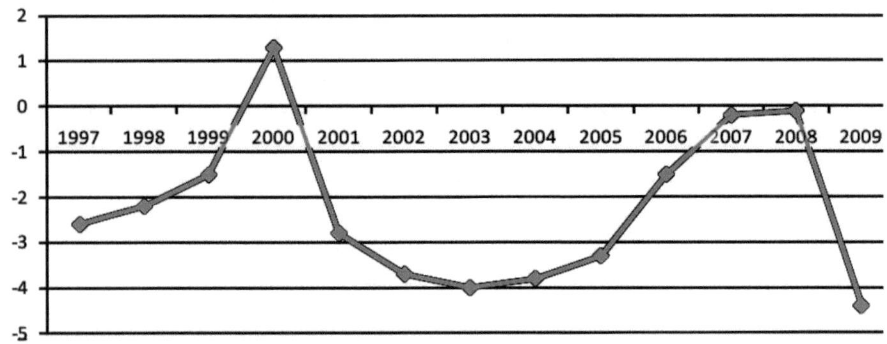

Source: Eurostat 2009, Projections; The Economist.

Figure 6: Social expenditure as percentage of GDP

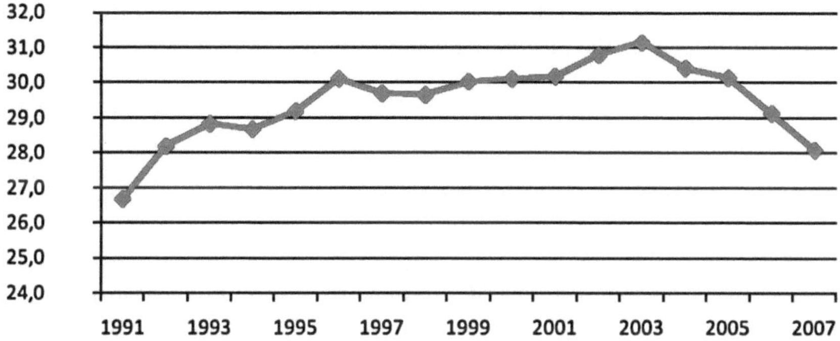

Source: BMAS 2008.

To summarize: Starting 2005/06 Germany began to make significant progress in achieving economic growth as well as reducing its unemployment rate and high budget deficit. Looking back at the situation in the first half of this decade, the current economic and fiscal situation of Germany does not seem that bleak, especially with regard to unemployment.

Welfare State Arrangements

In order to understand the impact of the current economic crisis on social protection it seems necessary to briefly sketch the normative underpinnings of the German welfare state as well as to analyse the reforms of the late 1990s and early 2000s.

Historical and Institutional Foundations

The historical development of the German welfare state during the 'golden age' of welfare capitalism led, on the one hand, to a wage earner-centred social policy (applying de facto largely only to male breadwinners) and on the other hand, to a sphere of unpaid welfare work provided by married women. The leitmotiv of post-war social policy expansion was to secure the 'achieved living standard' of the male breadwinner and his family during old age, disability, sickness, and unemployment. Accordingly, the pension reform of 1957 raised the old-age benefits on average by about 65% and indexed them to future increases in gross wages. In this way, retirees would benefit from any future increases in living standards which unions had subsequently achieved through collective bargaining. In short, pensions were locked to the development of gross wages (Schmähl 1999). The central aim of the 1957 pension law was – in the words of Josef Schüttler, the CDU politician and responsible committee correspondent to the

German Parliament – "to achieve a clear distinction between insurance and social assistance. … [The old-age insurance benefit] was to be transformed from a minimal allowance of the past into a benefit for the future which could maintain the living standard." (Bundestag, Stenogr. Prot. 2/184, p. 10181) By the mid-1970s, the net-income replacement ratio reached 70 per cent for a standard pensioner (*Eckrentner*), i.e. a person with a prior average income and a work history of 45 years (Schmähl 1999, p. 405). The decreasing proportion of senior citizens dependent on social assistance highlighted the overall success of the reformed pension insurance system (Leisering & Leibfried 1999).

If we examine the institutional arrangements for insuring against the risk of unemployment, we uncover a similar design: The unemployment insurance system was normatively bound to insure the worker's standard of living should he lose his job. This normative view dominated the political debates as well as the various policy measures up until the mid-1970s. In the late 1960s, for example, even members of the Liberal Party (FDP) in Parliament supported substantial increases in the level of unemployment benefits. Once again, the unemployment benefit was intended to replace wage income and was supposed to be clearly separate from social assistance benefits (Bundestag, Stenogr. Prot. 5/95, pp. 4335 ff). By the mid-1970s, the replacement income for those individuals receiving the regular unemployment insurance benefit reached 68% of prior net earnings. This level was to ensure a relatively stable income for workers during spells of unemployment. 'Suitable work' was defined in such a way that an unemployed worker did not have to accept a job which either paid less or was in a different occupational field to his previous job (Clasen 1994, p. 101).

In the 'golden era' of post-World War II capitalism, social policy experts were convinced that an improved social insurance system would eventually cover the standard social risks of workers to the point whereby social assistance in terms of providing a minimum level of subsistence would ultimately become residual. Although the reformed social assistance law of 1961 entitled individuals to a minimum cash benefit, it was not designed to cover general risks, but to primarily focus on helping persons with individual problems living on the fringes of society (Giese 1986).

Since it was the responsibility of the 'non-working' mother to provide the necessary social services for family members,[1] – and thereby forgoing paid employment – the male breadwinner's wage had to be high enough, in principle, to support the whole family above the subsistence level (family wage). If a mother had young children, employment outside the family or outside the family business was only considered legitimate if the woman was 'forced' to work out of economic necessity. Based on these normative principles, the state largely refrained from providing social services; moreover, state childcare facilities were

---

1 For an overview of the family ideology and family policies until the 1970s see Neidhardt 1978.

considered to be harmful to the personal development of children, especially pre-school children. They were even viewed as an attempt to rob parents of their children while forcing women into wage labour (Moeller 1993, pp. 179 f). Because women with small children were expected to fulfil their role as mothers, it seemed impossible to significantly expand the female labour force participation in the 1960s, even though Germany's booming economy was crying out for workers. In the early 1970s less than one per cent of all children below the age of three and about 30% of children between the ages of three and six had access to publicly financed childcare (Kolbe 2002).

To summarize: During the 'golden era', social policy intervention by the state was characterized mainly by statutory insurance schemes, which aimed to allow the worker and his family to enjoy their former standard of living during the worker's retirement and during spells of unemployment and sickness. The insurance schemes also aimed to grant derived social benefits to the worker's family members. The decommodifying potential of the social insurance system depended largely on the status of the individual worker in the employment system and on his achievements. The family played an important role as the primary provider of social services, which meant that the role of married women was largely limited to that of housewife and mother, the party responsible for providing unpaid welfare work and for bearing and rearing children. Hence, the 'public' sphere of the social insurance system was heavily dependent on the hidden 'private' sphere of unpaid housework and childrearing duties. The extent of defamilialization was very low. Finally, the German welfare state was based on the principles of social integration and cohesion, not on redistribution between classes, or the alleviation of poverty (Goodin, Headey, Muffels & Dirven 1999).

Reforming the Welfare State

Over the years the German welfare state has undergone a major transformation. The sum of the numerous policy changes in the unemployment and the old-age insurance programmes have amounted to a withdrawal from the principle of guaranteeing the achieved living standard. At the same time, the Government has significantly expanded family policies.

Withdrawing from the Publicly Guaranteed Achieved Living Standard

Pension Reforms

For most of the period, changes in the statutory pension programme have been incremental and without these changes the net replacement rate for a standard pensioner would have risen from about 70 to about 90% (Alber 2001). Nevertheless, substantial changes have been implemented since the late 1990s. The Pension Reform Act of 1999, enacted in 1997, included significant benefit reductions for future retirees. Although, the implementation of this law was suspended after the Red-Green coalition Government gained power in 1998, a major reform was enacted in 2001. This reform included a partial privatization of the public pay-as-you-go system combined with a significant reduction in the replacement rate, which was scheduled to decline from 70 to 64% by 2030. The introduction of an additional sustainability factor in 2003, will lead to further substantial benefit reductions. According to the pension expert and former Government adviser Winfried Schmähl the net replacement ratio for a standard pensioner will decline to about 54% by 2030, forcing once again an increasing number of pensioners to have to rely on means-tested old-age benefits (Schmähl 2007).

In order to compensate for these severe reductions in the statutory pension programme, the state introduced tax-financed subsidies for workers who voluntarily enrol in certified private or occupational pension programmes. Only those workers who enrol in these programmes will be able to enjoy a retirement income at about 70% of previous net wage based on certain Government assumptions with regards to contributions, demographic development and the rate of return on private investments (ibid.). Within the last years, this change in policy, especially the entitlement to convert wage into occupational pension entitlements via salary sacrifice schemes, has triggered a significant overall increase in occupational pension coverage. Although coverage of workers in all sectors has increased, the level of coverage varies greatly according to sector with especially high levels of coverage in financial services, medium to high levels of coverage in manufacturing and low coverage in real estate, renting and business services as well as hospitality services (see table 1).

Table 1: Percentage of employees in the German private sector covered by occupational pension plans by industry (2001-2007; in per cent)

Industry	*2001*	*2002*	*2003*	*2004*	*2005*	*2006*	*2007*
Manufacturing							
Production/Intermediate Goods	43	49	55	56	73	73	74
Consumer Durables	58	57	59	60	62	63	62
Food, Alcohol & Tobacco Goods	30	45	57	58	62	64	61
Consumer Goods	24	29	39	40	53	53	53
Mining, Quarrying & Energy Serv.	63	66	72	73	71	71	73
Financial Intermediation	76	76	83	84	89	89	90
Real Estate, Renting & Business Services	16	19	25	25	28	29	29
Hospitality and Food Services	10	20	25	25	26	26	28
Wholesale/Retail & Repair	27	33	39	40	47	46	46
Total Private Sector Coverage	38	42	45	46	52	52	52

Source: TNS Infratest Sozialforschung 2008, p. 42.

If we place the potential outcomes of the various reforms into an international comparative perspective, it becomes obvious that for the 'average worker' the German old-age income security system of the future is very likely to become less generous than for her/his British or American colleague with an additional occupational pension (see table 2).

Unemployment Insurance Reforms

Within the field of unemployment insurance, policy changes since the mid-1970s have not primarily focused on reductions in the wage replacement ratio, but much more importantly included re-definitions of the reference wage, contribution periods, and suitability requirements. In addition to these explicit measures, implicit disentitlement (mainly through a significant increase in long-term unemployment) has led unemployed workers to being increasingly dependent on tax-financed, means-tested benefits instead of on contribution-based benefits designed to guarantee the previously achieved living standard (see figure 7).

Table 2: Prospective pension minima and replacement rates for current workers (2004 baseline)

Country	*Minimum income for pensioners as % of average earnings*	*Gross replacement rate of public system (AW)*	*Net replacement rate of public system (AW)*	*Gross replacement rate of public and voluntary occupational pensions (AW)*
France	24.0	64.7	78.1	N/A
Germany	19.3	39.9	58.0	56.0
U.K.	20.0	30.8	41.1	67.0
United States	22.0	41.2	52.4	81.2

Note: Minimum income provisions are based on means-tested programmes available to pensioners. All replacement rates are based on the assumption of a full career. Gross replacement rates of public and voluntary occupational/private pensions are based on assumed contribution rates of 9% (currently the mean) for occupational pensions in the United Kingdom and the United States. For Germany the assumed contribution rate is 4%, currently the maximum contribution to receive the full tax incentive.

Source: OECD (2007), *Pensions at a Glance*. Paris: OECD.

Furthermore, a number of important policy reforms which have been undertaken since the mid-1990s have significantly reshaped the nature of German unemployment compensation. The Labour Promotion Reform Law of 1997/98 vastly curtailed the ability of those receiving benefits to be selective in their choice of prospective employment opportunities. Whereas in the past an unemployed worker could have rejected job offers which were 'below' his or her former occupational status, under the new law any job that paid up to 20% less than the previous job would be deemed suitable within the first three months of an unemployment spell. From the fourth to the sixth month, any job offer paying up to 30% less would be considered suitable. From the seventh month of receiving benefit, any job with a net wage equal to the unemployment compensation payment is defined as suitable. In addition, some reductions in the maximum duration of unemployment insurance benefit receipt were enacted. In 2004, the German system of unemployment protection experienced its most comprehensive institutional reform with the integration of the unemployment and social assistance schemes into a single flat-rate and means-tested programme for the long-term unemployed and for those ineligible to receive earnings-related benefits due to an insufficient employment history. This reform was complemented by a significant reduction in the regular maximum duration of unemployment benefits to 12 months. Older workers are currently entitled to maximum benefit duration of 24 instead of the previous 32 months.[2] As shown in figure 7, the majority of unemployed workers have been reliant on means-tested benefits since the early 2000s (Bleses & Seeleib-Kaiser 2004; Seeleib-Kaiser & Fleckenstein 2007).

Figure 7: Percentage of registered unemployed receiving unemployment insurance and unemployment assistance benefits 1975-2007

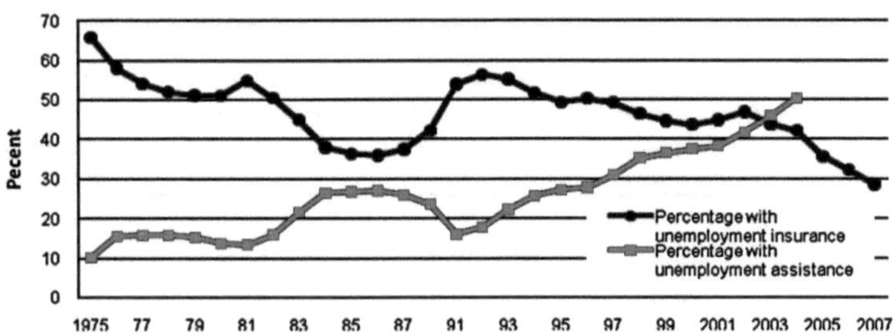

Sources: Author's calculations based on data from BMAS.

A similar shift in policy design characterized the active labour market policy (ALMP). Whereas in the past, (re)training and public employment measures were primarily aimed at status-equivalent re-employment of unemployed workers, now ALMP is increasingly geared towards a much more market-oriented policy dominated by 'activation measures'. These measures include subsidized re-employment in atypical employment relationships and subsidized self-employment (ibid.). Comparatively speaking, active labour market policies in Germany at the beginning of the 21st century have been changing in a way similar to those implemented in other West European welfare states a few years earlier. These developments in active and passive labour market policies fundamen-

2 Initially the maximum duration of benefit receipt for older workers was cut to 18 months, but was once again extended by the Grand Coalition Government in 2007.

tally contradict the key principle of an ideal conservative welfare state, namely preserving the socio-economic status.

Although the impact of these reforms has been overlooked in some quarters of the literature (Hall (2007), their potential significance has been taken into consideration in others. For instance, Soskice has noted that in Germany: "Employees with specific skills reacted with particular concern to the slowdown in growth, the rise in unemployment and the fear of welfare state reforms to unemployment benefits." (Soskice 2006, p. 432) The response of such workers to these changing economic and institutional conditions has been to forgo immediate consumption in favour of increased savings which has, in turn, had a significant cumulative impact on aggregate demand (ibid.). In other words, the policy reforms of the late 1990s and early 2000s have, according to this analysis, further contributed to the overreliance of the German economy on exports.

Expansion of Family Policies

The greater emphasis on market forces and the promotion of self-reliance within the unemployment and pension programmes are one side of the social policy reforms. Largely parallel to these changes new family policies were introduced and existing programmes expanded. Starting in the mid-1980s, family responsibilities were increasingly socialized. Family-oriented benefits have been introduced into the formerly strictly earnings-related pension system and were subsequently expanded. Instead of basing old-age pensions solely on social insurance contributions or on derived benefits for survivors (based on the earned benefits of a male breadwinner) – both core principles of a conservative pension system – benefits are now also dependent on the number of children an individual has raised. Currently, the time devoted to child rearing will be recognized as a fictive contribution to the old-age insurance system for the duration of three years per child – equivalent to 100% of an average contribution. Furthermore, if a parent should choose a part-time position to reconcile employment with the desire to at least partially care for the child personally, the state will contribute to the pension fund to make up for the 'lost' contribution up to a limit of 100% of the average contribution until the child is 10 years old (Bleses & Seeleib-Kaiser 2004). Through the recognition of (a limited) time spent as a caregiver, the state creates individual entitlement rights and reduces the dependence of the predominantly female caregivers on derived social insurance benefits of male breadwinners (Meyer 1998), while the level of derived benefits itself has been substantially curtailed over the years.

To reconcile employment with the desire to care for small children personally, the state enacted an entitlement to unpaid parental leave in 1986. Concomitantly the state introduced and subsequently expanded a flat parental benefit to two years (initially limited to 10 months) after the birth of a child. This benefit gave both fathers and mothers the opportunity to continue to work or opt out of the labour market and commit themselves to child rearing for a limited time period. The employer must guarantee the parent's reemployment in a similar position and with equivalent remuneration following the parental leave.

Declining birth rates, especially among academically educated women, has recently reinforced the perception among the elite of the need to expand family policies. This perceived need has triggered a substantial modification of the parental leave benefit along the lines of Social-democratic approaches in Scandinavia: Starting January 1, 2007, parents are entitled to an earnings-related parental leave benefit of 67% of their previous income (capped at a maximum of € 1,800 per month) for the duration of 12 months (with additional two months if the other partner takes these – in Scandinavia these are often referred to as 'Daddy Months'). This benefit is specifically focused towards the middle to high-income groups, as the parental leave benefit in the past was a flat rate, partially means-tested benefit. Under the new regulations all those parents not previously employed will be entitled to a flat monthly benefit of € 300. The parental leave benefit is financed through general tax revenues (BMFSFJ 2007).

Table 3: Supply of childcare facilities 1975-2006 (number of places as a percentage of age group)

Year	*Age*		
	0 <3 years	*3-6.5 years*	*6-12 years*
1975	<1	66	N/A
1985 [1]	1.6	69.3	3.0
1990	1.8 (54.2)	69.0 (97.7)	3.4 (32.4)
1995 [2]	2.2 (41.3)	73.0 (96.2)	3.5 (22.6)
1998	2.8 (36.3) *7.0*	86.8 (111.8) *89.5*	5.9 (47.7) [3] *12.6*
2002	4.2 (37.0) *8.6*	90.6 (105.1) *92*	6 (67.6) [3] *14.3*
2005/06	9.6 (39.8) *13.7*	N/A	N/A

Notes: [1] 1986; [2] 1994; [3] Ages 6-10. The numbers in brackets are for the territory of the former GDR, and the numbers in italics are for unified Germany. Data over the years are not fully comparable.

Source: Seeleib-Kaiser 2007.

In 1992, the Government introduced the right of every child between the ages of three and six to a place in a childcare facility. However, because of implementation problems at the local level, the entitlement only became effective in 1999. Although 600,000 new childcare places were created for children in this age group during this period, problems in coverage for children at other ages persisted. Beginning in 2002, improving day care facilities for children under the age of three became a priority. By 2004, the federal Government had allocated € 1.5 billion annually. Complementing efforts to improve childcare facilities, the Government furthermore allocated € four billion to support the *Länder* and local authorities to establish all-day schools (Bleses & Seeleib-Kaiser 2004, pp. 82 ff). Finally, based on a compromise between the political parties of the Grand Coalition Government in 2007, the capacity of publicly subsidised childcare is anticipated to fully meet demand by the year 2013. By this point, the Government has agreed to introduce an individual entitlement to childcare for every child. It is estimated that the number of places will reach 750,000 by 2013, increasing coverage for that age group from approximately 14% in 2005/06 to 35% (Seeleib-Kaiser 2008).

From Conservative to Liberal-communitarian Welfare

Only few years before the economic crisis, the German welfare state has undergone a significant transformation, which I have characterized as a process from Conservative to Liberal-communitarian welfare. The guiding principle of unemployment insurance for the long-term unemployed as well as old-age insurance for future retirees was shifted from guaranteeing the achieved living standard towards providing a basic level of support, increasingly relying on means-tested benefits. At the same time, family policies were re-orientated from supporting the male breadwinner towards a policy supporting parental choice, which included an expansion and reform of parental leave arrangements as well as childcare facilities. This policy trajectory was initiated by the Christian Democrats in the late 1980s and 1990s, further accelerated by the Red-Green Coalition Government (1998-2005) and continued by the Grand Coalition Government. Although the German welfare state for a long time had been identified of being unable to reform, it was substantially 'modernized' during the past decade. Based on these substantial reforms, it seems unlikely that any party will propose further comprehensive reforms any time in the near future.

The Global Crisis and Social Protection

As indicated in the introduction, the global crisis has not yet triggered any substantial reforms in social protection. However, it has to be emphasized that a considerable amount of the fiscal stimulus bill is targeted for improvements in infrastructure, especially schools and universities. Thus, in a sense the Government continues on the path of 'modernization' by investing in social infrastructure and is not reverting back towards an approach of increasing compensatory measures.

From a social policy perspective it can be argued that there is no immediate need for significant reforms as a result of the current recession: 1) The pension benefits for the current standard pensioner have not yet been significantly impacted by the reforms of the early 2000s. The overwhelming majority of pensioners rely on the statutory pension system; additional income from occupational or private pensions is rather residual. The fact that the poverty rate among pensioners is still below average, demonstrates the overall generosity of the pension system for current pensioners.[3] Furthermore, the grand coalition Government has agreed a provision that will prevent reductions in pension benefits, which might be triggered by declining wages due to the linkage of pension benefits to the wage development (cf. Bundestag 2009). 2) Despite the reforms of the late 1990s and early 2000s, the unemployment insurance system continues to be relatively generous for the short-term unemployed and functions as an automatic stabilizer. Unemployment insurance provides a net replacement ratio of 60% (67% for those unemployed with children) for duration of twelve months. Older workers are entitled to two years of receipt. Even as the global economic crisis has not yet had a significant impact on unemployment, those becoming unemployed can rely on the functioning of the welfare state.

As part of the stimulus package parents receive an additional one-off payment of € 100 per child in 2009. The benefits for low-income families were significantly expanded in 2005. In addition to the universal monthly child allowance of € 164 per child, raised by € 10 effective January 2009, parents with low incomes are entitled to an additional € 140 per month. Furthermore, the social assistance benefit for children (age 6 to 13) increased from € 211 to € 246 per month, effective July 1, 2009 (Bundesregierung 2009).

Perhaps the most significant policy change has been an expansion of the short-time work allowance (*Kurzarbeitergeld*). Short-time work allowances, that have been available for most of the post-WW II era, have the aim to support employment in companies facing cyclical and structural difficulties. To be entitled to short-term work allowances at least one third of employees at a company must have a reduced monthly income of at least 10%, due to a reduction of working hours. Either the company or the works council can apply for the allowance at the local office of the Federal Employment Office. Once the Federal Employment Office has ascertained whether all qualifying conditions are met, it will grant the affected employees a benefit of 60% (67% for employees with children) of the lost net income. The federal Government has extended the maximum duration of benefit receipt from 6 to 18 months, effective January 2009. In April 2009 the maximum duration was further extended to a total of 24 months (BMAS 2009). As part of the stimulus package the 30% condition has been suspended; in addition the Federal Employment Office reimbursed 50% of the employer's contributions to the various social insurance schemes of certified com-

3 At the end of 2006, only 2.6% of women and 1.8% of men and thus a total of 2.3% of all persons aged 65 and over were in receipt of benefits under the scheme for basic protection in old age and in the case of reduced earning capacity. See Bundesregierung 2008.

panies in the years 2009/2010. For those employees on short-time work engaged in further training the Federal Employment Office reimbursed 100% of the employer's social insurance contributions. The costs of this measure are estimated to be € 1.8 billion.[4] In December 2008, about 270,000 workers received the short-time work allowance; compared to the previous year the number of recipients was up by 193.000. Based on FTE, the short-time work allowance 'saved' 99,000 jobs in December. Newer figures are not yet available, but the number of companies that have applied for the short-time work allowance has significantly increased in the first quarter of 2009 (Bundesagentur für Arbeit 2009).

As the finances of the social insurance schemes are largely dependent on employment, a rise in unemployment will significantly impact the resources available. However, as social insurance contributions have declined over the past couple of years (see figure 8), the Government could once again opt to increase contribution rates or to increase subsidies to these schemes from general revenues, before having to revert to benefit cuts.

Figure 8: Social insurance contributions: 1975-2008

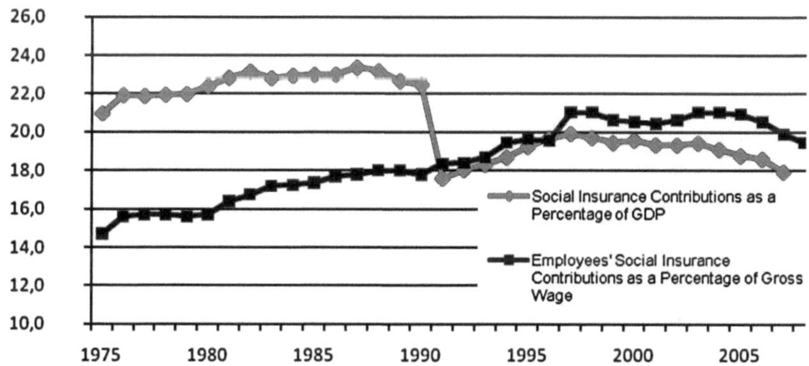

Source: BMAS 2008.

Conclusion

The German welfare state has a number of programmes and instruments in place that ameliorate the impact of the economic crisis. Overall its social insurance schemes are robust and their financial condition seems to be healthier than only a few years ago. Nevertheless, the current economic recession constitutes a 'stress test' for welfare state arrangements. Should the recession last long and lead to a considerable increase in unemployment, the Government will be forced to increase social insurance contributions, raise the subsidies to the social insur-

4 For details of the stimulus package see: http://www.konjunkturpaket.de/Webs/KP/DE/Homepage/home.html.

ance funds from general revenues or cut entitlements. For those ineligible for the earnings-related unemployment insurance benefits the Government provides a monthly means-tested unemployment assistance benefit of about € 350 (for an individual) plus housing allowance.

However, it has to be mentioned that the poverty rate has increased from 12% in the late 1990s to 18% in 2005. A more differentiated analysis shows that low-wage work has increased significantly; furthermore, the percentage of poor among the unemployed had risen by almost 15 percentage points, i.e. even before the comprehensive reform of the unemployment insurance scheme was implemented in 2004, whilst the poverty rates for pensioners and single parents have only 'marginally' increased or stayed constant (see table 4). It remains to be seen whether the current recession will lead to a further increase in relative poverty or inequality, or whether the recent increase in inequality will even decline, during the current recession.

Table 4: Poverty rates 1998-2005 (60% of median income)

Socio-economic group	*1998*	*1999*	*2000*	*2001*	*2002*	*2003*	*2004*	*2005*
Employees	6	6	8	9	9	10	10	12
Unemployed	30	31	36	40	42	44	47	53
Pensioners	10	12	13	14	13	13	13	13
Single parent households	36	35	36	37	39	36	37	36
Children below 15	16	16	18	20	22	23	25	26
Total before transfers	*21*	*22*	*22*	*23*	*23*	*24*	*24*	*25*
Total after transfer	*12*	*12*	*13*	*15*	*16*	*16*	*17*	*18*

Source: Bundesregierung 2008, p. 306.

References

Alber, Jens (2001), *Recent Developments of the German Welfare State: Basic Continuity or Paradigm Shift?* ZeS-Arbeitspapier 6/01. Bremen: Zentrum für Sozialpolitik der Universität Bremen.

Bleses, Peter & Martin Seeleib-Kaiser (2004), *The Dual Transformation of the German Welfare State*. Basingstoke: Palgrave.

Bundesagentur für Arbeit (2009), *Der Arbeitsmarkt- und Ausbildungsmarkt in Deutschland. Monatsbericht April 2009.* Nürnberg. http://www.pub.arbeitsagentur.de/hst/services/statistik/000000/html/start/monat/aktuell.pdf

BMAS/Bundesministerium für Arbeit und Soziales (2008), *Statistisches Taschenbuch 2008: Arbeits- und Sozialstatistik*. Berlin.

BMAS/Bundesministerium für Arbeit und Soziales (2009), http://www.bmas.de/coremedia/generator/33050/2009_04_29_ zusaetzlich_stabilisierende _massnahmen_arbeitsmarkt.html.

BMFSFJ/Bundesministerium für Familie, Soziales, Frauen und Jugend (2007), *Elterngeld und Elternzeit*. Berlin

Bundesregierung (2008), *Lebenslagen in Deutschland. Der 3. Armuts- und Reichtumsbericht der Bundesregierung*. Berlin [an abridged English-language version is available at http://www.bmas.de/coremedia/generator/27506/property=pdf/dritter_armuts _und_reichtumsbericht_englisch_kurzfassung.pdf].

Bundesregierung (2009), 'Konjunkturpaket: Soziale Aspekte', *Magazin für Soziales, Familie und Bildung*, number 073-03/2009.

Bundestag, *Stenographisches Protokoll,* 2/184, p. 10181; 5/95, pp. 4335 ff.

Bundestag (2009), *Änderungsantrag der Fraktionen der CDU/CSU und SPD zum Entwurf eines Dritten Gesetzes zur Änderung des Vierten Buches Sozialgesetzbuch und anderer Gesetze*. BT-Drucksache 16/12596, May 6.

Clasen, Jochen (1994), *Paying the Jobless. A Comparison of Unemployment Benefit Policies in Great Britain and Germany*. Aldershot et al.: Avebury, p. 101.

Eurostat 2009, 2010 projections [http://epp.eurostat.ec.europa.eu/portal/page/portal/structural_indicators/introduction].

Giese, Dieter (1986), '25 Jahre Bundessozialhilfegesetz. Entstehung – Ziele – Entwicklung', *Zeitschrift für Sozialhilfe und Sozialgesetzbuch*, 25, part I, pp. 249-258; part II, pp. 305-314; part III, pp. 374-382.

Goodin, Robert E.; Headey, Bruce; Muffels, Ruud & Henk-Jan Dirven (1999), *The Real Worlds of Welfare Capitalism*. Cambridge: Cambridge University Press.

Hall, Peter A. (2007), 'The Evolution of Varieties of Capitalism in Europe', in Bob Hancké, Martin Rhodes & Mark Thatcher (eds.), *Beyond Varieties of Capitalism*. Oxford: Oxford University Press, pp. 39-85.

Hamann, Götz & Rüdiger Jungbluth (2009), ‚Die Menschen machen das Geschäft', *Die Zeit*, May 7, p. 24.

Kolbe, Wiebke (2002), *Elternschaft im Wohlfahrtsstaat. Schweden und die Bundesrepublik im Vergleich 1945-2000*. Frankfurt a.M.: Campus.

Leisering, Lutz & Stephan Leibfried (1999), *Time and Poverty in Western Welfare States*. Cambridge: Cambridge University Press.

Meyer, Traute (1998), 'Retrenchment, Reproduction, Modernization: Pension Politics and the Decline of the German Breadwinner Model', *Journal of European Social Policy,* vol. 8 (3), pp. 195-211.

Moeller, Robert G. (1993), *Protecting Motherhood. Women and the Family in the Politics of Postwar West Germany.* Berkeley: University of California Press.

Neidhardt, Friedhelm (1978), 'The Federal Republic of Germany', in Sheila B. Kamerman & Alfred J. Kahn (eds.), *Family Policy – Government and Families in Fourteen Countries.* New York: Columbia University Press, pp. 217-238.

Niejahr, Elisabeth (2009), 'Lob des Sozialstaats', *Die Zeit*, April 30, p. 1.

OECD [http://stats.oecd.org/WBOS/index.aspx].

Schmähl, Winfried (1999), 'Rentenversicherung in der Bewährung: Von der Nachkriegszeit bis an die Schwelle zum neuen Jahrhundert', in Max Kaase & Günther Schmid (eds.), *Eine lernende Demokratie – 50 Jahre Bundesrepublik Deutschland.* WZB-Jahrbuch 1999. Berlin: Edition Sigma, pp. 397-423.

Schmähl, Winfried (2007), 'Dismantling an Earnings-Related Social Pension Scheme: Germany's New Pension Policy', *Journal of Social Policy*, vol. 36 (2), pp. 319-340.

Seeleib-Kaiser, Martin (2007), *From Conservative to Liberal-Communitarian Welfare: Can the Reformed German Welfare State Survive?* Barnett Papers in Social Research, University of Oxford, No. 4/2007.

Seeleib-Kaiser, Martin (2008), 'Social Democratic Reforms of the Welfare State', in Martin Powell (ed.), *Modernising the Welfare State*, Bristol: Policy Press.

Seeleib-Kaiser, Martin & Timo Fleckenstein (2007), 'Discourse, Learning and Welfare State Change', *Social Policy and Administration*, 41 (5), pp. 427-448.

Soskice, David (2006), 'Skill Specificity and the Modern Macroeconomics of Unemployment: Using the Iversen Tool-Kit', *Labor History*, vol. 47 (3), pp. 429-439

The Economist.

TNS Infratest Sozialforschung (2008), *Situation und Entwicklung der betrieblichen Altersversorgung in Privatwirtschaft und öffentlichem Dienst 2001-2007.* Untersuchung im Auftrag des Bundesministeriums für Arbeit und Soziales, Endbericht. München, 30. Oktober.

Part III

6 Crisis Governance in Denmark: Is Flexicurity Delivering?

Peter Abrahamson

Introduction

Currently the effects of what started out as a financial crisis in the United States in 2008 is now affecting the whole world in the form of a global economic crisis. Denmark is no exception to this, but perhaps it was better prepared or constituted than most states. In Scandinavia, there is a very long tradition for public intervention into societal settings in order to increase citizens' welfare *and* create social cohesion and integration. Hence fiscal and social policies and labour market measures were already very well developed in the whole region, when the crisis appeared. Another important precondition was that even when the Scandinavian welfare model has its specific features it is constantly developing, and the various Governments have often created commissions of experts to produce reports to advise them on feasible changes of welfare arrangements.

In the Danish case the Danish centre-right Government formed a so-called *Welfare Reform Commission* in the fall of 2003 with the aim of suggesting changes to provisions in Denmark that would make them stand the foreseeable future in- and external pressures. The Government was concerned about the prospect of the age structure, i.e. the unfavourable development in the demographical support ratio; the high rates of unemployment among immigrants; the expected increase in health care expenditure when people live longer etc. Consequences of globalization and Europeanization could add further to future problems for Danish welfare society and the Commission was instructed to come up with tangible reform proposals. The commission was announced as 'broadly composed of knowledgeable experts' (Ministry of State 2003); but it actually consisted of eight economists and a lawyer, which is as narrow as it gets. The mandate stated that "in the first part of the 21st century Denmark will be facing serious challenges following for instance from the changes in composition of the population. … The aim is to secure the basis for social security and social balance and a well-functioning welfare system in the future. Taxes cannot be increased since they already are at a high level, then consequences will be 'that the welfare systems to a higher degree must be targeted those groups most in need of help, and the policies must support the greatest possible labour market participation." (Ministry of State 2003) From these premises the Commission should investigate the possibilities of financing welfare provisions into 2020 given unchanged tax levels, and it should consider various ways of financing the provisions.

After having published its suggestions for welfare reform in December 2005 (*Velfærdskommissionen* [Welfare Reform Commission] 2005), the Commission officially forwarded the report (in three volumes) to the Government in January 2006, and somewhat surprisingly, it found the suggestions to be too radical or far reaching. Especially were the suggestions concerning a reform of the tax system rejected completely and right away by the then Prime Minister Anders Fogh Rasmussen. The Government had from the outset announced that it wanted a broad agreement in Parliament behind a welfare reform and negotiations were opened with all parties. On June 20th 2006 the Government (the Liberal Party and the Conservative Party) together with the Social Democrats, Danish Peoples Party and the Radical Liberals agreed on a welfare reform. This coalition only left out the Peoples Socialist Party and the Unity Group (Communists, Radical Socialists, and Trotskyites). The most important element in the agreement was the increase of retirement age. From 2019 to 2022 the voluntary early retirement age will be increased to 62 and the retirement age to 67 from 2024 to 2027. This means that people that were 48 years-of-age or older by the end of 2006 will not be affected. It is foreseen that from 2025 every fifth year there will be an adjustment of the retirement ages according to longevity for a 60 year-old. In the long run the average years spend in retirement will approach 19 and half years (Ministry of Finance 2006).

The agreements also contained initiatives concerning getting unemployed faster back in to employment, especially unemployed immigrants, and efforts will be made to get students faster through their studies, and to have more young people take an education. Finally, it was agreed to increase public investment in research to one per cent of GDP by 2010. As a result of the reform it is expected that employment will have increased by 110,000 people by 2025 and by 125,000 people by 2040 [in 2005 the workforce consisted of 2,759,392 people] (Ministry of Finance 2006).

Another important recent change within the Danish welfare state was the implementation of the so-called *structural reform*. June 2004 the Government made an agreement with the Danish Peoples Party (its parliamentary safety net) concerning a governance reform which drew a radically new map of Denmark with much fewer and bigger administrative units. The motivation and aim was to secure the public administrative structure against future challenges, which according to the Government meant that municipalities should have about 30,000 inhabitants to be big enough for handling the complex issues and problems at hand (Ministry of Interior and Health 2004). The number of municipalities was to be reduced from 271 to about 100, and the counties were to be dissolved and replaced by five regions. Since January 1st 2007 there are 98 municipalities with new responsibilities within special social care which used to be the responsibility of the counties and the five regions will only be responsible for health care, i.e. hospitals and agreements with general practitioners. Hence the former responsibility for upper secondary education (*Gymnasium* = high school) has been transferred to the state (Ministry of Interior and Health 2004).

The outcome of the reform can in one perspective be viewed with reference to the time glass metaphor: Competences are being concentrated more on the top (state) and bottom (municipal) levels, while the regional (county) level is being thinned out. In another perspective the reform can be seen as a centralization of public authority: After the reform there will be a longer distance between citizens and authorities since the municipalities have in average tripled with respect to number of inhabitants, and the regional level has had to pass over jurisdiction to the state. The philosophy behind the reform has clearly been that bigger is better, and that the central state wishes to be in control of more areas of intervention. Hence, Danish local governance structure has in less than 40 years changed from being composed of 1.388 municipalities to presently being composed of only 98 municipalities; simultaneously, the regional governance structure was reduced from 25 counties to five regions.

The most recent initiative of this kind was the Government setting up the so-called *Labour Market Commission* in December 2007 (Ministry of finance 2007). Its mission is to come up with suggestions for an increase in employment and man power in the long term. The ageing of society is viewed as a challenge to Danish society which, everything else being equal, points in the opposite direction. The Commissions consists of nine experts (economics professors and CEOs) chaired by the Director for the National Institute of Social Research, Jørgen Søndergaard. Among other things it shall analyse possibilities of increased employment through "a more spacious labour market for persons who today are outside the labour force; through better structures in the labour market, which enables shorter unemployment spells: through better integration of immigrants and second and third generation immigrants: through continuous employment of senior workers; through transferring part-time workers to full time; through measures that ensure that the average working time does not decrease". (Ministry of Finance 2007, p. 1) The Commission shall submit its report by summer 2009. According to the Commission's homepage it expects to submit the final report by August 20th 2009. But on request from the Government the Commission already in September 2008 published an interim report entitled *Work, Growth and Welfare* containing suggestions for changes within four areas: unemployment insurance; activation; foreign labour power; and voluntary early retirement pension (*efterløn*). Regarding unemployment insurance the Commission suggested a substantial shortening of the period during which one is entitled to benefits: down from the current four years to two and a half years in bad times and only one year and a half in good times. The judgement is that this would increase employment with about 20,000 people in the longer term. If implemented quickly it might mean an increase of 4-5,000 people in one or two years' time. It may improve the public finances by about DKK six billion per year. With respect to activation it is suggested that the activation offer comes earlier, namely after six months of unemployment, and not after nine months as it is presently. In the longer run this is expected to increase employment by 7,000 people, and it may increase the public finances by about DKK two billion. It is also suggested to increase the number of immigrant workers especially from the new Member States of the European Union by changing the income threshold for the so-called job cards from the existing DKK 375,000 down to 300,000.[1] Finally regarding the voluntary early retirement pension scheme it is suggested to move up in time the already decided extension of the age at which one can access the scheme by ten years. So instead of waiting to 2019 it should already be in effect from 2009. It is expected that after two years employment will have increased by 25,000 and in the mid- to longer term as many as 80,000 more people will be employed. The public finances could be improved by DKK five billion yearly (*Arbejdsmarkedskommissionen* 2008, pp. 5, 7, 8, 10, 11).

In the most recent document from the Labour Market Commission it is recognized that a significant shift in the business circle has occurred which has redirected the current political attention away from problems of lack of labour power and onto problems of increasing unemployment. Nevertheless, the Commission found that "increasing unemployment does not remove the need for reforms that strengthens public finances in the long run. … The increase in the official unemployment rate does not mean that many people will be permanently unemployed. The large majority will even in the current situation quickly return to employment. … The Commission strongly discourages that there with reference to the contemporary situation measures are taken that permanently or for a period of time reduce the effective supply of labour power." (*Arbejdsmarkedskommission* 2009, p. 2; author's translation)

Even if the particular suggestions presented by the various expert commissions are not immediately accepted by the Government, they nevertheless feed into the political debate over the development of the Danish welfare state, and, often, central suggestions are implemented at a later stage of having 'matured' in the public sphere.

Finally, an important background factor is that the period of time immediately prior to the crisis was one that saw the highest employment rates and the lowest unemployment rates ever recorded. Hence, the Government's primary concern was in the first place to take measures against an 'over heating' of the economy, because of lack of labour power, resulting in upward pressure on

1 The job card is a permission that employers can apply for in order to employ skilled EU workers earning at least DKK 375,000 yearly. So, essentially it is a means to by-pass the ban on importing East European labour that was established with the latest extension of the European Union.

wages and salaries and subsequently on consumer prices, leading to an acceleration of inflation relative to other European Union countries. When it became clear that Denmark experienced the world wide phenomena of declining exports, a 'freezing' of the housing market, bank collapses and an increase in unemployment, the Government's initiatives have been mainly of a fiscal policy nature and less so of social policy interventions. The most important interventions have been the introduction of aid packages toward the financial sector and a tax reform aiming at increasing private consumption by reducing personal income taxes. Some of the initiatives taken through the Ministry of Social Affairs have also been predominantly of a fiscal nature, e.g. the proposed measures to increase the construction of more public housing units. However, some social problems have increased in recent years – without being an effect of the economic crisis, but aggravated by it – particularly what by the press has been labelled 'gang wars' between different ethnic groups, leading to, among many other things, a number of incidents of shootings, predominantly in a few neighbourhoods in the capital city of Copenhagen. The Minister of Justice has suggested a number of initiatives to try and deal with this issue.

It is impossible to understand the current reaction to the crisis in Denmark without some insight into the institutional and social setup of the Scandinavian welfare regime. Thus this article starts out by providing such an overview. It then goes on to describe the particular Danish system of so-called *flexicurity*, the combined effect of a very flexible labour market and a high degree of social security facilitated by active labour market measures. The contemporary crisis governance measures are taking place within a certain socio-economic environment, which thus must be outlined before the presentation and discussion of the actual Government initiatives. The article concludes by stressing the preconditions existing for crisis governance in Denmark in order to accommodate the inspiration it may provide for the Korean Government.

The Scandinavian Welfare Regime

The Scandinavian model of welfare is: universal and (therefore) expensive; tax financed; based on public provision of both transfers and services; emphasizing personal social services vis-à-vis transfers; provides high quality provision; has high compensation rates and is therefore egalitarian; and is based on a high degree of labour market participation for both sexes. Viewed in an international perspective many observers pointed to those major characteristics. The Swedish sociologist Joakim Palme (1999, p. 15) summed it up thus: "The Nordic model is about ... universalism, generous benefits, social citizenship rights, dual-earner model, active labour market policies, and extensive social services." Duane Swank included tax policies and full employment:

"The Nordic countries are generally characterized by publicly funded and administered programmes that have comprehensive and universal coverage and relatively egalitarian benefit structures. Traditionally, they have been supported by redistributive general taxes and strong work orientations, in terms of both programmatic emphasis on work and economic policies that stress full employment." (Swank 2000, p. 85)

However, these generalizations have been challenged recently, and it was argued that the Scandinavian welfare regime is still distinct, but less so than previously because of Europeanization leaving more provision of services to the market and the voluntary sector (Abrahamson 2003). In what follows Denmark shall represent the Scandinavian welfare regime.

Viewed from a relative financial perspective not much has happened in terms of the size of the Danish welfare state. Total social expenditure as share of Gross Domestic Product (GDP) has been oscillating around 30%. Latest figures which are from 2007 indicate the share to be 28.7%, which is at par with a number of north western European states as is clear from the appendix table (OECD 2009; Statistics Denmark 2008, p. 18). The slight reduction in 2007 is a reflection of the increase in GDP. Because, in absolute terms social expenditure has increased since 2000 from around 7,500 purchasing power parity Euros to around 8,400 in fixed prices.

Table 1: Development of total social expenditure in Denmark, 1995-2006

	1995	*2000*	*2005*	*2006*
In % of GDP	31.9	28.9	30.1	29.1
Index 1995 = 100	100	90	94	91
Per capita at fixed 2006-prices PPP €	7,509	7,530	8,437	8,435

Source: NOSOSCO 2008, p. 197.

Like most other welfare states, Denmark spends most of its resources on old age and sickness. Housing and social assistance, only accounts for 0.7% of GDP, as indicated in table 2.

Table 2: Functional distribution of social expenditure in Denmark, 2007, as percentage of GDP

Sickness	*Invalidity*	*Old Age*	*Families*	*Employment*	*Housing*	*Social Ass.*	*Administration*
6.1	4.2	10.7	3.7	1.6	0.7	0.7	0.8

Source: Statistics Denmark 2008.

One of the major changes which occurred within the Danish welfare state over the last twenty years is the shifting of the burden of financing welfare. In 1987 the central Government covered 44% of total costs, municipalities 40%, employers 12% and employees only 5%. However, in 2007 the state had reduced its contribution to 21%, while employees had increased theirs to 21%. The burden has therefore been shifted from the state to insured workers, thus bringing

Denmark more in line with Continental Europe in this respect, as is shown in table 3.

Table 3: Share of financing of total social expenditure, 1987–2007(in %)

	State	*Municipality & Region*	*Employers*	*Employees*
1987	43.8	39.8	11.7	4.7
1990	49.3	36.6	8.4	5.7
1995	39.3	35.1	10.9	14.7
2000	28.6	39.8	9.8	21.8
2004	26.8	41.2	19.9	21.0
2007	21.1	40.7	17.3	20.9

Source: Statistics Denmark 2005, 2008.

What this simple overview shows is that the transfers and services directed directly toward the unemployed and/or poor only makes up a smaller part of the total social budget. Expressed differently, social policy in Denmark reaches out to the whole population not just the immediately needy. The fact that the middle and upper classes utilizes the health care system, have their children attend public day-care and receive old age pensions is probably the major explanation behind the success of the Scandinavian model. Everybody benefits, so everybody is willing to contribute. Welfare services enjoy a very high degree of legitimacy and have a high degree of support expressed now and again in surveys. These developments and expenditures are strongly related to movements and developments regarding the population (demography) and the labour market. In the section following the next one some central figures of magnitude and development are shown with respect to these two areas.

Flexicurity

In the Danish Government's report to the European Commission concerning the Lisbon objectives we can read the following (2005, p. 35):

"The Danish labour market has a favourable starting position. Denmark has an employment rate that is already higher than the joint EU objective of 70%, partially because of the high participation of women in the labour market. Furthermore, the Danish structural unemployment is relatively low, which is partially because of the Danish flexicurity model with flexible rules on hiring and dismissal, a well-developed unemployment benefit system and an active labour market policy-based on strict rules on availability, re-education, etc. Extensive reforms have been carried out, especially with regard to the development of the structural unemployment and to keeping persons with reduced working capacity on the labour market."

Flexicurity is here explained with reference to what has been labelled the 'golden triangle' – the relationships between a flexible labour market, where it is easy to hire and fire, and – therefore – where there is a high flow of workers in and out of employment (high level of external numerical flexibility); a generous welfare system which guarantees income security; and active labour market policies (activation) aiming at upgrading workers' skills. This is illustrated in figure 1 below:

Figure 1: The 'Golden Triangle' of flexicurity

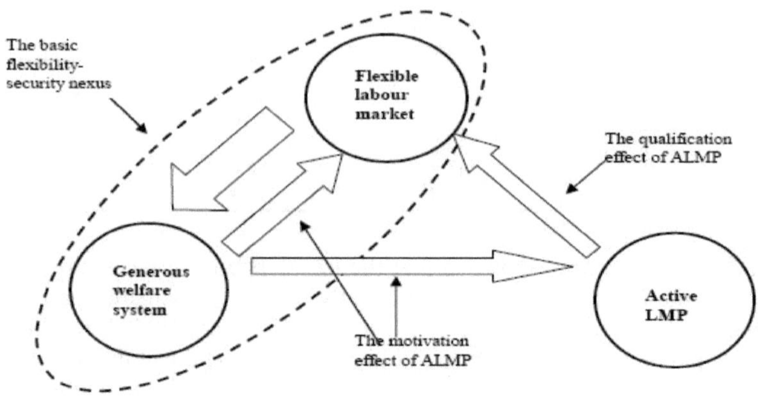

Source: Developed by the then Ministry of Labour (now: Ministry of Employment) and adapted by Madsen 2006, p. 354.

The idea is that if employers can easily get rid of workers in bad times, they are more inclined to hire workers in good times, and workers when fired, are still able to maintain a reasonable life because of relatively generous unemployment benefits. Finally, activation – either because of the scare/motivation effect (see below) or through skills upgrading – helps unemployed getting back into employment. Let us look a little more closely at these elements in turn.

A Flexible Labour Market

One way of measuring the degree of flexibility in the labour market is to calculate the percentage of all employees who changed to another firm each year. The figure below shows that from 1980 to 2002 10 to 15% of all employees changed to another firm each year.

Job changes may involve spells of unemployment. Hence, Ibsen and Westergaard-Nielsen (2005, p. 28) have calculated that "more than two thirds of all workers who leave an employer each year will have found a new job before next year and less than one third ends up in no employment the next year. A little more than half of these become unemployed while the rest is either retiring, in education or out of the labour force due to sickness or another reason." One such other reason could be activation. These job changes reflect the massive job creations and destructions taking place in the economy and shows up in figures

Figure 2: Numerical flexibility, 1980-2002
(the percentage of all employees who change to another firm each year)

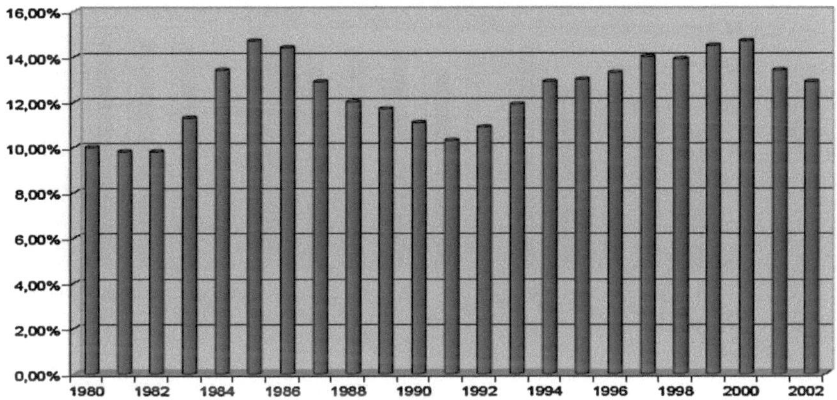

Source: Bredgaard, Larsen & Madsen 2006, p. 11.

for job tenure. Figure 3 below gives the share of the workforce that has less than one year's tenure:

Figure 3: Less than one year tenure in current job, 1981-2003 (%)

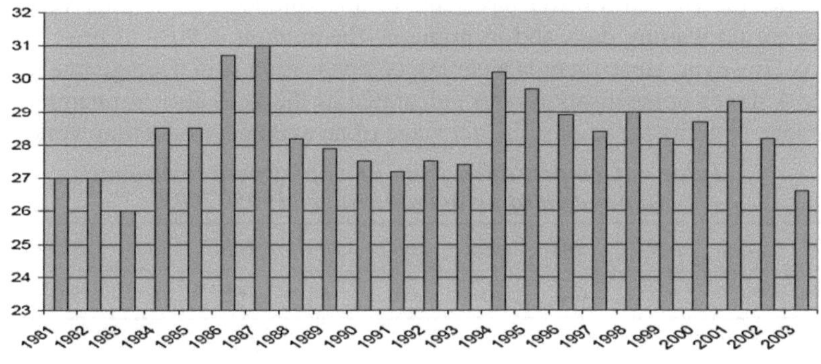

Source: Bredgaard, Larsen & Madsen (2006, p. 12).

Depending on the business cycle somewhere between 26 and 31% of the workforce have held their jobs for less than one year, and average job tenure is eight years, which is relatively low compared to most other countries (Ibsen & Westergaard-Nielsen 2005, p. 4). This is demonstrated in figure 4 below. It has been pointed out that job tenure is much lower in Denmark than in Sweden and Finland, hence leading some observers to talk about the Danish labour market regime being a 'hybrid' between a liberal and a Scandinavian regime (see, e.g. Madsen 2006).

Figure 4: Average tenure in years for employees in some OECD-countries

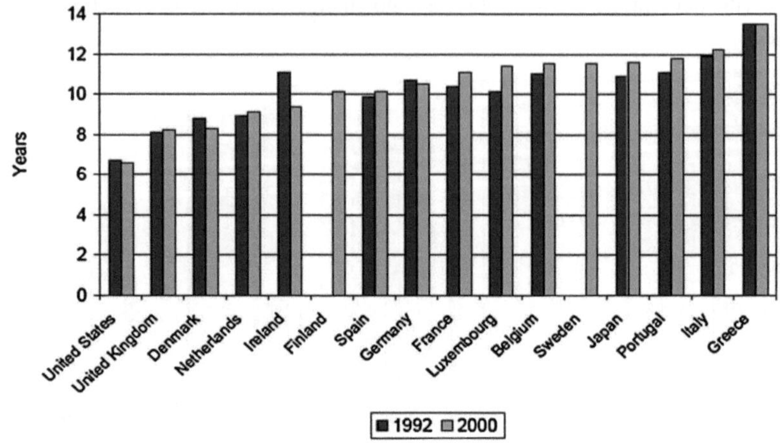

Source: Madsen 2006, p. 332.

A Generous Unemployment Benefit System?

On paper the Danish transfer payments to unemployed people look very good. There are no waiting days and in principle the amount is 90% of prior wage or salary. However, since there is a ceiling compensation is in average much lower. Table 4 shows compensation rates calculated as the net value of unemployment insurance benefits set against the net wage of an average production worker.

Table 4: Compensation from unemployment insurance in per cent of an average wage (1995- 2005)

1995	*1996*	*1997*	*1998*	*1999*	*2000*	*2001*	*2002*	*2003*	*2004*	*2005*
67	66	65	64	65	64	64	63	63	60	62

Source: NOSOSCO 2008.

Compensation was around two-thirds of an average worker's income in 1995, but has fallen back to 60% in 2004 (and the slight increase in 2005 is due to a change in the method of calculation). This can hardly be called generous, and it looks even worse when replacement rates for social assistance are calculated, as shown in table 5 below:

Table 5: Compensation in case of unemployment, non-insured, single, no children (1995- 2005) Source: NOSOSCO 2008.

1995	*1996*	*1997*	*1998*	*1999*	*2000*	*2001*	*2002*	*2003*	*2004*	*2005*
47	46	45	44	44	44	44	43	43	41	42

The value of social assistance benefits is equivalent to 42% of an average worker's wage, which – probably – nobody would label generous. What is furthermore clear from tables 4 and 5 is that not only are compensation not very generous it is also less so over time: down from 67 and 47% respectively to 62 and 42% respectively. However when the various child allowances are taken into account plus the possibilities of extra allowances and housing allowance, the single social assistance recipient with a child is raised above the poverty line.

Table 6: Compensation in case of unemployment, non-insured, single parent with one child 1995-2005

1995	*1996*	*1997*	*1998*	*1999*	*2000*	*2001*	*2002*	*2003*	*2004*	*2005*
77	77	76	74	71	73	73	71	72	69	72

Source: NOSOSCO 2008.

Nevertheless, the benefit period may be said to be generous in international comparison. Within the unemployment insurance system one can receive benefits for a total of four years including periods of activation, and in principle social assistance can be received indefinitely.

Evaluating Activation Measures

The National Institute of Social Research has carried through a thorough evaluation of these latest experiences of the compulsory active labour market policy. One investigation was done in the beginning of the 2000s by Henning Bach and reported in 2002. Here it was measured how various forms of municipal activation influenced the degree of self-sufficiency/dependency among activated persons during the period of time from 1995 to 1998 and the overall conclusion was that effects were, at best, very modest. Dependency was measured as the number of weeks in a year where the person was dependent upon one of the following transfer schemes: social assistance, unemployment insurance benefits, activation benefit, rehabilitation allowance, leave allowance, sickness benefits, early retirement pension, 'transfer' allowance (*overgangsydelse*, a scheme making it possible for mature workers ages 55-59 to receive unemployment benefits without actively seeking employment; the benefit was meant to take these workers over from long-term unemployment to voluntary early retirement; subsequently it was phased out during the 1990s), and voluntary early retirement. Dependency was calculated as 0% if the person was not relying on any of these benefits throughout the year and as 100% if the person was dependent upon one of them for the whole year. The situation before receiving an activation offer and after was then measured for each category of activation measures based on register data calculations. About one third of municipal activation consisted of sheltered employment and about one fifth of individual job training within the public sector. Unfortunately, they had very little effect: Sheltered employment reduced the dependency of transfers with only three percentage points, while individual job training within the public sector reduced dependency by six percentage points. The biggest effect was calculated for individual job training within the private sector; in those cases dependency was reduced by 16 percentage points, but only 12% of clients received such an offer (Bach 2002). Interviews with the clients revealed that half of them did not see any aim of going through activation other than they had to in order to keep their benefits. When they were to judge the effects of activation they more often pointed to issues such as improvement of their everyday life and self-confidence than to issues of being qualified for regular employment.

Similar to the study on municipal activation the institute carried out a study on municipal rehabilitation. Rehabilitation is substantially congruent with activation but is based on different legislation and presupposes some kind of reduced work capacity among the recipients. Physical problems dominate, but often there is a combination of problems. Approximately 25% of those starting a process of rehabilitation drop out of the programme; but among those completing, the large majority found a job afterwards. It is, however, difficult to determine whether this is a direct consequence of the rehabilitation measures the study shows. Hence it is demonstrated that the average reduction in dependency is very limited (Filges, Harsløv & Nord-Larsen 2002).

Presumably reflecting the above documented (lack of) effect a project called 'Company rehabilitation as the road (back to) employment' was started by the Social Democratic led Government and placed under the Ministry of Social Affairs in 2000, and after the change of Government continued under the newly created (or at least renamed) Ministry of Employment (former Ministry of Labour). More than 400 companies, of which 77% were private and 611 rehabilitees, participated in the project from 2000 to 2002. The National Institute of Social Research evaluated the project and reported this in 2004 (Harsløv et al. 2004). Participants in the project had no or very limited affiliation to the labour market. They were primarily social assistance recipients (57%) or recipients of sickness benefits (37%). Nearly half of them completed a rehabilitation programme within one of the companies during the observation period. 80% of those who had completed the programme were in employment immediately after its termination; two-thirds in subsidized employment, for the most part flexi-jobs. The research team concluded that positive effects are associated with two things: focus and meaning. This means that the activities must be organized so that they consciously and explicitly aims at the goal (employment), and that the person to which the activity is directed experiences this as meaningful whereby he or she becomes motivated for participation and makes an effort to reach the goal. The effects of company rehabilitation were summed up as threefold: there was found to be a *liaison-effect*, meaning that the long-standing relationship between the client and the company may result in subsequent employment, subsidized or regular; there was also found to be a *qualification-effect*, meaning that the client actually acquired skills and other competences during the programme; and a *developmental-effect*, meaning that the client to an increasing degree was able to handle his or her own situation and take responsibility for his or her own future and self-reliance (Harsløv et al. 2004).

Nevertheless, the unemployed have been supposed to be more flexible with regard to which kinds of job they would accept, and at what wages etc. The National Institute of Social Research investigated the flexibility among 1,500 unemployed persons via questionnaires in autumn 1994, and then traced their labour market performance via register data in the three following years (Bach 1999). Surprisingly it was found that there was no positive correlation between the degree of flexibility and the degree of employment.

What has been demonstrated in this overview are rather limited effects of activation measures; but one 'curious' effect has been identified by economists; one which they have labelled the 'motivation effect', or as it would better be understood by sociologists: the 'scare effect.' What has been discovered is that unemployed people significantly increase their job search and hence employment when they approach the time of activation (Geerdsen 2003). So, e.g. Geerdsen (2003) tentatively concluded that the prospect of activation may be more effective than activation itself. When it is only a tentative conclusion it is because there is the issue of selection effects. It may be so that the most employable of the unemployed are those who manage go get a job before they otherwise have to go into the activation measure. Larsen and Mailand recently summed up activation policies thus: "Throughout the period [from 1994 and onward] the policy has included complementary elements of social disciplining and social integration. There is no doubt, however, that developments have been shifting from a significant focus on social integration to a much stronger emphasis on social disciplining." (2007, p. 3)

Recent Socio-Economic Developments

From a social point of view the existence of and increase in unemployment is the worst thing about an economic crisis. Increasing unemployment is also a clear empirical indication of crisis, and the current situation is no exception. Yet, in October 2008 when the unemployment rate started to increase, it did so from an historical low level of 1.7% of the workforce as recorded in table 7 below. Already by April 2009 it had climbed to 2.9% (Statistics Denmark 2009), and it is expected to have doubled (i.e. having reached 3.5%) by December 2010 (Ministry of Finance 2008, p. 16). Still, a level far lower than December 2003 when unemployment had reached 6.2%, which initiated the first so-called Spring Package of 2004 (see the next section).

Table 7: Unemployment rates in Denmark, monthly (2001-2009) in %

Year	*Jan*	*Feb*	*Mar*	*Apr*	*May*	*Jun*	*Jul*	*Aug*	*Sep*	*Oct*	*Nov*	*Dec*
2001	4.8	4.8	4.8	4.7	4.7	4.7	4.6	4.6	4.5	4.5	4.5	4.5
2002	4.6	4.6	4.6	4.6	4.7	4.7	4.8	4.9	4.9	5.0	5.0	5.0
2003	5.2	5.4	5.4	5.5	5.7	5.8	5.8	5.8	5.9	6.0	6.1	6.2
2004	6.1	6.0	5.9	6.0	5.9	5.9	5.8	5.7	5.7	5.7	5.7	5.7
2005	5.5	5.3	5.4	5.4	5.2	5.2	5.2	5.0	4.9	4.8	4.7	4.6
2006	4.4	4.3	4.2	4.1	4.0	3.9	3.9	3.8	3.7	3.6	3.5	3.4
2007	3.2	3.2	3.2	3.1	3.0	2.9	2.8	2.7	2.5	2.4	2.3	2.1
2008	2.1	1.9	1.8	1.8	1.7	1.7	1.7	1.7	1.7	1.8	2.0	2.2
2009	2.3	2.5										

Source: Statistics Denmark 2009

Even if one unemployed person is one too many, an unemployment rate around 6% is not high relatively speaking in Denmark in a longer time perspective, as shown in figure 5 below:

Figure 5: Unemployment rates for men (blue), women (grey) and both (black) 1979-2006

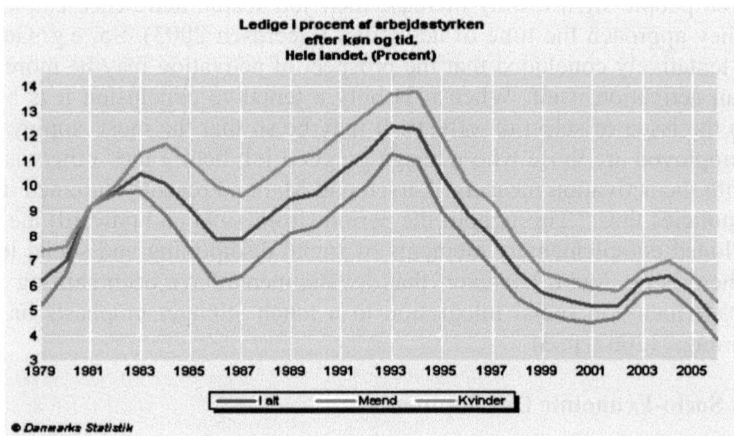

From 1979 to 1998 unemployment oscillated between 6 and 13%, and since the early 1980s women were hit harder than men often by two to three percentage points.

Although Denmark is a small country both geographically and population wise (5.5 million inhabitants) there is a considerable variation in unemployment across regions. The northern (*Nordjylland*) and the south eastern (*Storstrøm*) regions have higher rates of unemployment and the region north of the capital of Copenhagen (*Frederiksborg*) has considerably fewer unemployed as is clear from figures 6 to 8 below:

Figure 6: Unemployment rates in Nordjylland region 1986-2006

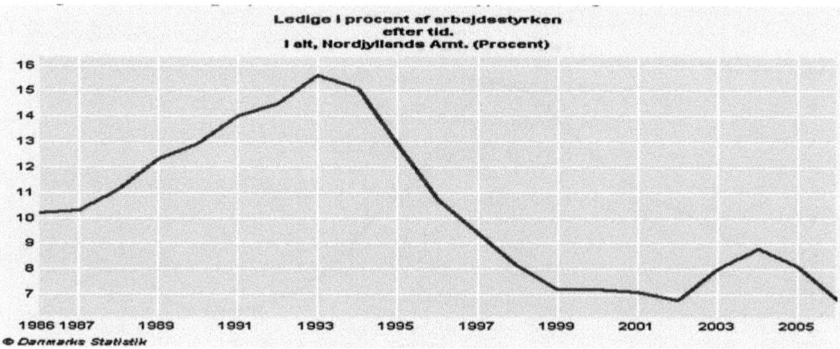

Figure 7: Unemployment rates in Storstrøm region 1986-2006

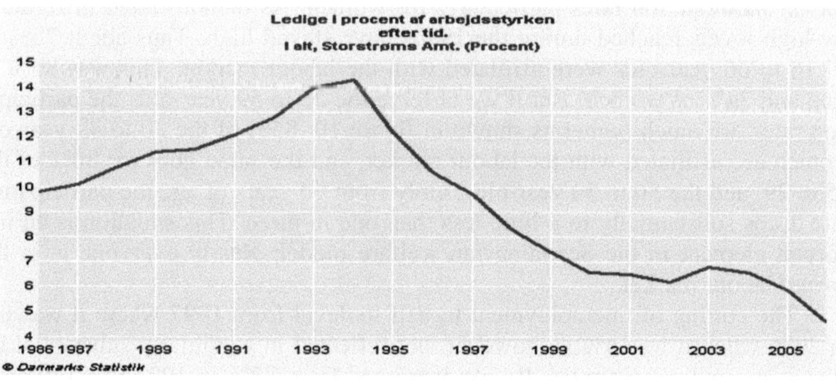

The shape of the curves is similar, but the levels are different. In the north and to the south east unemployment peaked at 16 and 14% respectively while the country average was 12%. Differently north of the capital: Unemployment when it was highest was 'only' less than 10%. The same differences appeared at the end of the period: In the north unemployment stood at 7% when it was at its lowest and the south east it was around 5%, while in the region north of the capital it was only 3%. These regional differences meant that when the average unemployment rate fell to 3% in 2006 and decreased even further in 2007 and 2008 there was a shortage of labour in many places, particularly north of Copenhagen. Hence the considerations made by economists in general and the Government in particular has been more oriented toward preventing the economy from 'overheating' than reducing unemployment even further as discussed in the following section.

Figure 8: Unemployment rates in Frederiksborg region 1986-2006

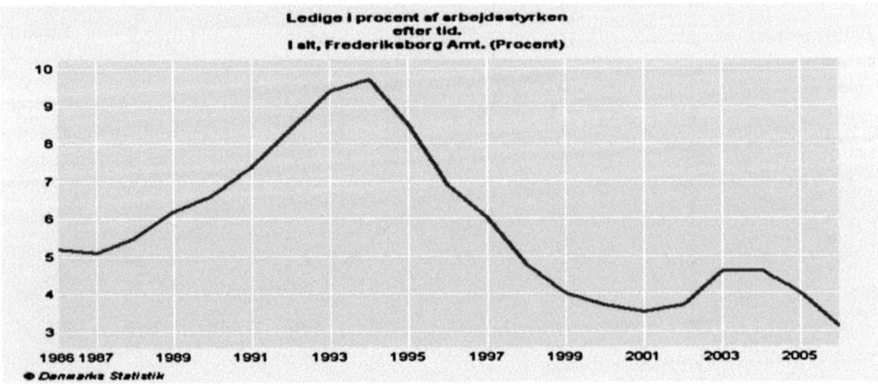

One of the peculiarities of the Scandinavian societies is the relative high labour market participation rates particularly for women. As demonstrated in figure 9 the high levels reached during the 1980s have stayed high. Thus about 77% of all 16 to 66 year-olds were affiliated with the labour market: This was 80% of men and 74% of women. But if we observe the 25 to 59 year-olds the participation rates are much higher as shown in figure 10: 85% of the 30 to 49 year-old women are affiliated with the labour market, and the same goes for 80% of the 25 to 29, and the 50 to 54 year-olds: Only from 60 years of age the participation rate drops substantially to a little less than one in three. This situation is an important element in the Scandinavian welfare model: Nearly everyone is in the *formal* labour market.

The cutting of unemployment to half its level from 1997 where it was 8% to 2006 when it was 4% is, however, not reflected in a similarly substantial increase in employment rates. It only increased from 72% in 1997 to a little less than 74% in 2006. Particularly for men hardly any development occurred. They had the same employment rate in 2006 as they had in 1997, and during this period of time they only increased their employment to 78% between 1999 and 2002. This is an illustration of the issues discussed as reclassification. Many unemployed people have been *reclassified*: They have *not* gone back to work.

The phenomenon of reclassification is summed up by Statistics Denmark by the concept of 'persons without ordinary employment' and as demonstrated in figure 12 above in the first quarter of 2007 there were more than 300,000 such persons, which was roughly equivalent to 10% of the work force. If we add to this figure the number of people of working ages that are receiving sickness benefits for at least half a year, those on early retirement and long-term unemployed we end up with about 20% being marginalized.

Figure 9: Participation rates for men (blue), women (grey) and both (black) 1997-2006

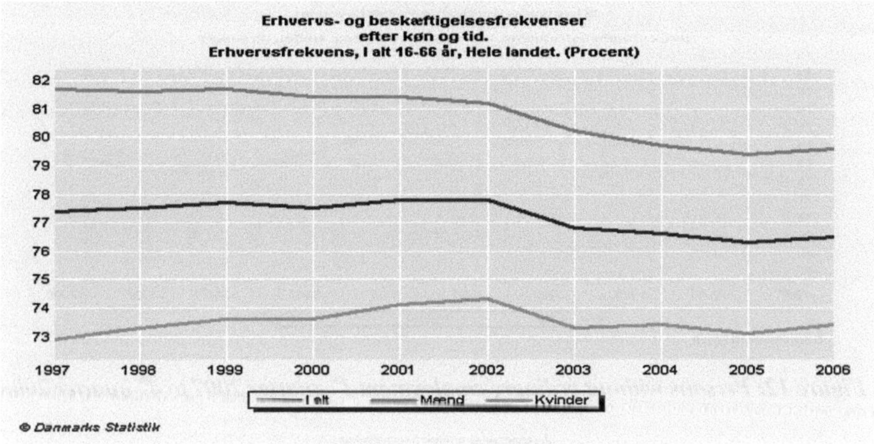

Figure 10: Participation rates for women various age groups 1997-2006

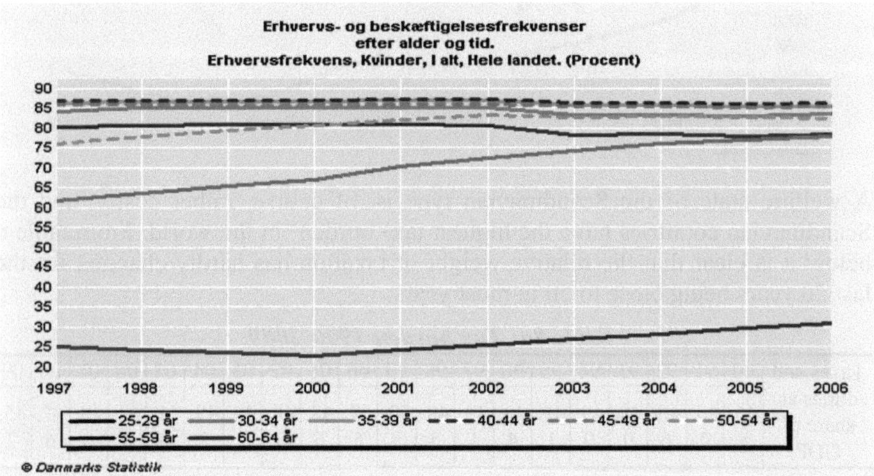

Figure 11: Employment rates men (blue), women (grey) and both (black) 1997-2006

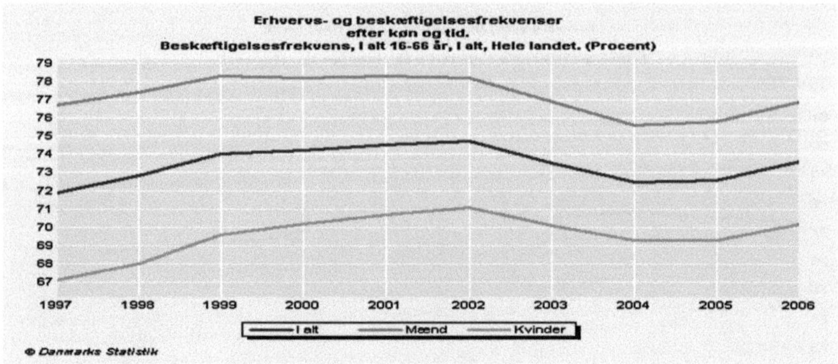

Figure 12: Persons without ordinary employment 1st quarter 2007 to 4th quarter 2008

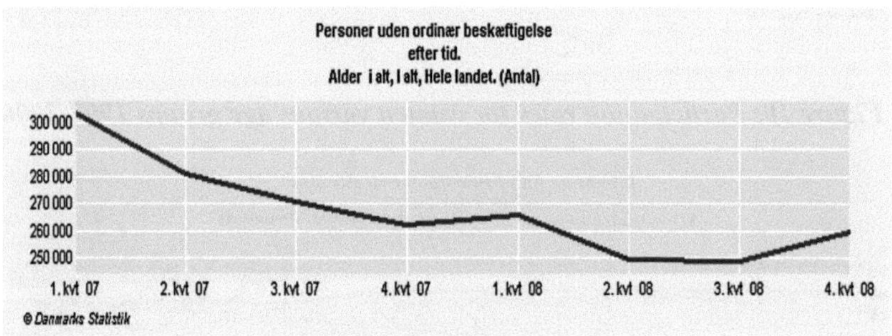

A welfare state of the Scandinavian type is, of course, rather costly, and the Scandinavian countries have the highest tax 'burden' in the world. From table 8 below it is clear that the relative weight of taxation has hardly changed for the last 20 years being close to 50 in most years:

Table 8a: Tax burden 1990-2009

Taxes and	90	91	92	93	94	95	96	97	98	99	00	01	02	03	04	05	06	07	08	09
duties as share of GDP	46.8	46.2	46.6	48.0	49.0	49.1	49.4	49.1	49.5	50.3	49.5	48.6	48.0	48.1	49.2	51.0	49.8	48.8	47.6	45.7

Table 8b: Tax burden 1971-1989

Taxes and	71	72	73	74	75	76	77	78	79	80	81	82	83	84	85	86	87	88	89
duties as share of GDP	41.4	40.9	40.3	42.1	38.4	39.4	39.8	41.0	42.1	43.0	42.8	41.6	43.6	44.7	46.1	48.2	48.9	49.4	48.3

Source: Statistics Denmark and Ministry of Finance (2008).

However, the tax structure has changed. This is described in table 9 below:

Table 9: Development in the tax structure in Denmark 1983-2009 (selected years)

Per cent	*1983*	*1986*	*1993*	*1994*	*1997*	*1998*	*2002*	*2006*	*2007*	*2008 **	*2009 **
Income tax to Government	24.2	23.3	23.8	19.0	14.5	12.7	11.7	10.5	19.8	19.4	18.6
Income tax to municipality, church and county (-2006)	28.0	24.7	28.9	29.4	29.5	30.0	31.0	29.1	21.2	21.9	22.7
Labour market contribution	0.0	0.0	0.0	5.5	8.8	8.9	9.3	8.8	9.2	9.6	10.0
Social contributions [1)]	3.9	3.0	2.3	2.2	2.1	2.1	2.5	2.1	2.0	2.1	2.2
Property taxes, value tax [2)]	2.2	1.9	2.4	2.2	2.0	2.0	3.9	3.7	3.7	4.0	4.2
Real interest/pension returns tax	0.0	2.3	4.1	3.7	2.8	2.0	0.2	1.5	0.5	0.0	0.2
Business taxes	2.9	6.2	4.2	4.0	5.4	5.7	6.0	8.8	7.4	7.0	5.3
VAT & payroll tax	21.1	19.4	20.2	20.0	20.2	20.3	20.6	21.3	21.9	22.3	23.1
Green taxes	7.4	9.7	7.3	8.2	9.3	9.9	9.9	9.4	9.3	9.0	9.2
Other taxes on goods & services	7.1	6.8	4.0	3.7	3.3	3.8	2.8	2.7	2.6	2.4	2.2
Other taxes and duties [3)]	3.2	2.7	2.8	2.1	2.0	2.6	2.2	2.1	2.2	2.3	2.4
Total/per cent	100	100	100	100	100	100	100	100	100	100	100
Total taxes & duties (DK billion)	238	338	437	478	553	575	658	810	823	835	823

Notes: The figures from 2000 and onwards are based on Statistics Denmark's figures from the new revised national accounts.

1) ATP (the labour market supplementary pension scheme), unemployment insurance funds etc. From 1999 the figures include contributions to early retirement schemes.

2) The years before and after 2000 are non-comparable. The figures exclude taxes on rental value from 1983-1999 but include property value tax from 2000.

3) Capital tax, inheritance tax and gift duties, fees etc.

Source: Statistics Denmark and the Danish Ministry of Finance, December 2008.

One central 'innovation' is the so-called labour market contribution, which currently contributes with one tenth of total taxation, and compensates for the reduced share of income tax to central and local Governments. To all employees this change is purely cosmetic; it is a deduction from salaries and wages parallel to the personal income tax.

Every year in December the Ministry of Finance publishes an Economic Outlook for Denmark in which it is stipulated how the Danish economy is expected to fare in the short to midterm future. The 2008 edition was, of course, reflecting the world wide crisis and under the heading sharpened challenges for the Danish economy stated that "probably in 2010 there will be a considerable public fiscal deficit for the first time since the mid-1990s" (Ministry of Finance 2008, p. 7; author's translation). A marginal drop in production is expected for 2009 and a very moderate growth of 0.75% is expected for 2010. All in all, weak growth is expected for the coming three to four years. Interest rates are expected to decrease and the fiscal policy is expected to be loosened through more public spending and reduced taxation. This is viewed to result in an increase of 3.75% in real disposable income, even when unemployment increases. The report is very critical when considering policies to keep unemployment at the current very low level:

"Attempts to keep unemployment at the contemporary level will lead to increased imports, an additional reduction in competitiveness and a weakened public fiscal situation and an upward pressure on interest rates, and will therefore lead to an even bigger increase in unemployment in the longer run, compared to what can be expected now." (Ministry of Finance 2008, p. 29; author's translation)

Hence, the suggestion is not to do anything in particular to keep unemployment at the historical low level; but instead do something for everybody, and that will be reducing taxation and expecting an increase in household consumption. However, why that is *not* expected to increase imports is somewhat puzzling.

One thing which is of great concern in Korea is fertility. Allow me, therefore to show the development in absolute fertility in Denmark (figure 13 above). The overall trend during the 20th century was one of decline, especially following the strong increase in female labour market participation rate from 1960 and onward. Absolute fertility (the number of children women are having during their life time) reached an all-time low of 1.4 in 1983; but has steadily increased since and was in 2008 standing at 1.9, which is one of the highest levels within the European Union. The increase coincides with an increase in public day care for children and elderly care, and we are convinced that there is a strong connection between collective high quality care and women's willingness to be both workers and mothers.

Figure 13: Absolute fertility 1901-2008

Government Initiatives

On April 21st 2009 the newly appointed Prime Minister, Lars Løkke Rasmussen,[2] presented the Government's work programme for the coming six months, and stated that "handling of the crisis is of course the totally dominating objective" (Prime Minister's Office 2009, p. 1; author's translation). He mentioned the tax reform negotiated with Danish People's Party as a good example of this (see below) and said that the Minister of Taxation now will propose to the Parliament (*Folketinget*) the 13 Acts that it comprises, and the expectation is that the whole reform package will be accepted before the summer break 2009, and, as planned will take effect from January 1, 2010. It was also mentioned that the Minister of Social Affairs and Interior, Karen Ellemann,[3] will propose an act strengthening the public housing sector. An initiative against gang crime was also stated but not specified (but see below).

In March 2009 The Danish Government and the Danish People's Party agreed on a tax reform and additional measures to stimulate activity in the Danish economy. The tax reform continues in the direction set out in the *Spring Package* from 2004 and the agreement on *Lower Tax on Earned Income* from 2007 by substantially reducing tax on work, including marginal income taxes. The agreement is entitled *Agreement between the Danish Government and the Danish People's Party on Spring Package 2.0: Growth, Climate, Lower Taxes*. It is expected that the tax reform will reduce income taxes (including the 'green cheque') by more than DKK 28 billion (1.5% of GDP) (long-term, permanent effect). The tax reform has the following elements:

- The middle-bracket tax is abolished.[4]

---

2 Lars Løkke Rasmussen, the previous Minister of Finance was appointed Prime Minister on April 5th 2009, when the former Prime Minister, Anders Fogh Rasmussen had made public that he was applying for the post of Secretary General of the North Atlantic Treaty Organization (NATO). Both belong to the so-called Liberal Party (Venstre), a traditional conservative party historically originating as the well-off farmers representation. The Liberal Party is forming a minority Government in alliance with the so-called Conservative People's Party (Konservativt Folkeparti) which historically represented the (urban) bourgeoisie. The Government has achieved parliamentary majority for its policies through an agreement with the so-called Danish People's Party (*Dansk Folkeparti*), a rather recent populist, xenophobic party, leaning to the left of the political spectrum on social issues, and leaning to the right on value issues, such as migration.

3 Karen Nellemann was appointed Minister of the Interior and Social Affairs on April 7th 2009. Prior to that she was Member of Parliament representing the Liberal Party (since November 2007). She succeeded Karen Jespersen who was Minister of Social Welfare until the 'reshuffling' of the Government. She held that post from September 2007.

4 For many years the progressive income taxation was created through a three tier system where income up to a level currently of DKK 290,000 is taxed 44%, the income from that

- The bottom-bracket tax rate is reduced.
- The income threshold for the top-bracket tax is raised.
- An income-graduated 'Green cheque' is introduced (to compensate households for increases in duties that are levied on them).
- In addition, the pension supplement is increased by DKK 2,000.

On the other hand, taxes on pollution and energy consumption are raised. That will presumably raise incentives to protect the climate and the environment. The agreement is expected to underpin economic activities in the Danish economy at a time when the international economy is hit by a severe crisis. According to the Agreement:

- The tax reform implies that tax reductions kick in quickly in 2010 and 2011 while the financing elements are implemented gradually until 2019, thus boosting household incomes in the near term.
- Households are allowed in 2009 to withdraw all savings in the compulsory Special Pension scheme, implying a potential increase in liquidity by DKK 25-30 billion (around 1.5 per cent of GDP).
- Funds amounting to DKK 1.5 billion (0.1 per cent of GDP) are set aside to subsidies for maintenance and construction works, including energy savings in owner-occupied housing.
- The Government and the Local Governments Association will discuss ways to increase investments in construction in 2009.

The agreement states that the tax reform is fully financed. Furthermore, the reform is estimated to raise labour supply by 19,000 fulltime persons. That will boost the longer term growth potential of the Danish economy. And it also implies a marked improvement of public finances by DKK 5.5 billion (0.3 per cent of GDP) in the long term, which strengthens fiscal sustainability. (Ministry of Finance 2009a)

Needless to say, the effects are calculations, and there is no certainty that things will turn out as stipulated. When the first *Spring Package* was introduced the Economic Council of the Labour Movement published a study indicating that the population in total had its consumption increased by DKK eight billion from June to December 2004. However, an analysis of consumption and import data suggested that the tax reductions resulting from the Spring Package to a high degree increased imports and only marginally increased production and employment in Denmark (Pedersen 2005, pp. 1-2).

Regarding the possible withdrawal of savings in the compulsory Special Pension (SP) scheme the Ministry of Finance have had a survey conducted which showed that more than half of Danes will withdraw their SP savings. 20%

level and up to DKK 390,000 is taxed by 49% (the middle bracket) and the additional income is taxed 63%.

will not, and the rest does not know. Of those that wish to withdraw their savings six out of 10 will use the money for consumption, while one in three will save the money in another form or reduce debt. If Danes do that, consumption will increase by DKK nine billion (Ministry of Finance 2009b). This is considerably less than the estimated DKK 25 to 30 billion.

As with the first Spring Package the Economic Council of the Labour Movement has again conducted a number of analyses on the possible consequences and, again, the Council is sceptical concerning the distributional effects of Spring Package 2.0. Their calculations show that the average gain for the richest decile will be DKK 18,300, while the poorest decile will gain DKK 800 from the package (Juul 2009a, p. 1). In other words, the better off will benefit disproportionately from the tax reform. Because people live segregated, the inequality in distribution will also be reflected spatially. Hence Jonas Juul (2009b, p. 1) calculated that inhabitants in the rich neighbourhood of Gentofte municipality in average will gain DKK 12,600 from the tax reform, while the inhabitants in the poor municipality of Langeland in average only will gain DKK 2,600. Furthermore, since men have higher incomes than women the distributional effect of the Spring Package 2.0 will disproportionately benefit men. They will on average gain DKK 2,000 more than women (Juul 2009c, p. 1).

The Ministry of the Interior and Social Affairs has taken a number of initiatives which directly or indirectly relate to the current crisis. On March 27th 2009 it was announced that an agreement between the Government, Danish Peoples Party and the so-called Radical Party (Det Radikale) was made concerning housing which was intended to fight ghettoization. By ghettoization are understood public housing estates where a large group of citizens are unemployed or otherwise outside the labour market. There has been an unfortunate concentration of ethnic minority marginalized people in many public housing estates. Part of the agreement consisted of de-bureaucratization measures, which will enable the municipalities and the housing associations to more quickly change and experiment with the development. They will also be allowed to leave apartments empty until so-called resource strong tenants want to move into the estate. "The many and rigid rules will be substituted by dialogue and collaboration" a communiqué from the Ministry of the Interior and Social Affairs said (2009a, p. 1). The agreement supposedly makes it cheaper to rent apartments within the public housing estates. The demands for the new apartments to be 'energy friendly' were specified and increased. It is expected that in total the agreement will lead to some 4,000 to 5,000 more units per year (Ministry of the Interior and Social Affairs 2009a, p. 1).

On July 1st 2009 a new act became effective. Its objective is to reduce the number of citizens being evicted from their apartments because of arrears. The tenant will then have a longer period of time between notification of behind payment of rent and actual eviction. The municipality will also be notified earlier that something is wrong. After notification the municipality must contact the tenant and judge if and eventually what it can do to help. Furthermore, the Ministry speculates that some tenants have a too high rent in relation to their income and should receive assistance in finding a cheaper apartment. As a new thing the municipality in those cases can help out with the moving costs. (Ministry of the Interior and Social Affairs 2009b, p. 1)

On April 30th the Ministry announced that it will support five voluntary organizations with DKK 16 million in order for them to establish debt counselling toward socially marginalized people in a number of cities across the country. They will be performed by people with a background from the financial sector such as bank clerks and accountants. People with debt, low income and low net disposable income may contact the new created debt counselling services and receive advice free of charge on how to get rid of debt and to create a personal/family budget. (Ministry of the Interior and Social Affairs 2009c, p. 1)

From a financial point of view the largest initiative taken by the Ministry was the creation of funds amounting to more than DKK 850 million which shall enable the municipalities to move investments up in time, i.e. carry them out earlier than otherwise expected. The funds are a combination of grants (DKK 212 millions) and loans (DKK 649 millions). They can be used for renovation of existing institutions such as schools, kindergartens and old-age homes, or to build new such institutions which 'are close to the citizens' (Ministry of the Interior and Social Affairs 2009d, p. 1). The Minister Karen Ellemann expressed that she expects this initiative to strengthen employment.

On April 29th 2009 the Minister of Justice, Brian Mikkelsen, presented to the Parliament a Bill which – if accepted – will lead to a number of initiatives to combat the increasing gang violence. Particularly in the capital of Copenhagen, and often in one neighbourhood (*Nørrebro*) there have been a number of shooting incidents which are viewed as a gang war between certain biker groups (Hells Angels) and certain ethnic groups. On a number of occasions completely innocent by-passers have been hit and killed. The Government has considered that this is a threat to "normal societal life in the particular neighbourhoods" and suggested that the punishment for possession of illegal weapons and ammunition in the street doubles to minimum one year imprisonment. It shall also be made easier for the police to investigate and it will have easier access to telephone tapings among many other changes which all amount to a considerable sharpening of the measures. (Ministry of Justice 2009, p. 1) The social problems which the Government tries to tackle with these initiatives are not directly related to the present economic crisis; but they may very well be aggravated by it. The predominantly younger and male people involved in the 'gang' activities are among the least skilled and most marginalized segments of the Danish population; and these segments are the first to feel the negative consequences of crisis in the form of unemployment and/or reduced financial resources.

Conclusion

The well preparedness and the robustness of Danish welfare society is one important backdrop for the way the economic crisis was met. The well preparedness was in no small way a result of very recent welfare reforms that have meant significant changes in both labour market policies and social policies. The robustness is a reflection of many years of commitment to a public responsibility for citizens' well-being. Advice given to the Danish Government from the various expert commissions and its own civil servants has been rather uniform. The concern has been about labour shortage *not* about unemployment. Hence, suggested changes have gone in the direction of increasing work incentives by rolling back social entitlements, which is a continuation of what happened with the labour market reform in the mid-1990s and the reform of social assistance during the 2000s (Abrahamson 2006). With respect to unemployment insurance the benefit period was then reduced from nine to four years, and recently the Labour Market Commission suggested reducing the period to about two years, arguing that a long benefit period might reduce job seeking and thus prolong unemployment spells. As demonstrated above the value of both unemployment benefits and social assistance have decreased over the last ten years. Furthermore, early retirement has been made more difficult, and it has been decided to increase retirement age to 67 from the current age of 65, but this is not expected to take place before 2019, unless a majority in Parliament listens to the advice given by the Labour Market Reform to having it being effective already from 2009. The recent changes and the suggested changes cannot, however be interpreted as a rolling back of the Danish welfare state. Total social expenditure is not decreasing, relatively speaking, as share of GDP, it is stagnating, but in absolute terms, per capita spending, and social expenditure has increased every year since it has been measured. What is important to keep in mind is that the Danish welfare state is, quantitatively speaking, not so much about supporting the poor and/or unemployed through targeted measures, but rather about supporting the population as a whole through universal services such as high quality health care free of charge, education including higher education free of charge, heavily subsidized day-care, comprehensive elderly care also free of charge, family allowances to all families with children irrespective of their income, and old age pension to all seniors irrespective of their income and wealth. A precondition for this is a tax burden of about 50% of GDP and a very high level of formal employment. Especially female employment is very high in Denmark and is interlinked with the comprehensive care services provided by various welfare state institutions. As a consequence of this Danish women are both able to raise children and be formally employed, which shows up in a relatively high absolute fertility rate of currently 1.9.

Together with a highly organized labour market[5] with working conditions and wage negotiations institutionalized through agreements between the social partners Denmark has developed a very flexible labour market as demonstrated above. There is a high degree of mobility and short job tenure in Denmark. Supposedly this leads to a very dynamic labour market where it is not risky for employers to hire in good times, since they can easily fire in bad times. Coupled with an extensive system of social security and facilitated by active labour market policies the Danish model has been dubbed *flexicurity*. The title of this article asks the question whether this system stands the test of the current crisis, and the answer is a limited yes. Yes in the sense that unemployed people are being taken care of either through benefits from the voluntary unemployment insurance, or through social assistance benefits, and yes because long-term unemployment was, is and is expected also in the foreseeable future to be low. However, the answer is also a limited yes, because the systems are less generous over time and are expected to be even less generous in the future, and activation which predominantly works via the scare or motivation effect is a very costly way of scaring or motivating unemployed people to go out of their way to seek and find whatever kind of employment under whatever conditions wherever in the country.

Given the situation of historically high employment and historically low unemployment at the point in time when the international crisis hit Denmark the Government in accordance with advice given by both groups of experts and its own civil servants decided to tackle the crisis through macroeconomic interventions which supposedly will benefit the whole population rather than focusing on the increasing but small group of unemployed people through new social policy measures. Hence the major intervention comes in the form of a tax reform which is expected to significantly increase private consumption from 2010 and the coming years. The reduction in personal income tax is coupled with an increase in environmental taxes which is expected to motivate companies to change their production and organization toward less energy consumption, less waste and less pollution. That it probably will. However, the critical point seems to be whether the increase in private consumption will lead to an increase in domestic demand and thus help to increase domestic production and growth, as expected by the Government, or whether the accelerated private consumption predominantly will lead to an increase in imports, hence benefitting production elsewhere, but not domestically. Probably, part of the increase in disposable incomes will be spent on consumption of locally produced services and goods and this way contribute to an increase in growth, but some of the additional disposa-

---

5 The Nordic countries have the highest trade union membership rates in OECD. Even if declining since the highest rate in 1982 of 82%, in 2007 69% of Danish workers were members of a trade union (OECD 2009). Concurrently, most employers are also members of an employers association.

ble income is going to be spent on imported goods and consumption of services outside the country such as tourism. And since the benefits disproportionately go to the better off, an import bias in their consumption could be expected. There is therefore some uncertainty concerning the effects of the major Government crisis governance measure.

Other initiatives by the Government are certain to have an immediate effect on unemployment, and that goes for the initiatives directed toward building, renovation and construction sectors. As described above part of the tax reform package is grants to help private households renovate their homes, and the major initiative administered by the Ministry of the Interior and Social Affairs is to provide funds – partly grants, partly loans – to the municipalities to enable them to renovate and construct 'citizen near' institutions such as schools, kindergartens old age homes and so on. The same ministry is also administrating legislation which will help the municipalities in cooperation with the housing associations to construct more public housing units. The building and construction sectors were the first ones to feel the effect of the crisis in the form of declining demand and increasing unemployment, so relatively speaking; it is within these sectors we find the most unemployed, or more correctly the highest unemployment rates. Currently unemployment among skilled construction workers is 7%, while the average is a little less than 3% (Bjørsted & Pedersen 2009, p. 2). Everything else being equal, these Government initiatives will have a positive effect on unemployment. Furthermore, the construction sector has a high multiplier effect, so a publically initiated increase in activities there is likely to spill-over into other sectors.

Another certainty is that the major initiative, namely reducing personal income tax especially on the last earned *kroner* will contribute to more inequality in the Danish society. It will disproportionately benefit the better off and thus continue the increase in inequality which Denmark has experienced since the mid-1990s. From 1986 to 1996 the Gini-coefficient was steady at around 0.20, but has since equally steadily increased and stood in 2006 at 0.24 (Ministry of Finance 2009c, p. 13). The increase in income inequality is reflected in an increase in relative poverty. There is some disagreement among different sources about the level of relative poverty defined as the share of the population receiving less than 50 or 60% of the median income. According to Eurostat (2009) at-risk-of-poverty (60% cut-off line) in Denmark has increased from 10% in 1997 to 12% in 2007, while the Ministry of Finance has calculated that the development has been an increase from 7% in 1994 to 10% in 2006. Hence there is a bit of disagreement about the level but not on the trend, and the difference in levels is probably a reflection of applying the same methodology to different data sets. By the more conservative cut-off line of 50% of the median income, poverty has increased from 3.6% in 1994 to 5% in 2006 as calculated by the Ministry of Finance (2009c, p. 18). The Economic Council of the Labour Movement has calculated income poverty by applying the 50% cut-off line and using the same methodology and the same data set, so not surprisingly they reached the same number of poor Danes as was identified by the Ministry of Finance, and they calculated the increase from 2001 to 2006 to be 26%. But they also show that out of the 271,000 income poor Danes in 2006, 98,000 were students. Thus, if students are left out of the calculations income poverty in Denmark is reduced to in average 3.2% of the population and long-term poverty only concerns 0.8% (Dahl, Quitzau & Vilhelmsen 2009, pp. 1, 7, 8). Thus, there is widespread agreement that inequality is on the increase in Denmark and that the present crisis will increase it even more both because of increasing unemployment *and* because the Government chose tax reductions on marginal personal taxation as the major means of crisis governance.

The question is, however, whether increasing inequality and poverty is likely to threaten social cohesion? Over all, that is not to be expected because the increase was from such low levels. Denmark is still and in the foreseeable future continues to be among the most egalitarian countries in the world with the smallest share of the population living in poverty. Furthermore, those sectors most severely hit by unemployment such as construction are 'used' to periods of high unemployment, but trust that it is a temporary situation; and the sector will receive considerable public investment during the next years. Even if compensation within the unemployment insurance system is on the decline it still keeps recipients above the poverty line, and those who have to get by on the very modest social assistance benefit are the most marginalized and few in numbers with very little 'voice'. Having said that it remains to be seen if the Government's initiatives toward the so-called gang wars in Copenhagen have the intended effects.

In line with the general idea behind the universal welfare state that services should benefit all or most of the population the Danish Government has chosen to govern crisis intervention to the benefit of the population at large instead of targeting the unemployed and the marginalized. The philosophy seems to be that the rising tide will lift all ships, small as well as big ones. But it could only do so because of the very favourable situation which prevailed when the crisis reached Denmark.

Finally a word of caution. Crisis governance and assessment is a moving target: Many, about half of the sources for this article were published during April and May 2009, i.e. when writing. Perhaps its content and conclusions would have looked quite different had it been written in say six months' time, when other and different data will be available. Also, even if one is sympathetic to the institutional setup of the Danish welfare state and the current crisis governance, those measures are not easily exportable to different settings. The Danish experience is premised on a very long tradition for transparent democratic rule, a political culture dominated by consensus and compromise, a very high level of institutionalization and organization and a very high level of trust in Government. Furthermore, from the outset most people are in formal employment and are willing to pay half of their income through various forms of taxes.

References

Abrahamson, Peter (2003), 'The end of the Scandinavian model? Welfare reform in the Nordic countries', *Journal of Societal and Social Policy,* vol. 2 (2), pp. 19-36.

Abrahamson, Peter (2006), 'Welfare reform: renewal or deviation?', in John Campbell; John Hall & Ove K. Pedersen (eds.), *National Identity and the Varieties of Capitalism: The Danish Experience*, Montreal: McGill University Press, pp. 356-374.

Arbejdsmarkedskommissionen (2008), *Arbejde, vækst og velfærd.* Copenhagen.

Arbejdsmarkedskommissionen (2009), *Resume af oplæg til trepartsmøde.* Copenhagen.

Bach, Henning Bjerregård (1999), *Længerevarende ledighed – jobsøgning og beskæftigelses-chancer.* Copenhagen: National Institute of Social Research (Report # 99: 12).

Bach, Henning Bjerregård (2002), *Kontanthjælpsmodtagere – aktivering og arbejdsudbud.* Copenhagen: National Institute of Social Research (Report # 02: 3).

Bjørsted, Erik & Frederik Pedersen (2009), *Byggeledigheden tordner I vejret.* Copenhagen: Economic Council of the Labour Movement.

Bredgaard, Thomas; Larsen, Flemming & Per Kongshøj Madsen (2006), *The challenge of identifying flexicurity in action.* Paper for the workshop 'Flexicurity and Beyond' Aalborg, 12-13 October.

Dahl, Sigrid; Quitzau, Jarl & Jes Vilhelmsen (2009), *Fattigdommens Danmarkskort.* Copenhagen: Economic Council of the Labour Movement.

Eurostat (2009), *Statistics on-line.* Luxembourg. Accessed several times May 2009.

Filges, Trine; Harsløv, Ivan & Mogens Nord-Larsen (2002), *Revalidering: deltagelse, forløb og effekter.* Copenhagen: National Institute of Social Research (Report # 02: 2).

Geerdsen, Lars (2003), *Marginalisation Processes in the Danish Labour Market.* Copenhagen: National Institute of Social Research (Report # 03: 24).

Harsløv, Ivan; Jensen. Søren; Kruhøffer, Anette; Møller, Sanne Nissen; Hansen, Anders Ellegaard & Anders Rosdahl (2004), *Virksomhedsrevalidering.* Copenhagen: National Institute of Social Research (Report # 04: 2).

Ibsen, Rikke & Niels Westergaard-Nielsen (2005), *Job creation and destruction over the business cycles and the impact on individual job flows in Denmark 1980 – 2001.* Aarhus: Center for Corporate Performance, Aarhus School of Business (Working Paper).

Juul, Jonas Schyltz (2009a), *Fordelingeeffekter af aftale om forårspakke 2.0.* Copenhagen: Economic Council of the Labour Movement.

Juul, Jonas Schyltz (2009b), *Skæv regional fordeling i forårspakke 2.0.* Copenhagen: Economic Council of the Labour Movement.

Juul, Jonas Schyltz (2009c), 'Størst gevinst til mænd af regeringens forårspakke 2.0.' Copenhagen: Economic Council of the Labour Movement.

Larsen, F. & Mikkel Mailand (2007), 'Danish Activation Policy: The Role of the Normative Foundation, the Institutional Set-up and Other Drivers', in Amparo Serrano Pascual & Lars Magnusson (eds.), *Reshaping Welfare States and Activation Regimes in Europe.* Bern et al.: P.I.E Peter Lang (Quoted from manuscript).

Madsen, Per Kongshøj (2006), 'How can it possibly fly? The paradox of a dynamic labour market in a Scandinavian welfare state', in John Campbell, John Hall & Ove K. Pedersen (eds.), *National Identity and the Varieties of Capitalism: The Danish Experience*. Montreal: McGill University Press, pp. 323-355.

Ministry of Finance (2006), *Historisk aftale om velfærdsreformer*. Copenhagen.

Ministry of Finance (2007), *Kommissorium for Arbejdsmarkedskommissionen*. Copenhagen.

Ministry of Finance (2008), *Økonomisk redegørelse*. Copenhagen.

Ministry of Finance (2009a), *Aftale mellem regeringen og Dansk Folkeparti om forårspakke 2.0 – Vækst, klima, lavere skat*. Copenhagen.

Ministry of Finance (2009b), *Danskerne vil hæve SP-opsparingen*. Copenhagen.

Ministry of Finance (2009c), *Indkomstudvikling og – fordeling I Danmark*. Copenhagen.

Ministry of Interior and Health (2004), *Aftale om Strukturreform*. Copenhagen.

Ministry of the Interior and Social Affairs (2009a), *Nyt boligforlig bekæmper ghettoisering*. Copenhagen.

Ministry of the Interior and Social Affairs (2009b), *Færre lejere sættes på gaden*. Copenhagen.

Ministry of the Interior and Social Affairs (2009c), *Gratis gældsrådgivning til social udsatte borgere*. Copenhagen.

Ministry of the Interior and Social Affairs (2009d), *Tilskud og lån sætter gang i kommuners investeringer*. Copenhagen.

Ministry of Justice (2009), *Regeringen klar med bandepakke*. Copenhagen.

Ministry of State (2003), *Kommissorium for Velfærdskommissionen*. Copenhagen.

OECD (2009), *OECD Data base*. Paris. Accessed several times April and May 2009.

Palme, J. (1999), *The Nordic model and the modernisation of social protection in Europe*. Copenhagen: Nordic Council of Ministers.

Pedersen, Frederik I. (2005), *Forårspakken går til øget import*. Copenhagen: Economic Council of the Labour Movement.

Prime Minister's Office (2009), *Statsministeren om regeringens arbejdsprogramme frem til sommer. Fra pressemødet den 21. April 2009*. Copenhagen.

Statistics Denmark (2005), 'Udgifter til sociale ydelser 1999-2004', *Sociale Forhold, Sundhed og Retsvæsen*, p. 17.

Statistics Denmark (2008), 'Udgifter til sociale ydelser 2002-2007', *Sociale Forhold, Sundhed og Retsvæsen*, p. 16.

Statistics Denmark (2009), *Statistikbanken*. Copenhagen.

Swank, D. (2000), 'Social democratic welfare states in a global economy', in R. Geyer; C. Ingebritsen & J.W. Moses (eds.), *Globalization, Europeanization and the end of Scandinavian social democracy?* London: Macmillan, pp. 85-138.

The Danish Government (2005), *The Danish Reform Strategy. Contribution to EU's Growth and Employment Strategy (The Lisbon Strategy)*. Copenhagen: Ministry of Finance.

Velfærdskommissionen [Welfare Reform Commission] (2005), *Fremtidens velfærd - vores valg*. Copenhagen.

Appendix: Social expenditure as share of GDP OECD 1980 -2005

(Data extracted on 02 May 2009, 06:47 UTC (GMT) from OECD. Stat)

Year	*1980*	*1985*	*1990*	*1995*	*2000*	*2001*	*2002*	*2003*	*2004*	*2005*
Country										
Australia	10.6	12.5	13.6	16.6	17.8	17.3	17.5	17.8	17.7	17.1
Austria	22.5	23.8	23.9	26.5	26.4	26.6	27.0	27.5	27.3	27.2
Belgium	23.5	26.0	24.9	26.2	25.3	25.8	26.2	26.5	26.6	26.4
Canada	13.7	17.0	18.1	18.9	16.5	17.0	17.1	17.2	16.6	16.5
Czech Republic	..	..	16.0	18.2	19.8	19.8	20.6	20.7	19.7	19.5
Denmark	24.8	23.2	25.1	28.9	25.6	25.9	26.6	27.6	27.5	26.9
Finland	18.0	22.5	24.2	30.9	24.3	24.2	25.0	25.8	26.0	26.1
France	20.8	26.0	25.1	28.6	27.9	27.9	28.6	29.0	29.1	29.2
Germany	22.7	23.2	22.3	26.5	26.2	26.3	27.0	27.3	26.7	26.7
Greece	10.2	16	16.5	17.3	19.2	20.6	20.0	19.9	19.9	20.5
Hungary	..	..	..	..	20.0	20.2	21.4	22.2	21.7	22.5
Iceland	..	..	13.7	15.2	15.3	15.3	16.9	18.2	17.9	16.9
Ireland	16.7	21.3	14.9	15.7	13.6	14.4	15.3	15.8	16.2	16.7
Italy	18	20.8	19.9	19.9	23.3	23.5	24.0	24.4	24.7	25.0
Japan	10.6	11.4	11.4	14.3	16.5	17.4	17.8	18.1	18.2	18.6
Korea	..	..	2.9	3.3	5.0	5.4	5.3	5.6	6.3	6.9
Luxembourg	20.6	20.2	19.1	20.8	19.7	20.8	22.0	23.4	23.9	23.2
Mexico	..	1.9	3.6	4.7	5.8	5.9	6.3	6.8	6.7	7.0
Netherlands	24.8	25.3	25.6	23.8	19.8	19.7	20.5	21.2	21.1	20.9
New Zealand	17.2	17.9	21.8	18.9	19.4	18.6	18.7	18.2	18	18.5
Norway	16.9	17.8	22.3	23.3	21.3	22.2	23.6	24.5	23.2	21.6
Poland	..	..	14.9	22.6	20.5	21.9	22.3	22.3	21.4	21.0
Portugal	10.2	10.4	12.9	17	19.6	19.9	21.3	22.9	23.1	..
Slovak Rep.	..	..	..	18.6	17.9	17.6	17.7	17.1	16.5	16.6
Spain	15.5	17.8	19.9	21.4	20.3	20	20.4	21	21.2	21.2
Sweden	27.1	29.4	30.2	32.1	28.5	28.9	29.5	30.3	29.8	29.4
Switzerland	13.5	14.5	13.4	17.5	17.9	18.4	19.2	20.3	20.3	20.3
Turkey	4.3	4.2	7.6	7.5	..	..	..	..	..	13.7
U.K.	16.7	19.8	17.0	20.2	19.2	20.1	20.0	20.5	21.1	21.3
United States	13.1	13.1	13.4	15.3	14.5	15.1	15.9	16.2	16.1	15.9
OECD - Total	16.0	17.7	18.1	19.9	19.3	19.7	20.2	20.7	20.6	20.5

7 Policy Tasks for Social Integration in Times of the Economic Crisis: the Case of South Korea

Yong Chan Byun

Introduction

The global financial crisis triggered by the subprime mortgage loans in the U.S. has spilled over to other businesses. The UN World Economic Situation and Prospects 2009 showed negative projections for high-income countries such as the U.S. (-1.9%), Japan -0.6%, and the Euro zone (-1.5%) as well as the global economy (-0.4%) (UN 2009). Export-driven South Korea is also expected to decrease at -2% in 2009 due to the spread of the global economic crisis.

The potential growth rate of South Korea fell from 8.6% in the 1980s to 6.3% in the 1990s and again to the 4% range in recent years, and the growth of productivity of consumer spending, manufacturing, and service industries continues to be sluggish. South Korea's growth rate is estimated to have slowed down due to low consumer spending amid the deterioration of external economic conditions such as uncertainties in the global financial markets and global economic contraction. In addition, factors like persistent household debt, uncertainty about future income, worsening inequality of income, slow job growth will have an impact on domestic spending.

Such internal and external economic conditions are projected to be the major factor behind the slump in local consumption: slow job growth, and inflation, in turn causing instability of income and increasing the gap between social classes. As a result, the size of the underprivileged social layers is predicted to increase in the course of social development. If we define those in the 50-150% of median income as middle class, the real income of middle class South Koreans has grown from 1995 to 2005 to recover to the pre-1997 financial crisis level in 2003. In contrast, that of the bottom 20% (low-income bracket) are reported to have been lower than that of 1997 (You Kyung Joon 2008). Such stagnation of income was caused by the adjustment of global employment structure. In other words, the shrinking of manufacturing's share of employment has reduced the number of jobs for the low-income brackets.

In order to become a leader in the global community, the South Korean Government is working double time to build an effective and efficient social safety net that will speed up social integration based on growth-friendly policies for supporting market. Social integration is a major economic-political factor in spurring continuous development and essential in coping with new social risks and conflicts, ultimately overcoming economic recession. Social integration for creating an environment where understanding and cooperation transcends the class and generation gaps is crucial to ensuring the well-being of citizens as well as economic growth.

Korea has adopted active welfare as one of the national initiatives for achieving both economic growth and social integration. Active welfare is defined as a concept to provide a framework to address ineffectiveness of policy outcomes and inefficient allocation of resources and to proactively respond to socioeconomic conditions, ultimately establishing a virtuous cycle of economic growth and expansion of welfare benefits for a sustainable welfare system in the future. However, since this global economic crisis threatens both economic growth and social integration of countries around the world, Korea is going the extra mile to build an appropriate social safety net.

This study aims at examining the general economic conditions facing Korea and the underprivileged classes, on which, they have direct impact. Also, it will explore the concept of social integration and international trends concerning the concept and then discuss the strategies of the Korean Government for tacking the economic downturn.

Ripple Effect of the Economic Crisis

The economic slowdown is forecast to raise the poverty and unemployment rates and worsen the distribution index of Korea. According to estimates by the Korea Institute for Health and Social Affairs, if the GDP growth rate turns negative, absolute poverty rate reaches about 13-14%, the number of unemployed persons is likely to be more than 1 million, and Gini's coefficient is projected to go up again from the level of the 1997 financial crisis (Kim Mi Gon 2009; Choi Sung Eun 2009).

An economic downturn has a direct impact on unemployment, and is followed by increase in poverty rate. As shown in figure 1, growth rate hit bottom at -6.9% in 1998 and unemployment rate also peaked at 7.0% in the same year. Poverty rate topped out at 8.6% in 1999. Speed of recovery of social indicators like poverty rate and inequality is slower than that of economic indicators such as growth rate and unemployment rate. Financial woes tend to have a long-term impact in social terms than economic terms, and the ensuing changes in the structure of employment and income distribution may negatively affect a society for much longer periods of time. For example, the middle class tend to have much less financial wealth, the underprivileged, including low-income class, children, senior citizens, the disabled, and single-parent families might be the most negatively affected. Worse still, increase in unemployment and poverty may lead to a rising number of social pathological incidents such as suicide, breakup of family, and crimes caused by economic woes.

Table 1: Simulation of poverty rate based on economic growth rate (in %)

Assumption		*Estimation*	
GDP growth rate	Unemployment rate [1]	Relative poverty rate (based on 40% of median income) [2]	Absolute poverty rate [3]
4	3.40	12.42	11.85
3	3.50	12.79	12.24
2	3.70	13.20	12.63
1	3.80	13.57	13.03
0	3.95	13.96	13.42
-1	4.10	14.35	13.81
-2	4.25	14.74	14.20
-3	4.40	15.13	14.59
-4	4.55	15.52	14.98

Notes: 1) Job search duration of four weeks or more. Some data is quoted from KDI documents, and the others are assumptions. 2) Ratio of population whose disposable income is less than median income 40%. All households, except for farming and fishing. 3) All households except for farming and fishing households

Source: Kim Mi Gon, internal data, the Korea Institute for Health and Social Affairs, 2009.

Figure 1: Trends of growth rate, unemployment rate, and poverty rate in the aftermath of the 1997 financial crisis

Source: Kim, Yongha 2009.

The economic crisis is expected to wage a particularly severe attack on the working poor, credit delinquents, the elderly, the disabled, and children in terms of poverty rate and the number of people in the brackets. Individuals and families may began to default on their loans due to declining housing prices and rising interest rates, resulting in credit delinquency and household insolvency. If the working poor become poorer, the cycle of inherited poverty may become worse because they are so financially weak that they are unable to afford education for their children, making them even more susceptible to the downswing in the economic cycle, which, also, a sudden erosion of the middle class can cause people in the bracket to take extra risks.

Not only that. The economic downturn aggravates the economic conditions of not only senior citizens but also the base of economic security for older people. A sharp erosion of employment opportunities for prime age workers is coupled with contraction of work opportunities for senior citizens, reducing private transfer income of families. Worsening poverty of the elderly may limit their access to healthcare facilities, directly leading to deterioration of the health conditions of the elderly and ultimately burdening families and the overall national economy. In addition, the diminishing family support for the elderly could increase the rate of abuse and desertion of senior citizens.

Moreover, contraction of business activities caused by a recession would negatively affect the employment rate of the disabled workers whose productivity is relatively lower, ultimately aggravating their quality of life. Decline in national income is also likely to decrease private transfer income, a main source of income for the disabled families. Such decrease could even limit their spending on basic healthcare and daily life, again deteriorating their quality of life.

We can also predict that rising unemployment and breakup of families would raise levels of child poverty. The 1997 financial crisis saw a sharp increase in the number of children living in poverty, deserted or lost, sharply driving up the demand for social services, foster families and protection of abused children. The number of runaway children and joint suicides with children are expected to rise amid economic difficulties, leading to increase in personal loss and social cost. In addition, a dwindling capacity of families to sustain care giving responsibilities is likely to reduce advance rate to higher school level of children and pass down poverty to successive generations. Given that children are our future, it is imperative for us to push for early intervention and family support programmes for the children at risk in order to prevent the breakup of families.

Recession-triggered poverty coupled with increase in nuclear families tends to accelerate the breakup of families. As mentioned earlier, a family's capacity to protect older people, children, and the disabled members has weakened over the last few years, leading to a rising number of desertion and abuse, neglect of senior citizens and children, and diminishing private income transfers. As a result, the poverty rate of the underprivileged has also risen. Needless to say, a prolonged economic downturn could put those in the low-income brackets in a serious financial squeeze.

In the past, the primary reason for poverty was loss of the capacity to earn money such as aging, disability, or disease. Because there had been a high demand for labour for economic development projects, most of the workers did not live in poverty. So, the poverty of some workers did not garner attention because laziness was considered to be the biggest reason for poverty. However, the labour market has changed substantially since the 1997 financial crisis. New classes of people living in poverty started to emerge such as the working poor, long-term unemployed workers, unemployed prime age workers, female householders, and single-parent families with the main reasons for their poverty being the fierce competition in the global markets, increase of non-regular workers, corporate restructuring and streamlining, various types of families, and breakup of families.

Poverty triggered by these 'new social risks' is called new poverty. Thus, new classes at risk are created by shift of social structure. Classes at risk is also defined as poverty generated by crisis situations like a financial crisis or after a certain period of time (2007) probably because the new social phenomenon (new social risk) and incident (financial crisis) were happening at the same time. However, it would be more appropriate and meaningful to define classes at risk as "classes in poverty who were reduced to poverty due to unregulated new social risks" (Kim Yong Ha 2009). Thus, some of the existing classes in poverty may be included in the class at risk and new populations in poverty may also be included in the class. In other words, people became poor for typical reasons before the 1997 crisis, while new types of classes at risk started emerging on the surface for poverty after the period of time.

If we define new types of classes at risk as "those reduced to poverty due to new social risks out of the total population in poverty", the size of classes at risk can be defined as "the total number of family members of classes at risk". The estimated number of the working poor living below the minimum cost of living was 1.56 million in 2007. And the 2009 economic outlook forecast that the number of the working poor will grow from 1.79 million (growth rate assumed to be 4%) to 2.42 million (growth rate assumed to be -4%). Because the working poor refer to members of poor families who are physically capable of working, the main target of labour policy is to improve their economic conditions.

The size of the working poor class is not directly related to that of classes at risk because classes at risk include the number of family members who are not capable of working and living with the working poor. Therefore, classes at risk are the main target of welfare policy as well as labour policy. In terms of contingency plan, size of classes at risk before and after the 2007 financial crisis can be estimated as follows (cf. table 3). As of 2008, the number of people included in classes at risk caused by new social risks before the financial crisis were estimated to be about 2.82 million. And the number of new classes at risk for the same reason is estimated to be about 0.32-1.2 million.

Table 2: Estimates of the working poor in 2009 (in %; households: 1,000)

Working poor in 2007	*Assumption*		*Estimation*			
	GDP growth rate	*Unem-ployment rate*	*Increase in poverty rate* 1)	*Increase in number of poor households* 2)	*Increase in number of working poor households* 3)	*Increase in number of working poor* 4) *(1,000 per-sons)*
1.56 Million 5)	4	3.40	1.09	176,054	126,735	232
	3	3.50	1.44	233,283	167,933	308
	2	3.70	1.83	296,463	213,414	391
	1	3.80	2.19	353,692	254,611	467
	0	3.95	2.56	413,896	297,950	546
	-1	4.10	2.93	474,101	341,290	625
	-2	4.25	3.31	534,305	384,629	705
	-3	4.40	3.68	594,510	427,968	784
	-4	4.55	4.05	654,714	471,307	864

Notes: 1) Increase in absolute poverty rate in 2009 compared to 2007; 2) Number of nationwide households (16,158,334) multiplied by increase in poverty rate; 3) Multiplied by the rate of the working poor households out of those of 100-150% of the minimum cost of living (71.99%); 4) Apply the average number of capable workers per the second-lowest working poor families and the third-lowest working poor families (1.83); 5) The working poor of absolute poverty.

Source: Kim Yongha 2009.

Table 3: Estimates of classes at risk in 2009 (in %)

Class at risk in 2007	*Assumption*		*Estimation*			
	GDP growth rate	*Unemploy-ment rate*	*Increase in poverty rate* 1)	*Increase in number of poor house-holds* 2)	*Increase in number of working poor households* 3)	*Increase in number of classes at risk* 4)
	4	3.40	1.09	176,054	126,735	32.3
	3	3.50	1.44	233,283	167,933	42.8
	2	3.70	1.83	296,463	213,414	54.4
	1	3.80	2.19	353,692	254,611	64.9
2.82 Million 5)	0	3.95	2.56	413,896	297,950	76.0
	-1	4.10	2.93	474,101	341,290	87.0
	-2	4.25	3.31	534,305	384,629	98.1
	-3	4.40	3.68	594,510	427,968	109.1
	-4	4.55	4.05	654,714	471,307	120.2

Notes: 1) Increase in absolute poverty rate in 2009 compared to 2007. 2) Number of nationwide households (16,158,334) multiplied by increase in poverty rate. 3) Multiplied by the rate of the working poor households out of those living in 100-150% of the minimum cost of living (71.99%). 4) Apply the average number of family members per the second-lowest working poor households and the third-lowest working poor households (2.5). 5) Total number of households (16,158,334) × rate of households in absolute poverty (14.1%) × average number of family members (2.2).
Source: Kim Yongha 2009.

An economic crisis affects not only the low-income class but also the middle class as well. According to 'the Definition and Estimation of the Middle Class' released by the KDI (Yu Kyung Joon 2008), the size of the middle class of Korea diminished by about 10%, 10 years after the financial crisis. Specifically, the proportion of the middle class has continued to fall from 68.7% in 1996 to 61.1% in 2000, to 58.5% in 2006, and again to 57.6% in 2007. In contrast, that of the poor class has continuously increased from 11.2% in 1996, to 15.5% in 2000, to 17.4% in 2006, and again to 17.8% in 2007. That of the upper class has also risen from 20.1% in 1996 to 24.6% in 2007. From 1996 to 2007, the rate of middle class households moving up to the upper class was about 3.4%, while those moving down to the poor class was more than double the number to reach 7%. KDI analysed that the reasons for the worsening indicators were economic downturn, collapse of self-employed businesses, and increase of one-person households. That is why the Korean Government needs to take comprehensive action for the middle class. All in all, it is imperative for the Government to dispel concerns of citizens by setting up Government-level measures for protecting people from falling into poverty and supporting economic recovery of individuals after economic hardships, ultimately facilitating social integration. This also complies with the Governmental initiative of active welfare for improving the livelihood of social minorities and the underprivileged, and enhancing the quality of life of people.

Concept of Social Integration and International Trends

In Korea, the term 'social integration' is interpreted as one of the three concepts: Social Inclusion, Social Integration, or Social Cohesion (노대명 2009). The three sound similar but are different in many ways. First of all, social inclusion refers to the protection of those who are not covered by the social security system or more broadly, protection of the people from social risks including poverty and unemployment. Thus, this concept is more about embracing people than about integrating people. And social integration means pursuit of common social goals by providing equal opportunities to all people, but the concept is sometimes negatively translated as imposition of uniformity because it also has something to do with forced imposition of republican values based on the tradition of French republicanism. For instance, France prohibited Muslim girls from wearing head scarves in public schools in order to remove religious elements from education. Lastly, social cohesion is defined as the process of developing shared values, shared challenges based on a sense of trust, hope, and reciprocity among all citizens. Therefore, what we need right now are social initiatives under the concept of social cohesion.

Since the 1990s, countries around the world have been facing a rising number of unemployed or low-income workers and widening income inequality, leading to weakened social solidarity. Given the increasing number of social risks, it is inevitable to institutionalize a mechanism for mitigating social risks that directly affect social integration since the trend of increasing social threats will not be removed completely even though a society pulls out of a recession. This also means that social integration would not be solidified after a crisis without an institutional basis for integration (Rho Dae Myung 2009a). Social inclusion policies pushed ahead by the EU Member States established a framework for systematically establishing national action plans based on the agreed upon guidelines, and consistently evaluating their progress (Gang Sin Wook 2005; Mun Jin Young 2004). Indeed, Social Inclusion Indicators of the EU provide implications for the directions of social integration policies. The table below shows representative social integration indicators the EU suggested with regard to income, employment, healthcare, and housing.

National action plan for social integration means comprehensive and proactive measures set up by monitoring core policy areas that affect social integration (Roh Dae Myung 2009). Objectives of the national action plan are to lay the foundations for economic growth and political stability by mitigating conflicts between social classes and groups, to reassure citizens by providing specific plans for improving their livelihood and preventing risks, and lastly to fulfil policy goals more efficiently by establishing a framework for integration, monitoring, and adjusting the currently scattered policies.

The process of preparing the action plan for social integration policy is as follows: First of all, the current state of social integration should be accurately identified. To do that, you need to develop an analysis tool for generating social integration indicators and gathering required data. Secondly, you have to identify areas of problem and groups at risk by monitoring the current status. Thirdly, link the identified areas and groups to policies for supporting them. To this end, you have to first identify policy areas and then, the target groups. The final outcome would be a national action plan for social integration. Discussions and coordination play a crucial role in creating the plan. Fourth, evaluation of the executed policies is also an important procedure for assessment of the past performances could help address problems on the process of policy execution.
Organization in charge of such policy management should have the following qualifications: First, it should be a high-level organization that is able to govern individual divisions in order to coordinate tasks of various divisions and adjust

the budget. Second, it should be a stable organization, which means a standing committee that can ensure consistency of policy management rather than an ad-hoc committee. In summary, a dedicated organization is required to effectively control and adjust operations with relevant Government agencies for an effective national action plan for social integration.

Table 4: Social inclusion indicators of the EU

Category	*Area*	*Indicator*
Primary Indicators	Income	1. Poverty rate
		2. Income distribution
		3. Poverty duration
		4. Relative poverty gap
	Regional Solidarity	5. Employment rate at regional level (NUTS) [1]
	Unemployment	6. Long-term unemployment
		7. No. of unemployed family members
	Education	8. Loss of educational opportunity
	Life Span	9. Average life expectancy
	Health	10. Perceived health conditions by income level
Secondary Indicators	Poverty	1. Poverty dispersion
		2. Change of poverty rate at certain points
		3. Poverty rate before income transfer
		5. Persistent poverty rate
	Income Distribution	4. Gini's Coefficient
	Unemployment	6. Rate of long-term unemployment
		7. Rate of initial unemployment
	Education	8. Rate of low education level

Note: 1) NUTS classification divides up the territory of the EU Member States.
Sources: Bardone & Stanton 2003; Gang Sin Wook & Kim An Na 2005.

Challenges of Social Integration and Governmental Measures

Challenges of Social Integration

Over the past five decades, various desires have been exposed from a number of classes and groups in the Korean society. Among them, the most common desires like economic growth and democratic rights have been deemed to be satisfied to some extent by industrialization and democratization. In the course of economic growth, however, issues of social integration have been persistently raised and a number of social policies have been applied to tackle them. But none of them perfectly resolves the issues, and even new sources of conflicts appeared. More recently, the recession that started from the U.S. gave rise to new desires for social integration and the main goals of the recent social integration are to take the society to a new level of economic growth, improve quality of life, welfare benefits, and trust in the Government.

Desire for New Growth

One of the common desires of the Korean people over the last decade has been new development and growth. The phenomenon is probably associated with Korea's history of going through rapid industrialization in the 1960s and 1970s and democratization in the 1980s, and suddenly being hit by the 1997 financial crisis. Korea recovered from the shock of the currency crisis in a relatively short period of time compared to other East Asian countries.

However, unlike the rapid growth pattern of the past, equipment investment has contracted and productivity gains have slowed down since the end of the financial crisis. The so-called jobless growth, in which, economic recovery does not produce strong growth in employment is evident in Korea. Another problem of the job market is inequality between large companies and small ones. While the proportion of non-regular workers increases, and young job seekers have a hard time finding a job, small and medium-sized enterprises suffer from lack of human resources.

This implies that the Korean people have expressed their desires for a more stable workplace that appropriately rewards them, improving livelihood, more aggressive business activities, and the desires seem to have been strengthened in recent years.

Desire for Quality of Life

All human being have desires. When the average income level is low and most people are susceptible to poverty, improvement of income levels is considered the same as enhancement of quality of life. And when the basic rights and freedom are not protected, desire for freedom and civil rights erupts. But in the post-industrialization and democratization period, desires for quality of life are uncovered.

Quality of life includes various values that are different from material wealth such as environmental benefits, like clean water and fresh air. Though it has long been understood that the environment has a direct impact on quality of life, disputes over development vs. conservation more frequently attract the attention of social members in recent years as environmental values are related to economic values of individuals and regions. In addition, with an increased number of incidents concerning life environment and food safety, the two factors have become important issues of interest.

Demand for Welfare Due to Economic Crisis

Koreans have gone through a significant structural change in terms of the economy since the end of the 1990s. Nearly all barriers associated with trade and movement of capital have been removed and global issues have had direct impact on the Korean economy. Korean industries and enterprises are categorized into two groups: Those who are armed with global competitiveness by adapting to the trends of global markets and those who are not. The disparity between the two continuously widens with the passage of time.

Moreover, flexibility of the labour market in Korea has made employers no longer ensuring lifetime employment, and employment no longer acts as an effective mechanism for increasing income and providing social security. Disparity between industries and between enterprises led to that of employment conditions. And the gap of employment status again gives rise to the gap of income and wealth. More recently, income gaps of parents are likely to limit the social opportunities of successive generations.

As stated earlier, since the recent economic slump is expected to worsen stability of employment and distribution of income, we have to come up with strategies for meeting welfare requirements in order to promote social integration.

Lack of Credibility in National Governance

Social trust actually prevents loss of social capacity and encourages members to engage in more productive activities by reducing social conflicts or time and energy invested in dealing with them. That is why social trust is also called as social capital.

Governance is a set of processes of institutionalized resolution of conflicting desires and involves a variety of political, legal, and institutional systems. Ideally, conflicting desires should be addressed by discussion and agreement between stakeholders. But, if not, we have to resort to political or legal resolution, and one of the direct means of doing this is national policy.

Unfortunately, however, governance is not currently functioning well enough to address conflicts in the Korean society for a few reasons. Many Koreans still do not appreciate the value of complying with laws and principles and have negative sentiments against the enforcement of Government policies.

Governmental Response to Social Integration

Strategy for Addressing Desire for Growth

The South Korean Government recognizes the need for a paradigm shift in administration based on its understanding of the spirit of the times, integration and development. To summarize, Koreans call for reviving the economy by restoring growth engines ignored by the democratization process and for integrating society by overcoming all the festering conflicts in terms of regional development, ideological dispute, and economic gaps. That is why Korea needs a new creative paradigm that goes beyond that of industrialization and democratization periods. The South Korean Government is now pushing for a new development paradigm dubbed as 'advancement paradigm'.

Table 5: Comparison of development mechanisms

New development mechanism (advancement paradigm)	*Previous development mechanism (industrialization phase)*
Collaboration between nations and societies	Government-led development
Qualitative growth (Virtuous cycle of growth and welfare)	Quantitative growth (Growth-first and welfare-next)
Rule of law and respect for the constitution	Disparity between rule of law and reality
Nurture human resources which respect pluralism, innovations, and ingenuity	Mass production of human resources based on monotony
Harmony between global standards and national standards	Closed nationalism
High level of social trust	Low level of social trust

Source: Homepage of Cheongwadae (http://www.president.go.kr/kr/policy/principal.php).

As shown in table 5, Korea's advancement strategies are clearly distinguished from the past development initiatives. Though some of them are directly related to social conflict or social integration while the others are not, the ultimate goal of the advancement strategies is to take the level of social integration to a new height by helping people in all income brackets improve their standard of living.

Green Growth for Addressing Quality of Life

A way to restore Korea's growth potential is to revitalize the market. To do that, the South Korean Government pushes ahead with policies aimed at ensuring maximum freedom of economic activities while dealing with only undesirable outcomes in the market. To this end, South Korea is boosting corporate investments both at home and abroad by implementing tax reduction and deregulation, and also pursues qualitative growth rather than quantitative development by nurturing a number of high value-added industries.

Unlike the past economic development projects that destroy and deplete natural resources, initiatives currently pursued by the Korean Government are designed to improve the environment and save energy. This type of growth pattern is also referred to as 'green growth' aiming at exploring new industries by creating a key infrastructure for eco-friendly and energy-saving business and tackling climate change while increasing local development of energy sources and developing renewable and clean energy. Green growth is at the top of the national agenda as a strategy for achieving both growth and environmental preservation since the initiative helps minimize environmental degradation arising from development and reduce social conflicts over conservation.

Active Welfare to Meet Demand

Right after the 1997 financial crisis, the Government implemented a temporary social security scheme to address a sharp increase in the number of low-income families and transformed its public welfare benefits mainly for working populations into the National Basic Livelihood Security Scheme, designed to aid the livelihood of the poorest in 1999. The Scheme included those who are able to work as recipients and at the same time impose certain conditions for receiving benefits to assist self-support. In addition, it was designed to provide a more realistic social security plan by applying realistic standards, the minimum cost of living, and broadening its coverage to housing. About 1.5 million of the poorest Koreans are currently benefiting from the scheme.

Korea's social security net is evaluated to be well structured. Four social insurance programmes act as the primary safety net, followed by the National Basic Livelihood Security Scheme. And emergency relief programme is the last resort to support citizens in need. In 2008, in order to address the needs of ageing population, the Long-Term Care Insurance System for the Elderly was introduced. In the course of recovering from the 1997 crisis, Korea has reinforced its framework for a social welfare system as described above. The public support scheme has been significantly broadened, five social insurance programmes (old-age pension, health insurance, employment insurance, workers' compensation, and long-term care insurance) are in place, and services for vulnerable classes have been expanded.

However, there are still challenges ahead. The social safety net is focused too much on the privileged and after-the-fact measures and the main body of welfare services is confined to the Government. As for health insurance, over 1.6 million households do not have access to health benefits due to failure to pay health insurance contributions for six months or more. Also because insurance recipients have to pay about 40% of medical fees, low-income families may not be able to pay medical bills if they suffer from terminal diseases. With regard to the national pension, about 28% of the eligible households are exempt from payment. The same is true for workers' compensation. This covers only about 40% of the total population, leaving the remaining 60% exposed to the risk of job loss (Kim Yong Ha 2009). Meanwhile, the rate of recipients of the National Basic Livelihood Security Scheme who meet the eligibility criteria, such as minimum cost of living, the duty of support stands at 3.5% of the total population. But those who have supporting families or a certain level of property are excluded from social security though they desperately need assistance.

In conclusion, though Korea has an institutional framework of social security, the underprivileged are still at risk of falling into the poorest class due to inflexible criteria, lack of pension fund etc. And the recent economic downturn is likely to cause a sharp increase in unemployed workers and negatively affect the self-employed, leading to a rise in the number of people in need of social security benefits.

The South Korean Government is pushing for active welfare that targets all Koreans, is more proactive and appropriate, and makes the most of market functions. To this end, it plans to pave the way for a lifetime welfare system for all Koreans including the middle class, revamp its pension system, and strengthen the responsibilities of the Government for indispensible medical services. In addition, it aims at offering a preventive and customized service in the areas of child care, welfare for the aged and the disabled. More specifically, its ultimate goal is to improve employment support services and career development programmes and create jobs for vulnerable classes like women and senior citizens under the assumption that the best welfare system is designed to encourage people to work. The Government has already announced pre-emptive pump priming measures to cope with the recent recession and currently reduce taxes and expand spending. Also, under the theme of active welfare, it has announced initiatives for improving standard of living of the Korean people as follows:

Plan for Improving Livelihood of Citizens

When the economic crisis sharply increased the cost of living, the underprivileged and vulnerable classes would be hit the hardest, thereby raising the need for protection of the classes from job loss due to closure of businesses. Therefore, the Government decided to allocate an extra budget for providing more benefits to those at risk in terms of basic livelihood and emergency support and also improve the welfare system for stabilizing their livelihood in order to provide customized services to the underprivileged.

The plan also includes support for unemployed families, and workers with back pays, and will be expanded to the stabilization of educational tuitions. With regard to housing, improvement of facilities of public rental houses including

CCTV, parking lots, welfare centres will be improved and purchase or rent of multi-household houses will be expanded and financed at 50% of rent deposits of the underprivileged. Such rapid and systematic measures are taken to prevent further expansion of the size of the underprivileged. The Government expects these measures will help the low-income families improve their livelihood to some extent.

Humane New Deal Policy

In addition to the consistent reinforcement of the existing safety net for protecting low-income families, the Government announced the so-called Humane New Deal for protecting middle-income workers, so they have a foundation for recovery (Ministry of Education, Science and Technology, Ministry of Culture, Sports and Tourism, Ministry of Health, Welfare and Family Affairs, Ministry of Labour, Small and Medium Business Administration, Presidential Council on Future and Vision 2009). The reason for announcing the initiative was that the current safety net is focused on public support for low-income families and social insurances for regular workers, so it has limits in preventing the middle class falling into poverty and bringing them out of poverty when an economic crisis hits the nation. In other words, inflexible criteria of public support limit its response to a crisis, and recipients tend to continue to receive benefits regardless of change of their social status. And social insurances are not broadly applied to temporary, non-regular workers, and self-employed businesses, so they also have limits in supporting the working poor in times of crisis. In addition, the unemployment insurance and the National Basic Livelihood Security Scheme, which are designed to support unemployed workers, have a very low level of coverage rate for the marginal middle class. Thus, the Government has come up with Humane New Deal aiming at preventing middle and low-income families from falling into the lowest class.

The goal of Humane New Deal is to facilitate investment in human resources to enhance the national capacity to cope with future challenges and broaden the middle class by improving the growth potentials of the Korean society. In addition, the initiative is designed to ensure stability of livelihood of families and their right to pursuit of happiness with a proactive approach to financial crisis and economic recovery of individuals through labour.

The major policy direction of Humane New Deal is divided into three tasks: 1) prevention of contraction of the middle class, 2) facilitation of entry into the middle class, and 3) nurturing of the future middle class. The objective of the first task is to keep middle-income families from falling into the lower class because they are not likely to recover from a crisis once they fall into the lower class. The task includes tactics like support for the maintenance and increase of the number of jobs, creation of jobs for women, lessen the financial burden of housing, education, and medical costs on households.

The goal of the second task is to support the middle class for returning to its original social status by helping them develop competencies through employment when economic conditions turn better. This includes job training, career development programmes, incentives for low-income families to get out of poverty, encouragement of start-up of business. To this end, the model of '1 person start-up' is suggested where middle-income families can start a new business based on innovative ideas. The last task is for preventing inheritance of poverty and facilitation of children of low-income families to enter the middle class, which includes improvement of public education through increased investment in education and increased investment in children and adolescents.

Recovery of Trust in Government through Transformation into a Sincere Government

What is urgently needed for social integration is the recovery of trust in Government. This will directly lead to respect for the rule of law and public good. Trust in Government is directly related to respect for the rule of law and public good, further paving the way for preventing and coordinating social conflicts. The first step to restore trust in Government is to enhance competency and transparency of Government. One of the main goals of the South Korean Government is to become a small, competent, and transparent Government.

Also, Korea is making efforts to facilitate communication among different social groups along with spreading the culture of respect for the rule of law in order to address social conflicts. Social conflicts are not confined to certain areas but often caused by the clash of values of different sectors of a society. That is why Governmental effort for social integration requires cross-agency collaboration. A social integration committee needs to be installed to resolve these issues in a more comprehensive and effective way, thereby establishing a legal and institutional framework for improving competency of public agencies to predict, coordinate, and resolve social conflicts.

Conclusion

Though the Korean Government has continued its efforts to link economic achievements of the past to improvement of quality of life and standard of living of every individual, internal and external conditions facing South Korea have the risk of putting brakes on its sustained growth. Particularly, the current global recession is likely to increase the number of people in poverty significantly, and economic woes may negatively influence social integration in a country like South Korea that is not perfectly armed with a social security system. Worse still, the downturn has spread across the world at a time when South Korea has been recovering from the 1997 financial crisis. In other words, the economic slump adds new socioeconomic issues to the process of social integration.

To achieve both social development and growth, a certain level of equality and fairness should be ensured. Social integration is a prerequisite for joint growth and sustainable growth. The crucial challenge is how to overcome social exclusion and lay the foundations for future growth. Social integration requires a framework for ensuring rights to basic elements of livelihood such as housing, health, education, and social participation. Social integration is the starting point to create a competitive, stable, and flexible society.

Pursuit of comprehensive social integration policies is required to overcome the current crisis. The South Korean Government is pushing for a set of social policies such as green growth that satisfies desires for both growth and quality of life and active welfare that reinforces the safety net. Korea needs to create a virtuous circle of economic growth and welfare benefits by strengthening the social safety net.

Moreover, South Korea needs to push ahead with such social policies designed to bring Koreans from all income brackets together in order to overcome economic woes and enhancing social values. For establishing a systematic social integration action plan for both addressing economic problems and social integration similar to that of the EU, Korea needs to learn from the experiences of the leading countries in the world.

References

Bardone, L. & David Stanton (2003), *The Experience of Developing Indicators in the Social Protection Committee's Indicators Sub Group*. Lisbon: Paper presented to the 23rd CEIES seminar 'Social Protection Statistics' (Annex).

Choi Sung Eun (2009), *Priorities of Welfare under an Economic Crisis, Data from Conference on Challenges and Policy Directions in 2010*. Seoul: Korea Institute for Health and Social Affairs.

Gang Sin Wook & Kim An Na (2005), *Research on Social Exclusion Indicators and Application*. Seoul: Korea Institute for Health and Social Affairs.

Joint measures by relevant Government agencies to support livelihood. Seoul: March 2009.

Ministry of Education, Science and Technology; Ministry of Culture, Sports and Tourism; Ministry of Health, Welfare and Family Affairs; Ministry of Labour, Small and Medium Business Administration; Presidential Council on Future and Vision (2009), *Human New Deal for Supporting Middle Class*. Seoul.

Kim Mi Gon (2009), *Internal data from the Korea Institute for Health and Social Affairs*. Seoul.

Kim Yongha (2009), *Plan for Strengthening Social Safety Net at a Time of Economic Crisis, 2nd Seminar on Administrative Tasks*. Seoul: National Research Council for Economics, Humanities and Social Sciences.

Mun Jin Young (2004), 'Comparison of Social Exclusion among Nations – Centered around France, U.K., and Sweden', *Korea Social Welfare*, Issue 56 (3).

Roh Dae Myung (2009a), *Tasks and Strategies for Social Integration*. Seoul: Korea Institute for Health and Social Affairs.

Rho Dae Myung (2009b), *Current State and Future Challenges of Social Integration*. Health and Welfare Forum (KIHASA), vol. 150, April 2009: 6-19.

Yu Kyung Joon (2008), *Definition and Estimation of Middle Class*. Seoul: KDI Trend of Financial Policies.

UN (2009), *World Economic Situation and Prospects*. New York/N.Y.

8 The Relationship between the Economic Crisis, Non-regular Labourers, and Social Security in Present-day Japan

Takanobu Kyogoku

Introduction

Aiming at the construction of a new social security system for overcoming the unprecedented economic crisis. At present, in the midst of the worldwide financial crisis, Japan is also confronted with an unprecedented economic crisis. In the midst of this situation, the breaking down of the conventional social security system which is cantered on regular labourers is becoming increasingly noticeable, and the creation of a new safety net for non-regular labourers has an important meaning in the short term. Also, upgrading of long-term care services to cope with the advance of the super-aged society will perform a major role in the medium-to-long term. In any event, these two social security measures also have an extremely large economic effect for increasing domestic demand in the Japanese economy, and are also considered to perform an important role in coping with the economic down-turn for the time being. This article covers: (1) the actual situation and emergency measures for the economic crisis in Japan, (2) the relationship between social security and the increase in domestic demand, (3) the relationship among, economic growth, social security and employment, (4) the creation of a new safety net for non-regular labourers, and (5) the expansion of long-term care insurance, in that order.

Economic Crisis and Emergency Measures

The current economic crisis in Japan is the largest since the end of World War II. The situation of this crisis based on economic indexes is shown below. The features of this economic crisis are firstly the fact that it is a major structural economic downturn which had its beginnings in the financial crisis which occurred in the midst of globalization, secondly the fact that it is a long-term economic downturn in which the conventional heavy chemical industry, which was previously a star industry, is falling into a decline period in the industrial life cycle, and is at the stage where the rapid rise of 21st century type industries, such as IT and the environment, is insufficient. The third feature of this economic crisis is the fact that it has occurred in the absence of social security which can cope with social changes such as the advance of the falling birth-rate and the ageing society and also changing labour relations.

Table 1: Main economic indices (approx. %)

	Fiscal 2008		*Fiscal 2009*	
	Real likelihood	*Current estimation*	*Economic prospects*	*Current estimation*
Real gross domestic production	▲0.8	▲3.1	0.0	▲3.3
Nominal gross domestic production	▲1.3	▲3.2	0.1	▲3.0
Total unemployment rate	4.2	4.1	4.7	5.2
Number of persons employed	▲0.2	0.0	▲0.4	▲0.9
Mining industry production	▲5.5	▲12.9	▲4.8	▲23.4
Domestic corporate goods prices	4.1	3.3	▲2.1	▲5.5
Consumer prices (overall)	1.3	1.1	▲0.4	▲1.3
GDP deflator	▲0.5	▲0.1	0.1	0.3

Notes: 1) Taking into consideration the facts that civil activities constitute the mainstay of the Japanese economy and also that there are many factors which are difficult to forecast, particularly amid changes in the international environment, the various coefficients in the above table should be considered as rough guidelines. 2) With the exception of the total unemployment rate, the figures shown above represent the increase or decrease with respect to the previous fiscal year. 3) The domestic corporate goods prices for fiscal 2008 (current estimation) are the real achievement. 4) In the above estimations, the following assumptions were made based on the existing economic and financial policies. Note that these assumptions are assumptions for the work, and do not indicate predictions made, or the prospects determined, by the Cabinet Office.

Source: Concerning the provisional estimation (estimation made by the Cabinet Office) of the prospects for the economy in fiscal 2009 (April 27, 2009, Cabinet Office).

In the midst of this, in April 2009 the Japanese Government determined 'Economic Crisis Measures' as follows (refer to figure 1). The three main important pillars which support these measures are: I. Growth strategy – Avoidance of bottom deepening, II. Growth strategy – Investment in the future, and III. Actual reassurance and vitality – General mobilization of Government policies. As shown in figure 1, each of these pillars is supported by small pillars. An intimate relationship between social security and related measures exists in the shaded areas (I-1 Employment policy, II-2 Long and healthy life, and child rearing, and III-2 Acquisition of safety and peace of mind etc.).

Figure 1: Points concerning the main measures in the 'Economic Crisis Measures'

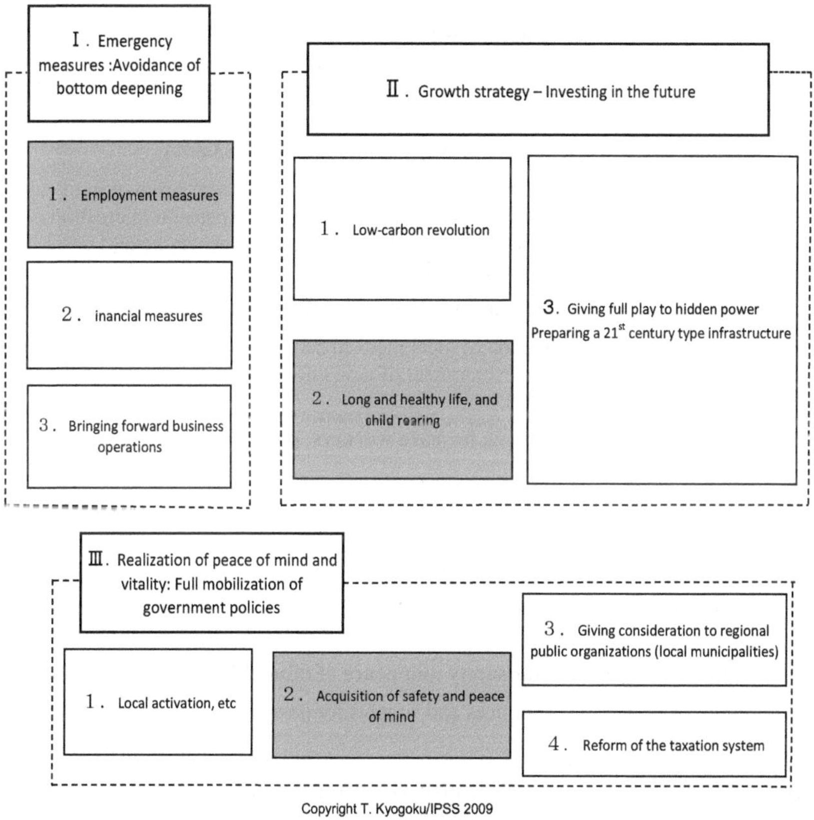

Note: The shaded areas indicate measures related to social security.
Source: Joint Government and ruling party conference and economic measures; Cabinet conference concerning Cabinet office's 'Economy Crisis Measures' in April 2009.

The Ministry of Health, Labour and Welfare's supplementary budget for fiscal 2010, which is based on these 'Economic Crisis Measures', is shown in table 2. Of the total of Yen 4.6718 trillion for related measures, the greatest portion is Yen 2.5123 trillion (53.8%) for emergency employment measures cantered on providing assistance to non-regular day-labourers. It includes the creation of a new safety net. The next largest portion is Yen 0.8443 trillion (18.1%) for improving the working conditions of long-term care workers and also preparing care homes and centres for the aged. These two departments account for Yen 3.3570 trillion (72%). As a result, it can be seen that the two major fields of social security mentioned at the beginning of this article are also important from the viewpoint of the economic crisis measures in Japan.

Table 2: The Ministry of Health, Labour and Welfare's supplementary budget for fiscal 2010 (draft)

Outline of measures related to 'Economic Crisis Measures', total 4.6718 trillion Yen

1. **Emergency employment measures 2.5123 trillion Yen (53.8%)**

   Expansion of Government subsidies for employment adjustment, promotion of support for reemployment and ability development measures, expansion of creation business for emergency employment, acquisition of unemployment benefit costs etc., home and living support costs, and others

2. **Local medical services and new medical technology 768.4 billion Yen (16.4%)**

   Overall support for revitalization of local medical services, strengthening of medical functions and facilities, etc., development of new influenza vaccines, strengthening of production setup, and others

3. **Improved working conditions for care workers, preparation of care centres 844.3 billion Yen (18.1%)**

   Improved working conditions for care workers, emergency preparation of a care infrastructure, earthquake-proofing of social welfare facilities, etc., and others

4. **Child-raising support 278.8 billion Yen (6.0%)**

   Expansion of special allowance for child-rearing support, support for single parent families, etc., and others

5. **Promotion of measures for safety and peace of mind 278.8 billion Yen (6.0%)**

   Promotion of measures for services and support for persons with disabilities, others

Source: Kyogoku 2009.

Relationship between Social Security and Increased Domestic Demand

I personally believe that if social security is considered to be a system for providing national living maintenance, the relationship between the national economy and social security can be expressed as shown in figure 2.

From figure 1, it is clear that social security possesses not only the functions of a safety net for national livelihood, but also functions which increase the demands on the national economy (figure 3).

Figure 2: Overall relationship between social security and the economy

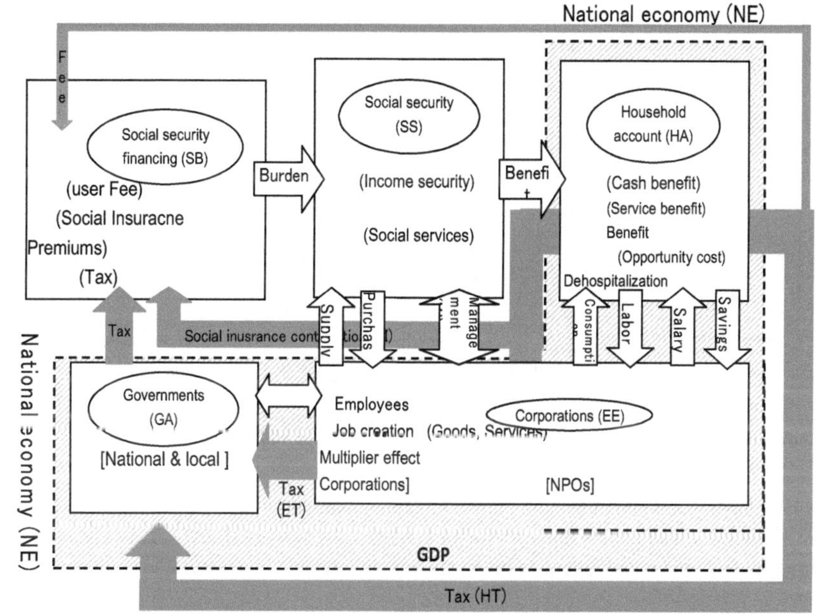

Notes: 1) Economic activities of local & central Governments are included in EE, and tax & premiums paid by civil servants in household accounts. 2) Goods and services of corporations include capital gains (MI) etc. 3) In developing countries, financing of social security includes ODA funds. 4) The user fee of social security is fairly small and thus is omitted in the diagram. 5) Figures are of long-term care insurance (FY 2003) in chapter 8 of the source document. *Source*: Kyogoku 2007, figure 4, p. 59.

Figure 3: Major economic functions of social security (economic effects)

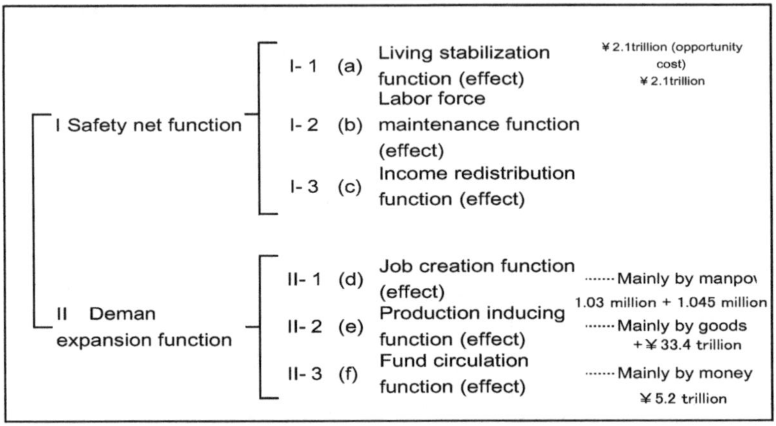

Note: 1) Figures are in chapter 8 of Long-term Care Insurance (FY 2003).
Source: Kyogoku 2007, p. 61, figure 5.

Here, the functions which increase demand are (d) an employment creation function (effect), (e) a production inducement function (effect), and (f) a capital circulation function (effect), which generate mainly workers, products, and money.

Firstly, regarding (d) the employment creation function, care is a maximum not only in the social security field, but also through all industries as well, and moreover is expected to steadily increase along with the ageing of the population.

Secondly, (e) the production inducement effect is not inferior in the overall field of social security, even as a public project. Particularly, medical care that necessitates drugs and medicines, medical appliances, and so on, is a maximum in the field of social security, and remains considerably larger than other industries.

Thirdly, regarding (f) the capital circulation effect, reserve funds amount to approximately Yen 150 trillion, which is a much higher figure than that of other advanced countries, partly because the period during which Japan's pension scheme used a reserve system was long, and it is worth noting that the reserve funds perform the role of a lubricant for the national economy through the purchase of Japanese and foreign stocks and bonds.

By not merely implementing such direct internal economic effects but also adding long-term care services and nurseries, for example, both micro and macro indirect external economic effects, such as the promotion of female workers, the acquisition of peace of mind by the public, and the activation of national consumption expenditure, will be obtained. Although this is not covered in this article, it is considered that these benefits will become immeasurably large.

Social Security, Economic Growth and Unemployment

At one time in Japan, arguments to the effect that social security would prevent economic growth predominated. However, as mentioned above, social security is effective for raising the level and stimulating growth of the national economy.

Here, I would like to add Germany, France and Sweden and observe the correlation between them. There are six countries including Japan, the U.K., U.S.A., Germany, France and Sweden.

Figure 4 shows the correlation between economic growth rate (5-year average) and the net national burden ratio (national burden ratio for each purpose – income insurance return ratio). Although it is by no means a high correlation (R^2 = 0.1957), it is at least rising slowly, and is not falling as is being emphasized in some quarters. 'The net national burden ratio' is the original term by myself, which consequently, looking at the situation subsequent to the year 2000, it can be seen approximately that the higher the net burden ratio, the higher is the economic growth rate.

Figure 4: Economic growth rate and real effective national burden

Vertical axis: economic growth rate; horizontal axis: real effective national (social) burdens

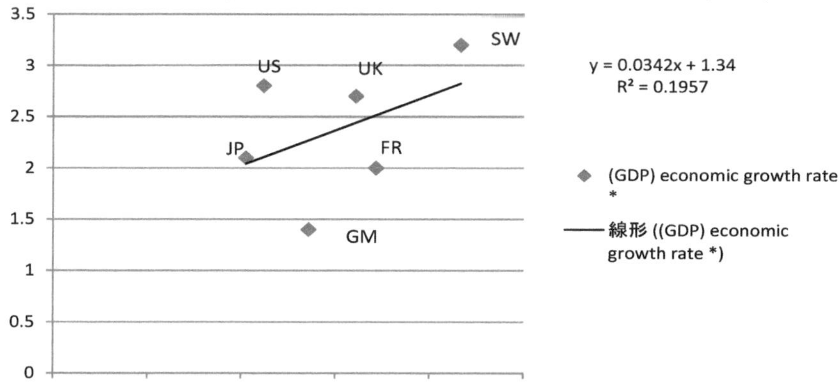

Source: Real effective social burdens are calculated by T. Kyogoku and Y. Kaneko based on the national birth-ratio 2005 estimated by the Ministry of Finance of Japan minus the ratio of cash benefits of social expenditures over GDP. The economic growth rate is the average rate from 2003 to 2007 based on the IMF World Economic Outlook.

However, as shown in figure 5, there is almost no correlation between the unemployment rate (5-year average) and the net national burden ratio. This is probably due to the fact that if income security is excluded, the unemployment rate will be high, so the net national burden ratio will not rise significantly, and conversely the real national burden ratio will be high, causing the employment opportunities to increase, and thus the unemployment rate will not rise.

Figure 5: Unemployment rate (1995-2007) and real effective social burdens (2005)

Vertical axis: Unemployment rate; horizontal axis: real effective national (social burdens)

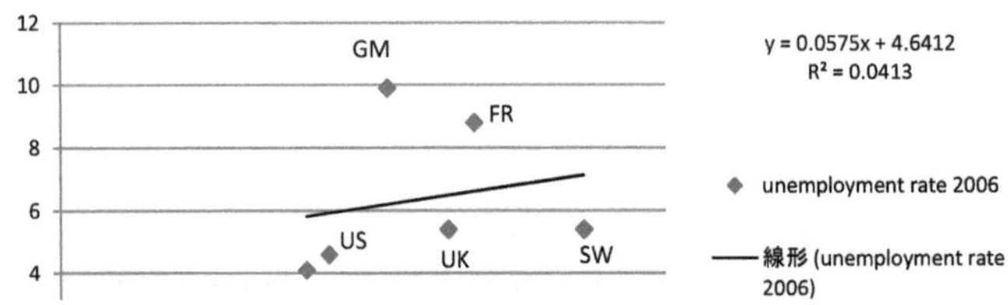

Source: Real effective social burdens are calculated by T. Kyogoku and Y. Kaneko, based on the national birth-ratio 2005, estimated by the Ministry of Finance of Japan minus the ratio of cash benefits of social expenditures over GDP.

Also, the correlation between the unemployment rate and the economic growth rate on a 5-year average basis can be seen, and a mild reverse correlation in which the unemployment rate falls as the economic growth rate rises (refer to figure 6).

Figure 6: Unemployment rate and real economic growth rate (1995-2007)

Vertical axis: unemployment rate; horizontal axis: economic growth rate

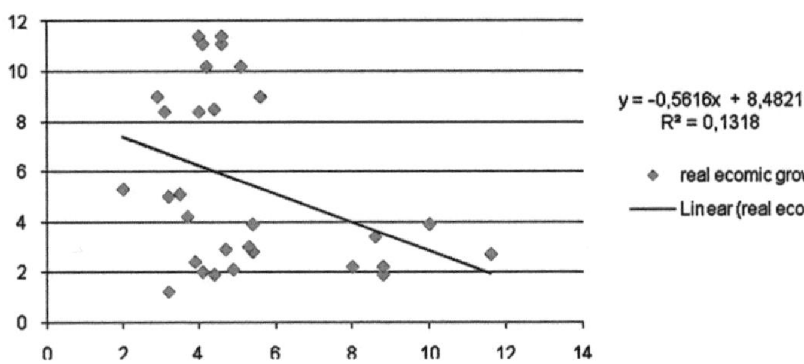

Source: T. Kyogoku's and Y. Kanako's tabulation based on the OECD Economic Outlook.

Finally, looking at the correlation between the Gini coefficient and the social expenditure rate (social expenditure ÷ GDP) among the OECD member countries, it can be seen that the inverse correlation is increasing more or less steadily as shown in figure 7, and that there is a very high inverse correlation ($R^2 = 0.3$, $r = - 0.6$).

Figure 7: Gini coefficient and social expenditure/GDP

(Vertical axis: Gini coefficient; horizontal axis: social expenditure/GDP)

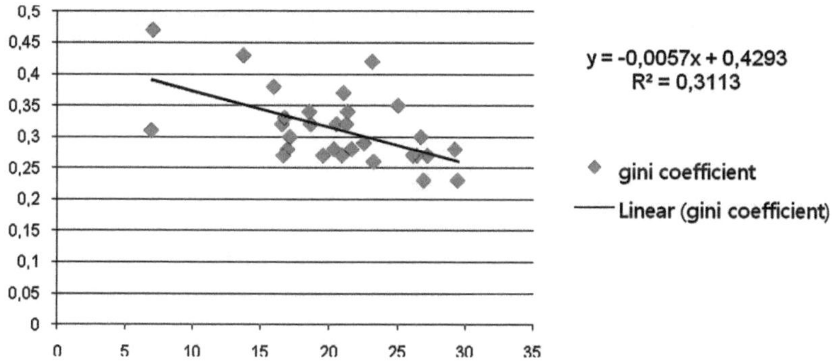

Sources: Kyogoku's and Kaneko's tabulation based on the Gini coefficient for the mid-2000s: *Growing unequal?* OECD ELSA, 2008, and Social expenditure/GDP: Social Expenditure Aggregated Data 2005; OECD Social Expenditure and OECD 2009.

It can be seen that the higher the percentage occupied by social expenditure in the gross domestic production, the lower is the Gini coefficient, and the more equal is the income redistribution in the country concerned. Summarizing the above, it can be said that in a welfare state the real national burden ratio does not necessarily impede the rise of the economic growth rate, and the high social expenditure lowers the Gini coefficient, thus making for a more equal income redistribution.

Construction of the Second Safety Net

The safety net for Japan's unemployed workers consists of two departments: (1) unemployment benefits (social insurance) due to unemployment insurance, and (2) livelihood assistance (public assistance) in cases where unemployment benefits are not provided. Particularly, unemployment insurance mainly in large corporations matches the features of the relationship between labour and management in Japan: (1) lifetime employment system, (2) age-based remuneration system, and (3) corporate-based labour unions. Under this system, the unemployment insurance burden is divided equally between the employee (worker) and the employer (manager), and used to provide unemployment benefits when the necessity arises. However, along with the rapid increase in the number of non-regular workers resulting from the effect of economization in the service section and also the changing labour environment in recent years, most of these workers cannot be covered by unemployment insurance, and a large number of unemployed workers are unable to receive the benefits of unemployment insurance (refer to figure 8).

Figure 8: The trend of regular and non-regular employees in Japan

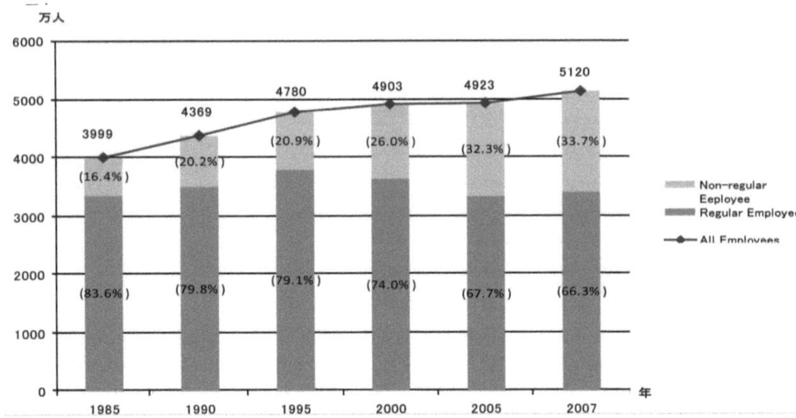

Note: Number of all employees is that excluding the number of executives. The number in ( ) is the share of each type of employees over all employees.
Source: The Special Survey in February of the Labour Force Survey (Statistics Bureau, The Ministry of General Affairs) from 1984 to 2001.

Consequently, in the first safety net, the function of unemployment insurance is lost, and non-regular workers who lose their jobs quickly become dependent upon livelihood assistance. However, as a result of moderation and constraint of health care costs, livelihood assistance is also significantly restricted. Consequently, the plight of non-regular workers is not redressed by the conventional safety net. There were 1.6 million receivers of public assistance and 0.8 million receivers of unemployment insurance in the 2009 fiscal year's budget

Accordingly, the Ministry of Health, Labour and Welfare has already devised various measures, however, now it has decided to newly construct a second safety net. This second safety net stands on two pillars: (1) the provision of support for securing housing, on-going livelihood consultation, loaning of living expenses, and so on, for persons who have lost their jobs and homes, and (2) the promotion of the provision of additional emergency temporary facilities by leasing existing buildings, aiming at providing more substantial assistance to homeless persons. A schematic outline of this is shown in figure 9.

The second safety net was constructed in the valley between unemployment benefits and livelihood assistance. Under this scheme, non-regular workers who are unable to receive unemployment benefits do not immediately receive livelihood assistance, but are saved at an intermediate point by the second safety net.

This second safety net consists of four elements: (1) employment stability fund loans, (2) provision of training and livelihood support, (3) housing allowance, and (4) loan (benefits package support loan). The combination of these four elements is expected to help unemployed persons to get back on their feet. This system avoids the necessity to provide long-term livelihood assistance, and provides emergency relief through the short-term provision of benefits in all cases.

Figure 9: Overall image of the second safety net

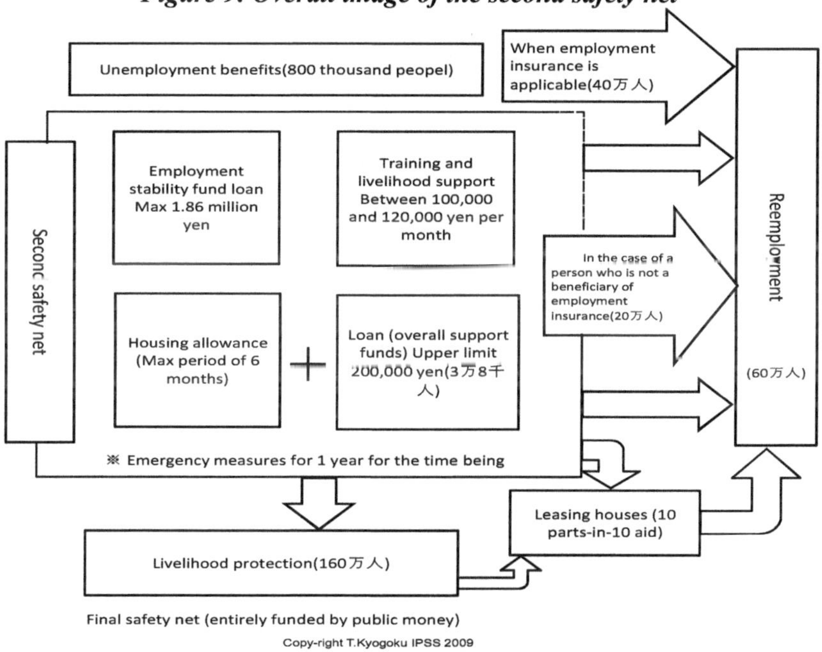

Note: The number of people in the brackets are those numbers, estimated approximately for 2009 by the author.

Source: National Institute of Population and Social Security Research, from 'Fiscal 2006 Care Insurance Business Situation Report (annual report)'.

Expansion of Long-term Care Services

Care services for the elderly persons in Japan expanded greatly subsequent to the enactment of the Care Insurance Law (1997) in 2000 (refer to figure 10).

Figure 10: Changes in care benefits (number of recipients and values)

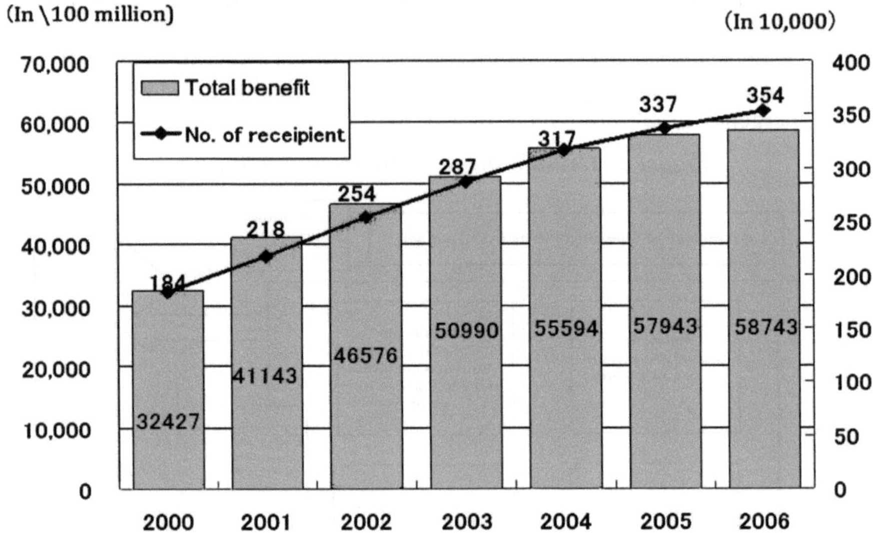

Source: Prepared by T. Kyogoku, National Institute of Population and Social Security Research from MHLW 2006, *Long-term care insurance business report* (annual).

Long-term care services were reorganized into a system which coordinates health care and welfare, and is based on social insurance. These care services respond directly to the trends of decentralization of authority and privatization. In the case of decentralization of authority, the local municipality (city, town or village) is the assurer, and systematically promotes long-term care services. In the case of privatization, the main provider of a service is not only a municipality (city, town, or village) or a social welfare body, as was the case in the past, but also includes companies, cooperative societies, agricultural cooperatives and NPOs. Particularly, approximately 49% of the organizations that carry out visiting care are profit-making corporations (companies etc.). Also, 76.1% of the organizations that carry out care of people living in specific facilities, and 87.1% of the organizations that lease welfare appliances, are profit-making organizations. In addition, as mentioned previously, the demand for care is steadily increasing along with the ageing of the population, so any Government investment in the care field is highly unlikely to be excessive. If anything it will probably be insufficient. Here, I will summarize the main economic results of care insurance, based on figure 3.

(1) If a female who was unable to work because of the need to care for an ageing parent becomes able to work as a result of care insurance, the opportunity costs will be approximately Yen 2.1 trillion, and the effectiveness of the use of care facilities in preventing social hospitalization will be Yen 2.1 trillion, result-

ing in a livelihood stability function of approximately Yen 4.2 trillion. (2) The employment creation effect is 1.045 million people, the production inducement effect is Yen 33.4 trillion, and the capital circulation effect is Yen 5.2 trillion.

By totalizing the above, the economic effect corresponding to the current investment scale will be Yen 147.3 trillion. If a further investment of Yen 1 trillion is added to this, each economic effect will further increase. Incidentally, if one half of the supplementary budget of Yen 0.84 trillion for 2010 were to be allocated for care (home care), and the other half were to be allocated for (B) care (facility), employment for a total of 168,840 persons consisting of (A) + (B) will be generated, where (A) is 0.248 persons/ Yen 1 million × Yen 0.42 trillion = 104,160 persons, and (B) is 0.154 persons/ Yen 1 million × Yen 0.42 trillion = 64,680 persons, and also a total production inducement effect of Yen 35.6250 trillion consisting of (A) + (B) will be generated, where (A) is 4233 × Yen 0.42 trillion = Yen 17.7790 trillion, and (B) is 4249 × Yen 0.42 trillion = Yen 17.8460 trillion (refer to table 3). The Japanese Government has a special plan to increase the number to 0.3 million care workers within three years, related to the 'Economic crisis measures in April 2009'.

Table 3: Major factors of industrial relations effects in the care service sector

(56 units in 2000)

	1) Internal and external multipliers			*2) Inverse matrix co-efficient (production inducing coefficient; (column marginals)*	*3) Employment inducing coefficient (person/ million)*	*4) Income = Production inducing coefficient, including ripple consumption effect (column marginals)*	
	Internal multiplier	*External multiplier*	*Total effect*			*Additional coefficient*	*Total expanding ripple coefficient*
Care (at home)	1.167	1.061	1.235	1.418	0.248	2.743	4.233
Care (institutional)	1.162	1.084	1.254	1.485	0.154	2.711	4.249
All industry average	1.477	1.061	1.563	1.791	0.095	2.409	4.067
Medical (simp. av.)[2]	(1.260)	(1.142)	(1.416)	(1.754)	(0.111)	(2.686)	(4.478)
(Public projects)	(1.067)	(1.067)	(1.528)	(1.874)	(0.099)	(2.364)	(4.090)
	Internal multiplier × external multiplier = Total effect (effect by industrial groups)			*(Effect by industrial group)*	*Inverse matrix coefficient × employment coefficient*	*[Inverse matrix] [1] ×[Additional ripple inverse matrix list] = [Augmented inverse matrix]*	

Notes: 1) [Income = Production inducing coefficient including additional ripple effect on consumption] is on an actual household consumption/total income basis; 2) Figures for medical care are obtained by simply averaging national/public, public-interest corporations' and medical corporations' figures.

Source: Institute for Health Economics and Policy, Analysis of Relations between Medical and Welfare Industries (2004), p. 10. However, numbers are truncated by this author to 3 decimal places.

Conclusion

As described above, at present the construction of a second safety net and also the enhancement of social security through the expansion of long-term care services perform an important role in Japan's economic crisis measures.

By way of conclusion, I have re-evaluated the concept of a 'social market' (which was founded by R. Titmuss in the 1960s, and was developed further by N. Gilbert in the 1980s), as a cluster of social exchanges. I consider social security not as an existing economic market, but as the core of a new social market based on taxes, social insurance and user charge, and also believe that a large mixed incorporated market is being formed as a result of the mixing of the social market with the economic market (refer to figure 6.1). This view was already presented as my discussion paper in IPSS in 2008. This situation will strongly impact the economic market, and cause the domestic market to become stronger and expand, and hence I am convinced that it is an important strategic issue concerning economic growth in Japan, a nation with a high percentage of elderly people, in the 21st century.

Figure 11: Effects of social and incorporated markets (α and β effects)

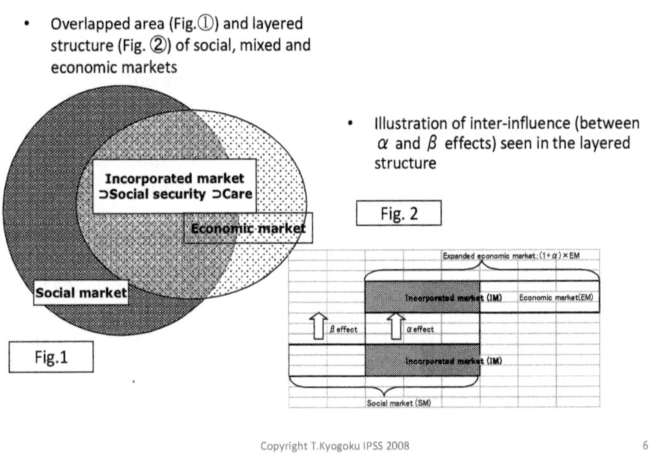

References

Gilbert, N. & Barbara Gilbert (1999), *The Enabling State: Modern Welfare Capitalism in America*. Oxford: Oxford University Press (The Japanese edition, translated by H. Ibe, Tokyo: Chuohoki Publishing Company).

Kyogoku, Takanobu (2005), *Long-term Care Insurance for All of the People*. Tokyo: Chuohoki Publishing Company (in Japanese).

Kyogoku, Takanobu (2007), *Social Security and Japanese Economy*. Tokyo: Keio University Press (in Japanese).

Kyogoku, Takanobu (2008a), *Introduction to the theories of social market*. Discussion Paper, No. 2008-E01, Tokyo: National Institute of Population and Social Security Research.

Kyogoku, Takanobu (2008b), *Reform of Public Assistance and Decentralization*. Minerva Publishing Company (in Japanese).

Annex: Employment Insurance in Japan

Source: Social Security in Japan 2007, National Institute of population and Social Security Research, chapter 6; http://www.ipss.go.jp/index-e.html.

General Characteristics

Japan uses the term "Labour Insurance" to mean both the Labour Accident Insurance and the Employment Insurance. The two are independent schemes, but in some respects, such as the collection of the premiums, are treated together. In this Annex, we shall introduce the outline of the Employment Insurance in Japan.

Employment Insurance has two functions. One is to provide employees cash benefit in case he/she loses the job. The other is to support employers to prevent them from laying off their employees. The former is called the Unemployment Benefits, and the latter consists of three components, namely: Services for employment stabilization, Services for developing human resources, and Services for employees' welfare. The Unemployment Benefits also include a variety of benefits such as the Job Applicants' Benefits, the Study and Training Benefits, and the Employment Continuation Benefits. The entire scheme is shown in figure 6.1.

Fig. 6.1 Employment Insurance

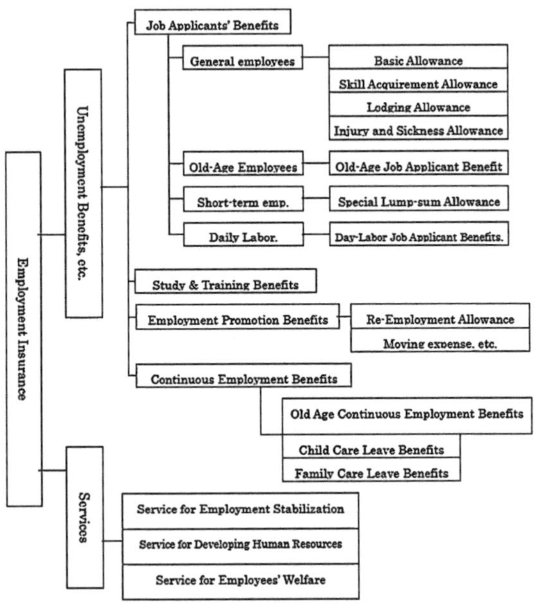

Employment Insurance System (the Unemployment Benefits)

The Basic Allowance for the Job Applicants

This is the most commonly referred to as the 'Unemployment Benefits'. For general employees, it is necessary to have been insured for at least 6 months within one year prior to leaving the job. The duration of the benefits ranges according to the age of the beneficiary and the years of being insured. Since April 2001, the duration of the benefits also depends on the reason of the unemployment, i.e. whether the termination was voluntary (including retirees) or involuntary and without enough time period to arrange re-employment (due to lay-off or bankruptcy of the firm). The Tables 6.1 to 6.3 show the number of days for each kind of recipients.

Table 6.1 Duration of Basic Allowance (General Employees)

(unit: days)

<table>
<tr><td></td><td colspan="4">Years of being insured</td></tr>
<tr><td></td><td>Less than 5 years</td><td>5<= and <10 years</td><td>10<= and <20 years</td><td>More than 20 years</td></tr>
<tr><td>General</td><td>90</td><td>120</td><td>150</td><td>180</td></tr>
<tr><td>Short-term</td><td>90</td><td>90</td><td>120</td><td>150</td></tr>
</table>

Data is effective starting April 1, 2001.

Table 6.2 Duration of Basic Allowance (Involuntary terminated Employees)

(unit: days)

<table>
<tr><td></td><td colspan="5">Years of being insured</td></tr>
<tr><td>Age of beneficiary</td><td>Less than 1 year</td><td>1<= and <5 years</td><td>5<= and <10 years</td><td>10<= and <20 years</td><td>More than 20 years</td></tr>
<tr><td>Less than 30</td><td rowspan="4">90
(90)</td><td colspan="2">90
(90)</td><td>180
(150)</td><td>--
--</td></tr>
<tr><td>30~44</td><td>90
(90)</td><td>180
(150)</td><td>210
(180)</td><td>240
(210)</td></tr>
<tr><td>45~59</td><td>180
(90)</td><td>240
(210)</td><td>270
(240)</td><td>330
(300)</td></tr>
<tr><td>60~64</td><td>150
(150)</td><td>180
(150)</td><td>210
(180)</td><td>240
(210)</td></tr>
<tr><td colspan="6">For those difficult to get employed(disabled, etc.)</td></tr>
<tr><td>Less than 45</td><td>150</td><td colspan="4">300</td></tr>
<tr><td>45~64</td><td>150</td><td colspan="4">360</td></tr>
<tr><td>Less then 30</td><td>(150)</td><td colspan="4">(240)</td></tr>
<tr><td>30~64</td><td>(150)</td><td colspan="4">(270)</td></tr>
</table>

* numbers in ( ) are for part-time workers

Data is effective starting April 1, 2001.

Table 6.3 Duration of Old-Age Job Applicant Benefit

(unit: days)

<table>
<tr><td></td><td colspan="3">Years of being insured</td></tr>
<tr><td></td><td>Less than 1 year</td><td>1<= and <4 years</td><td>More than 5 years</td></tr>
<tr><td>Continuously older workers</td><td>30</td><td>60</td><td>75</td></tr>
<tr><td>Short-term workers</td><td>30</td><td colspan="2">50</td></tr>
</table>

Old Age Continuous Employment Benefits

This is a scheme for old employees who are between ages 60 and 65 and continue to work at a salary lower than 85% of their salary at age 60. They have to be insured for at least 5 years before receiving the benefit.

Rise of Part-time and temporary employment in the young and the women

Partly due to high unemployment, and partly due to changing employment preferences (both by employees and employers), the number of part-time and temporary workers is rising, especially among young and women. Many of them do not or cannot participate in the Employment Insurance. This is due to the system's underlying concept that the Employment Insurance is security for livelihood for those who make their living with the wages received for their own labour, at the time they lose their jobs.

In response to the changing job market, the 2001 Reform of the Employment Insurance abolished some criteria for part-time and temporary workers to subscribe: the main one of them is the yearly income threshold (Yen 900,000/year). Now part-time or temporary workers working at least 20 hours per week, and works (or sent to work from temp agency) at a same workplace for more than 1 year are eligible to subscribe to the Employment Insurance.

Current Issues

The Increase of part-time and temporary workers

There has been a continuous shift of labour force from full-time permanent employment to part-time, temporary employment, especially among the young generation and women. In 2005, the Government has set the goal of shifting 0.2 million temporary workers to permanent workers per year. Training and job-matching programmes were put in place and the goal was met. In 2006, the goal of shifting 0.25 million workers has been set.

Treatment of elderly employees

However, the current system still favours old age employees in many respects (For example, the Old Age Continuous Employment Benefits and the insured period categorization of the Unemployment Benefits). The assumption of the Employment Insurance was that young people are hired easily and will continue to work full-time for the entire duration of their career. Some researchers believe these schemes distort the labour market. The treatment of old age employees must be re-examined closely in relation with the labour market and also other social security systems such as pensions.

Part IV

9 The Current Status of the Health Insurance and Tasks Ahead

Jinsoo Kim, Rah-Il Hwang and Kyungha Kim

Introduction

Health insurance is a system under which economic burden of all community members would be resolved collectively by all people. As such, it constitutes an integral part of the overall social welfare system of the country and strives for promoting social justice and solidarity. Though most countries with health insurance system have their own unique systems which incorporate unique historical, economic and social characteristics of their countries, medical insurance systems can be classified into four broad categories depending on the resource financing methods (contribution versus tax) and the mode of service provision (private provider versus public sector provider). In the case of South Korea, our health insurance system adopted so-called 'social insurance method' under which resources are financed through contributions, and medical services are provided mainly by private providers (Cho 2001).

In modern welfare states, health insurance is considered as a basic national right which should be protected by law. Likewise in South Korea, the Constitution stipulates that "all people are entitled to be protected by the State for their health" (Article 36). The importance of healthy life has emerged as a basic human right in recent years. (Lee 2003)

Since it was first introduced for workplaces employing more than 500 workers in 1977, the health insurance system in South Korea has come a long way with a long history of more than 30 years. Though the Korean health insurance system was introduced quite late compared with other advanced countries, lagging behind 100 years or at least 50 years, it has achieved the target of universal coverage within a short time and now it is contributing greatly for promoting health and medical advancement of the nation (Cha 2007). The health insurance system in Korea has been highly evaluated for its contribution for the continuous expansion of medical manpower and hospital beds, for facilitating easy access to modern medical services to all people, and for its successful effort to maintain medical service costs at an affordable level. One of another commendable achievement of the health insurance system in Korea was the introduction of the Long-term Elderly Care Insurance system which was initiated in July 2008. All of these truly commendable achievements were achieved by the Korean health insurance system during the past several years when there was strong pressure to raise medical costs arising from increasing demand for better services, problems arising from ageing population, changing patterns of diseases towards chronic diseases and demand for new medical technology. All these factors influenced adverse impacts on medical costs and the financial position of the health insurance system. Given the deteriorating environment and new challenges arising from ever increasing demand for better services, it is high time for the health insurance system to formulate a long-term programme and strategy to cope with these challenges more effectively.

In this study, the history and achievement of the Korean health insurance system will be critically reviewed and the new challenges facing health insurance arising from changed health environment will be diagnosed with a view to come up with a new direction of health insurance system to follow in the future.

History and Current Status of Health Insurance

As mentioned before, the South Korean health insurance system was introduced in 1977 to provide health insurance coverage to workplaces employing more than 500 workers. The medical benefit system, which provides medical services by the Government as a part of public support programme, was also initiated in 1977. Considering the poor health status of rural communities, the coverage of health insurance was extended to rural areas first in 1987, followed by further extension to urban areas in 1989. By 1989, the health insurance system achieved universal coverage within a short time of 12 years. This remarkable achievement was highly acclaimed by the WHO and the German Government. After carefully reviewing the development of Korea's health insurance system from its inception to the stage of achieving universal coverage, the World Health Organization (WHO) praised Korea's achievement as the fastest case to achieve universal coverage in record time in its report in 2004. Likewise, the German Government also commended the Korea's successful achievement in shortest time span in its report issued by the Federal Government in 2005 (Carrin & James 2004; GTZ 2005). Judging from the experiences of Germany which took 127 years to achieve universal coverage and Japan (36 years); therefore Korea's achievement was remarkable by any standard. In 2000, the management of health insurance by several divisions was integrated under a single entity and the name of the corporation was changed from 'medical' insurance to 'health' insurance to reflect the comprehensive health services the system was providing. Starting from July 2008, a Long term Elderly Care Insurance scheme was launched to provide care services to growing number of incapacitated elderly as part of its commitment to pursue social solidarity (see figure 1).

Figure 1: Chronological development of the health insurance system

Enactment of the Health Insurance Act (1963)

Year	Employee Insurance	Insurance for Self-Employed
1963	Survey data on Workplaces employing 300 workers completed	
1970		Data on self-employed prepared
1977	Automatic eligibility for workplaces employing 500 workers	
1979	- Automatic eligibility for civil servants & private school teachers - Automatic eligibility for workplaces with 300 workers	
1981	Automatic eligibility for workplaces employing 100 + workers	- 1st pilot project for self-employed coverage (Hong Cheon, Ok Gu, Gun Wi) - Establishment of occupational health insurance cooperatives
1982	Automatic eligibility for workplaces with 16 + workers	2nd pilot project for self-employed coverage (Gang Hwa, Bo Eun, Mok Po)
1988	Automatic eligibility for workplaces with 5+ workers	Automatic eligibility to rural self-employed persons
1989		Automatic eligibility for urban self-employed persons
	National coverage completed (1989) - Universal coverage completed after 12 years of operations; Germany required 127 years, and Japan 36 years	
1998	Enactment of the National Medical Insurance Act (integration of civil service personnel, private school teachers and self-employed health insurance)	
1999	Enactment of the National Health Insurance Act (integration of civil service personnel, private school teachers and self-employed health insurance)	
2000	Effectiveness of the National Health Insurance Act (integration of employee insured and self-employed in-	

	sured)
2003	Financial integration of employee insured and self-employed insured
2008	Introduction of Long-term Elderly Care Insurance System – universal coverage completed Countries with both health insurance & elderly care insurance systems: Japan, Germany (two countries)

This article would like to describe the operational status of the health insurance by presenting insurance eligibility, sources of financing, health insurance benefits and management and operational system of health insurance.

First, there are two groups of participants, i.e., employee and self-employed insured. Employee insured include employees and employers of workplaces, civil service personnel, private school teachers and dependents. Self-employed insured include all Korean nationals except for the employee insured and their dependents. Moreover, those persons who are participants of medical aid, the Government support programme that provides special medical services for special groups (including national patriots who had contributed for the independence of our country and their family members specified by law). In 2008, there were about 50 million participants of which 48.16 million (96.3%) were participants in the health insurance, and the remaining 1.84 million (3.7%) were participants of medical aid. As you may find in table 1, the number of beneficiaries of medical aid has been fairly stable at around 3.7%, except for 2002 and 2003 when it was 3.0%.

Second, main sources of health insurance are revenues from contributions and Government budget support. Contributions for health insurance are calculated by applying a fixed contribution rate (5.08% in 2009) to the salary for employee insured, and contributions are shared equally by employees and employers. In this case, salary means total remuneration received for work, but it excludes some income specified as non-taxable income in the Income Tax Law such as honorarium, prize money and translation fees (Article 63-3 of the Act, Article 33-1 of the Implementation Statute). On the other hand, the contributions of self-employed insured will be calculated on the basis of contribution points which, in turn, reflect the property of participant's household (including vehicles, house rent), participant's income and living standards. When the points are obtained, contributions will be calculated by multiplying points by a fixed amount (Won 148.95 in 2009).

Table 1: Population covered by medical insurance and aid
(in %; unit: 1,000 persons)

Year	*Health Insurance*			*Medical Aid*
	Total	*Employee insured*	*Self-employed insured*	
2000	45,890 (96.7)	22,400 (48.8)	23,490 (51.2)	1,570 (3.3)
2001	46,380 (96.9)	23,170 (50.0)	23,210 (50.0)	1,500 (3.1)
2002	46,660 (97.0)	23,750 (50.9)	22,910 (49.1)	1,420 (3.0)
2003	47,100 (97.0)	24,830 (52.7)	22,270 (47.3)	1,450 (3.0)
2004	47,370 (96.9)	25,980 (54.8)	21,390 (45.2)	1,530 (3.1)
2005	47,390 (96.4)	27,230 (57.5)	20,160 (42.5)	1,760 (3.6)
2006	47,410 (96.3)	28,450 (60.0)	18,960 (40.0)	1,830 (3.7)
2007	47,820 (96.3)	29,420 (61.5)	18,400 (38.5)	1,850 (3.7)
2008	48,160 (96.3)	30,420 (63.2)	17,740 (36.8)	1,840 (3.7)

Sources: Health Insurance Annual Statistics Report, 2007; Major Statistics on Health Insurance, 2008; National Health Insurance Corporation, 2009.

With respect to Government support, financial support will be made from both general accounts as well as from the National Health Promotion Fund. The total amount of the Government support would be 20% of contribution revenues, of which 14% would be provided by the general account (National Health Insurance Act, Article 92), and the remaining 6% will be charged to the National Health Promotion Fund (National Health Promotion Act, Addendum, Article 7).

As to the financial operation of health insurance, a modest surplus was recorded up to 2005, but some deficits were recorded in 2006 and 2007. In 2008, quite a large surplus of Won 1,366.7 billion was recorded in 2008 due largely to the less frequent utilization of medical facilities, reflecting economic slowdown (see figure 2).

Third, health insurance benefits are provided in kind in the course of diagnosis, consultation, test, pharmacy, treatment and hospitalization. Some exceptions are made for caretaker's expenses and a maximum limit of patient's share for which cash payments are permitted. The patient's share would be 20% in case of hospitalisation, and range between 30% and 50% in the case of outpatients. The share of the insurer in the total cost has been increasing from 61.8% in 2005, over 64.3% in 2006 and to 64.6% in 2007, respectively.

Fourth, the management and operation system of health insurance is as follows: There are three operators/managers (National Health Insurance Corporation, Health Insurance Review and Evaluation Board and health service providers) who are playing key roles in carrying out the health service on behalf of the Government under the overall supervision and direction of the Ministry of

Figure 2: Annual financial positions of the health insurance

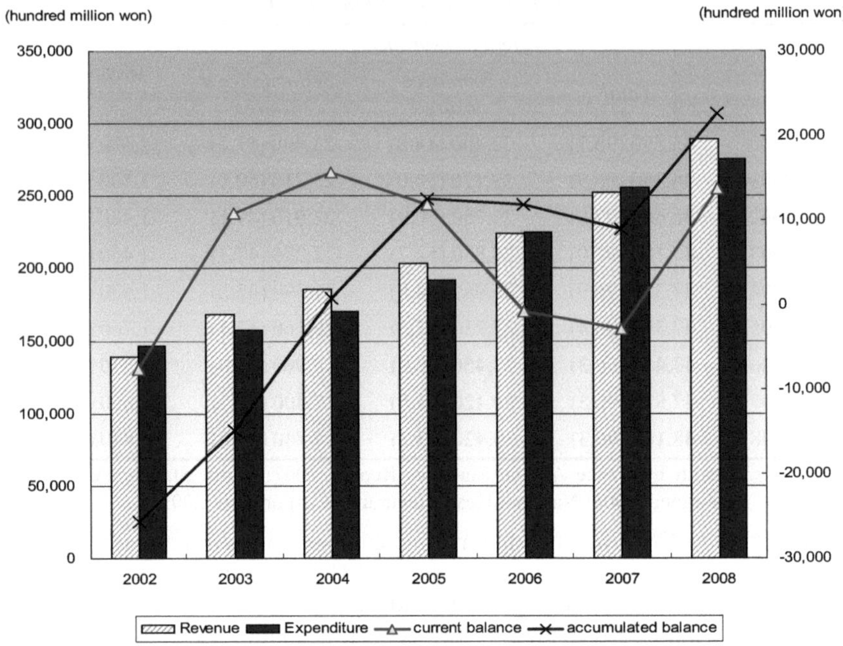

Health, Welfare and Family (see figure 3).

Figure 3: Health insurance management and operation system

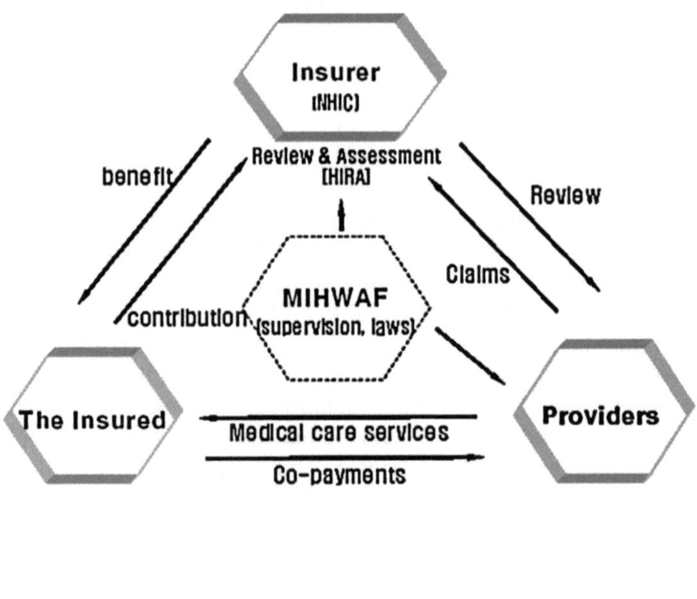

The National Health Insurance Corporation (NHIC – Insurer) is responsible for the overall management, coordination and supervision of health insurance activities including management of eligibility of participants and their dependents, contribution calculation and collection, execution of participant's health promotion activities and determination of fees to be paid to health service providers under the contracts. Health Insurance Review and Assessment Service (HIRA) is responsible for evaluating the appropriateness of health service quality and fees charged by health service providers and determine the rational fee structure to be charged by NHIC. Health service providers provide medical services to participants, and their service charges will be determined under the contract with NHIC.

Effect of Health Insurance and Evaluation

Effect of Health Insurance

Since its inception in 1977, Korean health insurance has performed remarkably as demonstrated by the fact that it has achieved universal coverage within a short time span of twelve years. By providing coverage to all people, the health insurance has contributed very much to achieve social solidarity and consolidation regardless of income levels, groups, regions and gender. In order to verify the income redistribution effect of the health insurance, contribution payments and benefits of all participants had been classified into 20 groups. The result of this exercise had been very striking. The participant who paid one-tenth of the higher paying participant had the same level of health service. This indicates that there was income transfer from high contribution paying participants to low contribution paying ones.

Second, the health level of people has been improved very much by improved access to health facilities and more frequent utilization of health services. According to the Report prepared by Korea Development Institute (KDI) (1975), about 40% of sickly patients in Korea had no access to health services at that time which led to deteriorating health level. During 1060-1970, well before the introduction of health insurance, the life expectancy in Korea ranged 50-55 in contrast to that of OECD countries where they had 70 years life expectancy in 1960 (Cha 2007). However, the introduction of health insurance in 1977 and the completion of universal coverage of health insurance in 1989 changed the picture completely. With the increased supply of health services, the utilization of health services increased drastically. The number of health service providers grew 12.3 times from 1979 (1,979 providers) to 2008 (78,407 providers). Similarly, the number of hospital beds increased from 287,040 in 2000 to 450,119 beds in 2007, while the number of doctors increased from 57,188 in 1995 to 91,475 in 2007. The number of nurses doubled between 1995 (120,415 nurses) to 2007 (235,687 nurses). The health service utilization rate has increased substantially from 0.1 day hospitalization per participant in 1977 to 1.7 days in 2008. Likewise, out-patient hospital visits also increased from 0.7 visit in 1977

Figure 4: Comparison of contributions and benefits: Self-employed insured, 2008

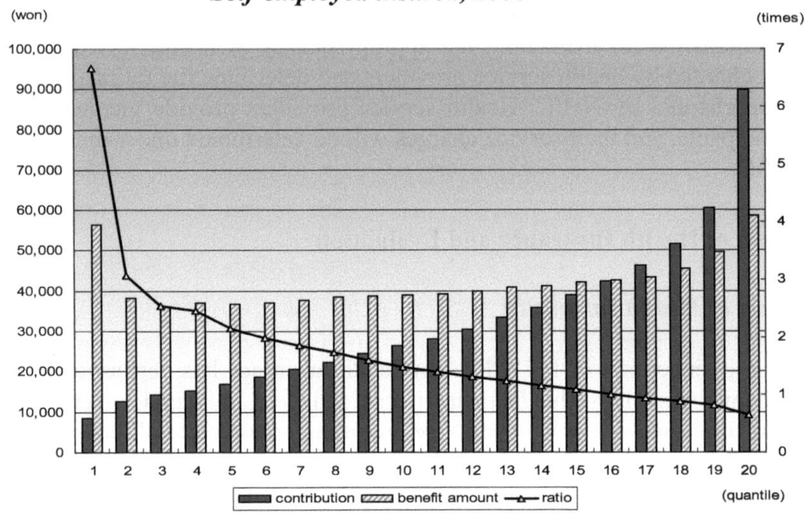

Figure 5: Comparison of contributions and benefits: Employee insured, 2008

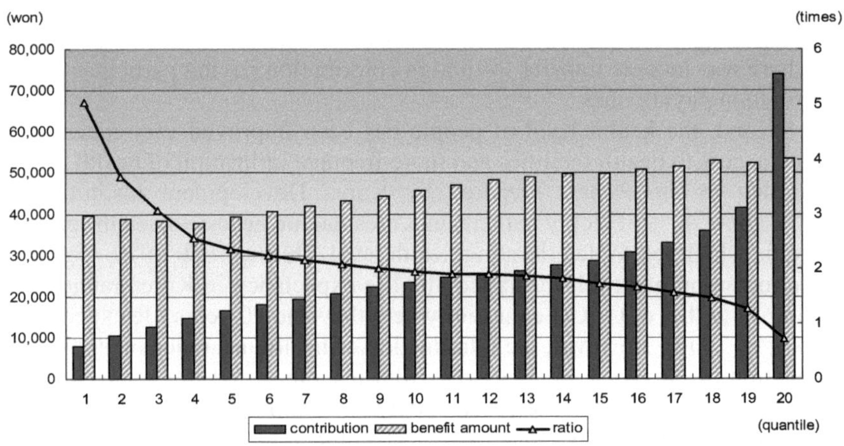

to 15.1 visits in 2008. This drastic change in visits raises some concern for over utilization of health services. When we compare with the OECD countries, Korea's hospitalization days and out-patient visit frequency were 1.09 times and 2.04 times of OECD averages, respectively, in 2006 (see table 2).

Table 2: Per-capita hospitalization days and out-patient visit frequency

Year	Per-capita hospitalization days		Per-capita out-patient visits	
	Korea	OECD average	Korea	OECD average
2000	0.88	1.18	10.8	6.8
2001	0.93	1.16	12.2	6.7
2002	0.97	1.15	13.0	6.8
2003	1.09	1.14	13.6	6.7
2004	1.13	1.14	13.8	6.7
2005	1.19	1.12	14.1	7.4
2006	1.32	1.21	14.7	7.2
2007	1.57	-	15.0	-
2008	1.74	-	15.1	-

Sources: Health Insurance Statistical Yearbook, 2007; Major Statistics on Health Insurance, 2008; NHIC 2009; OECD Health Data 2008.

Along with the drastic increase in health service utilization, life expectancy of Koreans rose rapidly as child mortality rates dropped considerably. Life expectancy of Koreans increased very fast from 52.4 years in 1977 to 79.1 years in 2006, recording an increase of 1.5 times during this period, surpassing the OECD average of 78.9 years in 2006 (see figure 6), while the child mortality rate declined very rapidly from 45.0 deaths per 1,000 live births in 1970 to 5.3 deaths in 2006, almost the same as the OECD average of 5.2 deaths in 2006.

Figure 6: Changes in average life expectancy

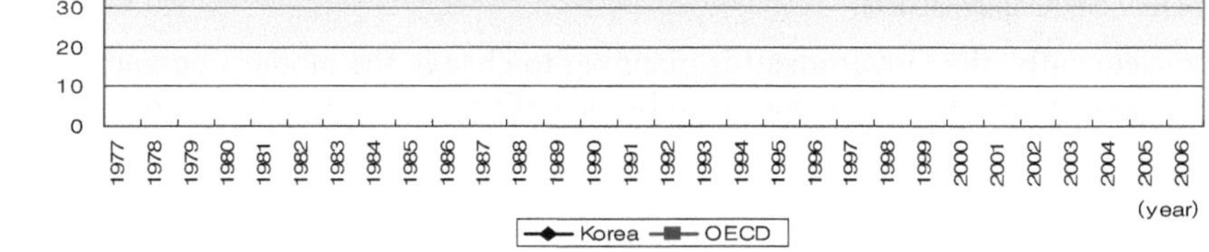

Third, the cost burden of patients has been continuously declining as the benefit coverage rate rose consistently. Starting from 1996, CT was covered under insurance benefits, and the 'National Health Insurance Development Committee' was constituted in 2003 to discuss benefit coverage issues in earnest. Meanwhile, the Government has taken steps to expand benefit coverage for the very expensive medicines as part of a concerted effort to reduce the cost burden of patients. In 2004, the Government decided to reduce the cost burden of patients who were suffering from cancer, Parkinson's disease and 62 other severe diseases to the level of hospitalized patients (i.e., 20% cost burden for patients). Furthermore, the NHIC introduced a stop-loss system (patient burden capping) in 2004 under which the NHIC would bear all excess costs if patient's cost burden exceeds 3 million Won over a six months period. Starting from 2007, the upper limit of the stop-loss system was further reduced to Won 2 million to diminish the cost burden of patients with severe diseases. However, as shown in table 3, the bulk of benefits went to higher income patients. Of the total benefit amount of the stop-loss system (Won 243.6 billion), only Won 92.7 billion (38.1%) went to lower income groups.

Table 3: Patient burden capping (stop-loss) system in 2008

Income brackets	*Number of beneficiaries (%)*		*Amount of benefits (Won million '00, %)*	
Total (1-10)	233,861	(100.0)	2,436	(100.0)
1	26,658	(11.4)	245	(10.1)
2	15,332	(6.6)	152	(6.3)
3	17,935	(7.7)	179	(7.3)
4	17,846	(7.6)	183	(7.5)
5	16,367	(7.0)	168	(6.9)
Sub-total (1-5)	94,138	(40.3)	927	(38.1)
6	15,989	(6.8)	172	(7.1)
7	17,767	(7.6)	191	(7.8)
8	19,047	(8.1)	202	(8.3)
9	24,207	(10.4)	258	(10.6)
10	62,713	(26.8)	686	(28.1)
Sub-total (6-10)	139,723	(59.7)	1,509	(61.9)

Source: NHIC Internal data.

Consequently, the Government is planning to change the modus operandi of the stop loss system so as to reduce cost burden of lower income groups by applying differentiated stop loss system in which income level (as expressed in terms of contribution amount) would be factored into the system from December 2009. The detailed content is presented in table 4.

The overall cost coverage ratio of NHIC had increased from 61.3% in 2004 to 64.6% in 2007. The increase in coverage ratio was very much pronounced in the case of cancer patients: coverage ratio of cancer patients increased from 49.6% in 2004 to 71.5% in 2007. Coverage ratios for high cost patient (over Won 5 million), heart disease patients and rare diseases patients increased also during this period as shown in table 5.

Table 4: Criteria of the stop-loss system by income brackets

Income Bracket	*Stop loss upper limit (patient burden)*
10-50% in contribution payment (low income)	Won 2 million per annum
Medium 50-80%	Won 3 million per annum
Top 20% (80-100%)	Won 4 million per annum

Note: Revision of the NHIC Act (announced on April 6, 2009), NHIC.

Table 5: Health insurance coverage ratios by year

Category/Year	*2005*	*2006*	*2007*
Total *61.3% (2004)	61.8%	64.3%	64.6%
Cancer patients *49.6% (2004)	66.1%	71.0%	71.5%
High cost patients *49.0% (2004)	59.6%	64.7%	67.6%
Heart patients (in-house)	65.7%	66.0%	69.4%
Rare diseases patients (out-patients)	71.1%	72.1%	74.2%

Note: Coverage ratio is ratio of patient-paid costs to total costs (including non-insured costs).
Source: Kim Jung-Hee et al. 2006-2008.

Fourth, another important achievement of health insurance is the launching of the Long-Term Elderly Care Insurance (LTECI) system. This system was designed to address the care needs of elderly and to mitigate the heavy burden of excessive long-term care costs. After a 3-year preparatory pilot project during 2005-2007, this system was launched in July 2008. As of December 2008, some 214,480 elderly (157,320 from NHIC and 57,160 from medical aid) were enrolled into this system. By participating in this system, care costs (monthly care costs ranged between Won 500,000 to Won 2.5 million) were substantially reduced to the Won 300-400,000 level. The benefits of this system are the reduced care-cost burdens to families in the short run. However, in the long run, there should be many more benefits such as improved physical condition and improved quality of life of elderly, employment opportunities for family members freed from care, and creation of jobs to provide care services for elderly. The social benefits of this system were calculated for both the econometric part as well as the non-econometric part. The outcome of the analysis indicated that social benefits were estimated to amount Won 4,621 billion (Won 4,382 billion minimum) in 2009 and Won 7,018 billion (Won 6,571 billion minimum) in 2012. Additional employment would be 106,634 persons in 2009 (76,854 persons minimum) and 149,819 (108,657 persons minimum) in 2012, respectively (see table 6).

Table 6: Social benefits of the LTECI system (2008-2012)

Category/year		*2008* [1)]	*2009* [2)]	*2010*	*2011*	*2012*
Social benefits	minimum	25,176	43,825	49,859	59,793	65,717
	maximum	26,205	46,210	52,634	63,523	70,182
Jobs created	minimum	63,818	76,854	83,694	100,116	108,657
	maximum	92,252	106,634	115,019	138,164	149,819

Notes: 1) This figure is the sum of the production and job creation effects arising from the 2007 project "Strengthening of Elderly Care Facilities", funded by the state budget.
2) Employment creation would be very active during 2008 and 2009 with the construction of facilities (architects, civil engineers etc. and nurses). Starting from 2009, job creation will remain unchanged.

Source: Noh Sang Yun et al. 2008.

Assessment of Health Insurance and Problems

Despite all the glittering achievements, the health insurance in Korea has internal problems to solve and tasks yet to achieve.

First, there exists some blind zone in health insurance. The health insurance had achieved universal coverage in 1989, and the low income group is covered with medical aid. However, while some 7-10% of the population is protected under medical aid in advanced countries, only 3.7% of the population in Korea was protected by medical aid in 2008. This implies that there is a blind zone in reality. It means that there are many people who do not enjoy the benefits of health insurance because they failed to pay a contribution. As of 2008, there were 2,006,000 households with overdue contributions of three months (25% of total participating households) and total overdue contributions amounted to Won 1,538 billion (the average household overdue contribution was Won 79,000), according to the internal data from NHIC. The blind zone in health insurance is caused by low income participants, when they have 6 months overdue contributions and when the NHIC denies any benefits to them. This blind zone may be attributable to some social problems such as unemployment, bankruptcy and broken families, but it can be also attributable to institutional problems such as inflexible criteria in selecting eligible beneficiaries (Cha 2007).

Second, there is some problem arising from inequitable contribution burdens among regions. In principle, the resource financing of health insurance is supposed to be equitably distributed to various regions, considering the nature of health insurance and the social solidarity principle. However, it is very difficult to estimate income levels of self-employed households correctly. As of May 2008, income surveys for self-employed households completed only 38.7% of households compared to 28.03% in 1997. In the absence of reliable household income data, contributions by self-employed insured are being determined by using non-income data such as property and vehicles. Therefore, there are two different criteria (dual structure) in determining contributions: one based on income for employee insured and another relaxed criterion applicable for self-employed insured. This dual structure in contribution determination has been causing many problems. In 2007, when one participant moves from employee to self-employed insured status or one moves from self-employed to employee insured, the contribution amount increased by 30.4% (from Won 41,414 to 53,988) or declined by 33.1% (from Won 56,019 to 37,504). Another problem is the increasing number of 'free riders' of employee insured, disguised as dependents. Despite the increasing number of unemployed persons, the dependent support ratio maintained the decreasing trend largely thanks to the NHIC actions to convert dependents with income to self-employed insured, and expanded self-employed insured by encouraging workers employed in small workplaces (less than 5 workers), part time workers (with 80 hours work record) and daily workers to join as self-employed insured. The fact that one-third of people are not paying any contribution to the health insurance hurts greatly the principle of social solidarity, and this problem must be urgently corrected (see table 7).

Table 7: Dependent support ratio by year (in %)

Year	*2000*	*2001*	*2002*	*2003*	*2004*	*2005*	*2006*	*2007*	*2008.3*
Support ratio	2.08	1.94	1.85	1.82	1.80	1.79	1.73	1.63	1.63

Source: NHIC 2009.

Third, the degree of coverage in health insurance in Korea is too low. Though the health insurance completed its universal coverage in 1989, and Korea joined the OECD in December 1996, our health insurance does not provide sufficient coverage as a safety net compared with other OECD countries. In 2006, the share of public health expenditure in total health expenditure in Korea was 55.1% compared with 73.0% of OECD average (see table 8). Though there had been some efforts to enhance coverage of health insurance such as the increased coverage applicable to cancer patients and patients with rare diseases, most of Koreans are still suffering from high prices of drugs, and many expensive drugs are excluded from insurance coverage. This creates unbearable cost burdens to households. Under these circumstances, health insurance in Korea is not fully performing its function as social insurance.

Table 8: Share of public health expenditure in total health expenditure (in %)

Year	*Korea*	*OECD Average*
2001	54.5	72.7
2002	53.1	73.0
2003	51.7	73.2
2004	52.4	72.7
2005	53.1	72.9
2006	55.1	73.0

Source: OECD Health Data, 2008.

Fourth, from the perspective of supplying health and medical services, the public sector does not own a sufficient number of hospital beds in Korea. In order to maintain the characteristics of the public nature of health services, it is important to own a sufficient number of hospital beds. The share of public in total hospital beds in Korea was 17.5%, which was very low compared to 62.3% in Germany, 33.7% in the U.S., 35.8% in Japan and 33.0% in Taiwan. This situation creates a big problem for the public health authority in carrying out its policy because it lacks leverage to influence private hospitals (see figure 7). In foreign countries, central and provincial Governments are operating many hospitals. The NHIC is currently operating one hospital, and it has plans to expand the hospital network to regional hubs.

Figure 7: Ratio of public hospital beds in some major countries (in %)

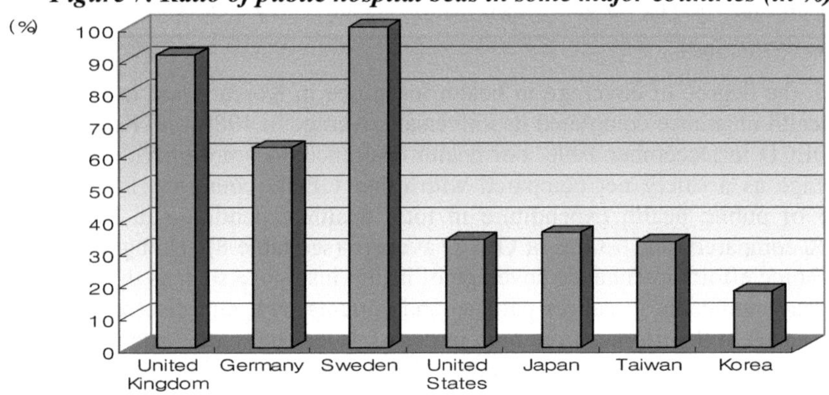

Changes in the Health Insurance Environment

Health insurance in Korea is now facing new challenge from changes in surrounding medical environment (see figure 8).

From the perspective of demand, the biggest change was the ageing population and consequent increase in elderly population. The elderly population of over 65 years more than doubled from 1.96 million (4.9% of health insurance eligible population) in 1990 to 4.6 million (9.6%) in 2008. The share of elderly health expenditure in total health insurance expenditure increased by more than three times from 8.0% in 1990 to 29.9% in 2008 (see table 9).

Figure 8: Changes in the health insurance environment

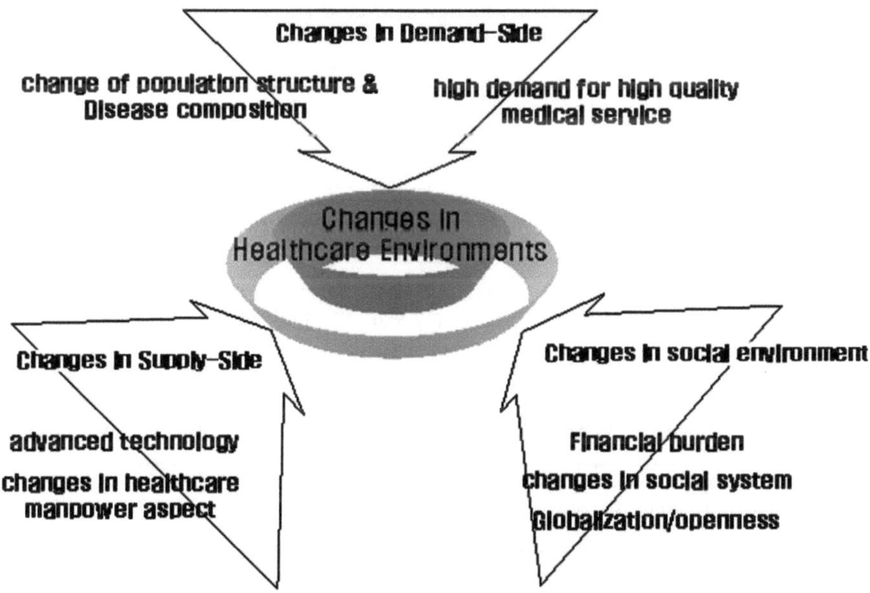

The changes in the population had resulted in changes in the disease composition, in which chronic diseases were increasing. The number of patients with chronic diseases increased by 30.7% during the period of 2002-2005 from 4.98 million in 2002 to 6.51 million in 2005. Medical expenses incurred for the elderly rose rapidly by 52.1% during this period (Health Insurance Statistical Yearbook). As income levels rise, there was a strong demand for high quality and even for individually tailored medical services.

Second, there were changes in the supply side too. As advanced and state-of-the-art technologies came to play a more important role in modern medical equipment, the demand for new technologies, new drugs and new equipment increased and this caused a substantial rise in medical costs. The utilization of new technology such as PET, gamma knife and operation with laparoscope became popular that also pushed up medical service costs. Another sensitive issue is the continued request from health service providers to raise fees. As the economic crisis deepens, it is expected that the request for fee increase would be resurfaced soon. During 2001-2007, there had been seven rounds of contract negotiations between the NHIC and representatives of health and medical and pharmaceutical industries, but all negotiations had failed, except for the 2006 negotiation. All other changes were approved through a voting process at the Health Insurance Policy Deliberation Committee of the Ministry of Health and Welfare (see table 10).

Table 9: Medical expenditures by age and year (unit: %, Won '00 million)

Year		*1990*	*1995*	*2000*	*2005*	*2006*	*2007*	*2008*
Eligible population	Over 65	1,957 (4.9%)	2,483 (5.6%)	3,019 (6.6%)	3,919 (8.2%)	4,073 (8.6%)	4,387 (9.2%)	4,600 (9.6%)
	Less than 65	42,223	41,533	42,877	43,473	43,336	43,433	43,560
	total	40,180	44,016	45,896	47,392	47,410	47,820	48,160
Medical expenses	Over 65	2,353 (8.0%)	7,385 (12.0%)	22,555 (17.5%)	60,731 (24.3%)	73,504 (25.9%)	91,189 (28.2%)	104,310 (29.9%)
	Less than 65	27,066	54,057	106,567	187,884	210,599	232,702	244,147
	total	29,419	61,442	129,122	248,615	284,103	323,892	348,457

Note: Eligible population – year end; medical expenses – payment date basis.
Source: Health Insurance Statistical Yearbook 2007; Major Health Insurance Statistics 2008.

Table 10: Trend in conversion index revisions

year	*Agreement*	*Adjustment rate*	*Conversion index*
2001	Failed *	7.08% ↑	55.4 Won
2002	Failed *	2.9% ↑	53.8 Won
2003	Failed *	3.0% ↑	55.4 Won
2004	Failed *	2.7% ↑	56.9 Won
2005	Failed *	2.99% ↑	58.6 Won
2006	Agreed	3.50% ↑	60.7 Won
2007	Contract OK *	3.50% ↑	62.8 Won

Notes: Health Insurance Policy Deliberation Committee (HIPDC) is a committee set up pursuant to provisions of Article 4 of the Health Insurance Act. * Decided by HIPDC.
Source: Kim, Jin-Soo et al. 2007.

Third, this is regarding the impact of changes in the social environment of health insurance. Even though the ratio of health expenditure to GDP (6.4%) in Korea is relatively low, compared to other OECD countries (9.1%), this ratio is expected to rise due to an ageing population. Regarding the possibility of setting up a private health insurance company and the establishment of profit-oriented hospitals, we recommend a cautious approach so as not to endanger the stability of health insurance. Most people demand an efficient management, adequate level of contributions and a higher benefit coverage.

Issues and Tasks for Developing Health Insurance

The health insurance should pursue tasks to develop and to adjust itself to the changing environment, based on lessons learned during its long history of thirty years.

Figure 9: Direction of development for the health insurance

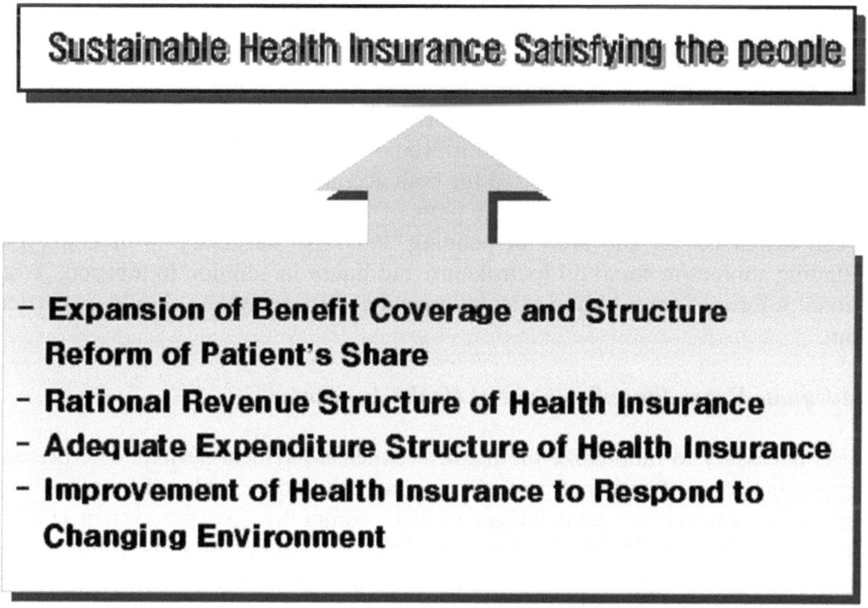

Expansion of Benefit Coverage and Structure Reform of Patient's Share

The first task should be an expansion of benefit coverage and a structural reform of patient's share. The NHIC should formulate a mid-term strategy to enhance a benefit coverage ratio target of 72% by 2013. In order to achieve this target, it should gradually expand coverage for high cost and severe disease patients and low income patients and health promotion, prevention of diseases, and rehabilitation should be covered gradually. Since some 24,412,000 persons visited clinics for common cold, and their medical cost amounted to 10.2% of out-patients costs, we should adjust the share of patients for light diseases like common cold and the resulting funds should be diverted to enhance the coverage ratio of severe diseases.

Rational Revenue Structure of Health Insurance

The revenue structure of the health insurance should be rationalized. In 2008, Korea's contribution rate of 5.08% was too low compared to 14.86% in Germany and 13.55% in France. As additional resources must be mobilized to expand the benefit coverage, it is necessary to increase the contribution rate to some adequate level. In order to facilitate a steady and timely funding from Government budget and from the National Health Promotion Fund, it is worthwhile to consider an ex-post settlement system for both accounts. During the six year period between 2002 and 2007, some large parts of funds (Won 2,831 billion) have not been disbursed yet and are still pending. It is also necessary to diversify the funding sources to fossil oil (petroleum) and liquor in addition to tobacco. A rational reform of contribution calculation and collection system should be carried out.

Adequate Expenditure Structure of Health Insurance

It is necessary to rationalize the medical expense payment system. The present spot payment system is not cost effective and should be replaced by more cost effective systems like total budget system, comprehensive fee system (DRG) and other systems. The medical service delivery system should be reformed by introducing an Integrated Care System which incorporates physical examination, treatment, rehabilitation, long term care and hospice under one umbrella. Another important reform would be the drug management system which creates the highest expenditure in the health insurance. In this regard, it is necessary to rationalize the drug pricing system by linking drug prices and quantities used. It is also desirable to monitor the trading flow of drugs to make drug trading more transparent.

Improvement of Health Insurance to Respond to Changing Environment

Lastly, prevention of diseases and health promotion should be given higher priority in reforming health insurance. For this purpose, it is necessary to introduce a lifetime cycle examination system as well as the U Health Care system to monitor chronic disease patients more effectively. We should also consider the possibility of sharing with individual insurance companies in promoting the expansion of coverage. For the effective management of the NHIC, it may be desirable to encourage internal competition and build up a basis for Global Health Care to promote green growth and green health.

Concluding Remarks

The health insurance in Korea has contributed very much for promoting health and medical development by continuously expanding medical manpower, hospital beds and by improving benefit coverage. And yet, the health insurance has many inherent problems such as the existence of blind zones, unfair contribution burden sharing among regions, a low benefit coverage and low public hospital beds ratios as well as other internal problems.

As expectations of a better health service are rising to reflect globalization and aspirations of better quality of life, an ageing population and the introduction of new medical equipment and technologies, these will create quite a formidable demand for the health insurance system and will push health costs upward. Moreover, a declining economically active population will aggravate the financial position of health insurance.

Consequently, in order to ensure a sound financial position of the health insurance, it is desirable to enhance the benefit coverage of certain group of patients (such as high costs, severe diseases and low income patients), reduce coverage for light patients (common cold for example), raise contribution rates, diversify revenue sources, rationalize the expense payment and drug management systems. These recommendations have been made several times in the past but no action could be taken so far, due to the conflict of interests and difficulties of reaching consensus.

Armed with thirty years history of achieving impossible tasks and know-how and supported by the consensus that health insurance in Korea must be sustained at any cost, we should explore ways to resolve all these problems.

References

Cha, Hung-Bong (2007), 'Ideal Direction of Health Protection', *Health Insurance Forum (NHIC)*, vol. 6 (2): 22-36.

Choi, Sook-Ja; Kim Jung-Hee & Lee Sang-Yee (2005), 'Strengthening of Benefit Coverage', *Health Insurance Forum (NHIC)*, vol. 4 (4): 2-13.

Choi, Won-Yung (2007), 'Health Insurance: 30 Year's Achievements', *Health Insurance Forum (NHIC)*, vol. 6 (2): 2-21.

GTZ/Deutsche Gesellschaft für Technische Zusammenarbeit GmbH (2005). *Social Health Insurance: A Contribution to the International Development Policy Debate on Universal Systems of Social Protection* Federal Ministry for Economic Cooperation and Development

Health Insurance Statistical Yearbook (2007), Seoul.

Kim, Jin-Soo & Noh Sang-Yun (2007), 'Process of Medical Fee Negotiations & Meaning of Fee Contract', *Health Insurance Forum (NIHC)*, vol. 6 (4), p. 28.

Kim, Jung-Hee et al. (2006-08), *Survey on Patient's Share in Medical Expenses*. Seoul: NHIC.

Korea Development Institute (1975), *Fourth Economic Development Plan*. Seoul.

Lee, Sang-Yong (2002), *NHIC: Its Birth and Growth path*. Seoul: NHIC.

Lee, Sang-Yong & Jin-Soo Kim (2003), *Health Insurance Contributions & Benefits: Equity Study*. Seoul.

Major Statistics on Health Insurance National Health Insurance Act. Seoul.

National Health Promotion Act & Implementation Statute (2008), Seoul.

National Health Insurance Act (Revised April 2009), Seoul.

Noh, Sang-Yun & Jin-Soo Kim (2008), 'Socio-economic Benefit Analysis on the Wake of Introducing Long-term Elderly Care Insurance System', *Health Insurance Forum (NHIC)*, vol. 6 (4): 2-8.

Noh, Sang-Yun; Jung-Hee Kim & Ho-Yong Lee (2008), *Application of the Stop Loss System by Different Income Groups*. Seoul: NHIC.

Yang, Bong-Min (2003), 'Issues and Tasks of Health Insurance Development for Korea', in *Proceedings to the Korean Society of Health Policy and Administration*, Seoul.

Yang, Bong-Min (2005), 'Forward Looking Health Insurance System', *Health Insurance Forum (NHIC)*, vol. 4 (2): 2-15.

10 Efficient Management of Medical Treatment Costs of the Health Insurance for the Elderly

Chong Yon Park, Min Jung Ko, Jun Tae Han and Jin-Hee Kwon

Introduction

Many countries throughout the world are feeling the strain of rising medical expenses triggered by their ageing population. In major OECD nations the ratio of medical expenditure incurred for senior citizens to total medical expenditure stands at around 40%. According to the OECD Health Data, as of 2005 Japan spent approximately US$ 300 billion for national health care, 47% of which was medical spending for senior citizens. In the United States, the biggest spender of medical expenses in the world, the medical expenses paid for elderly citizens accounted for 38% of the national medical spending of almost US$ 2 trillion. In most industrialized nations, medical expenses paid for the elderly are becoming an issue of grave concern.

Most of all, the level of ageing serves as one of the main reasons behind the increase in national medical spending, and it is shown in the relationship between the ratio of the aged population to the total population and the ratio of medical spending for seniors to total national medical expenses. In the United States, elderly people accounting for 9.4% of the total population spent 19.7% of total medical expenses in 1963, and 9.9% spent 27.5% in 1970, highlighting the fact that the increase in medical spending for the elderly was much greater than the increase in the aged population. In 2000, senior citizens accounting for 12.6% of the total population spent 39.2% of total medical spending of the nation (table 1).

Table 1: Relationship between the level of ageing and the medical expenses for the elderly: U.S.A. (1963-2000)

Year	*Per cent of population*	*Per cent of spending*
1963	9.4	19.7
1970	9.9	27.5
1977	10.9	34.7
1987	12.2	42.7
1996	12.7	41.5
2000	12.6	39.2

Source: Meara et al. 2004.

The reason behind the increase in medical spending – related to the increase of the aged population – can be more clearly seen by comparing the amount of medical spending per person by age group. According to a study on the trends in medical spending from 1963 to 2000 in the United States, when compared with those in the age group of 35 to 44-year old, those in the age group of 65 to 74 spent about thrice more; those in the age group of 75 or older five to seven times more (figure 1).

Figure 1: Medical spending by age group relative to the age group 35-44

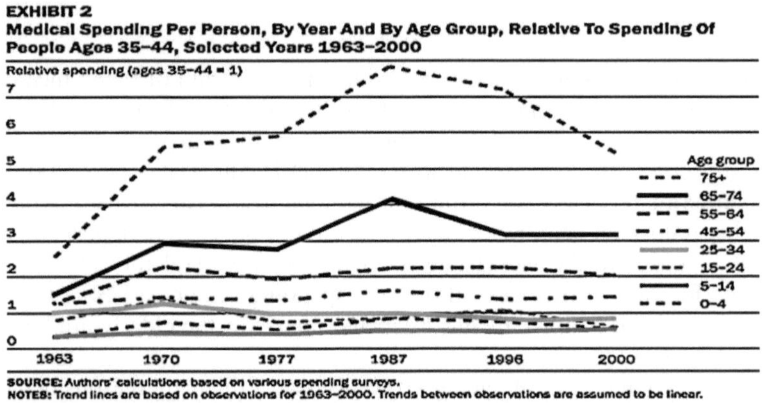

Source: Meara et al. 2004.

In order to cope with the national health care burden incurred by elderly people's medical spending, many nations that are faced with rapid ageing, skyrocketing national health care costs, and changes in people's lifestyle and mind-set are actively pursuing policies to curb the increasing medical spending for the elderly. Being a key policy tool to contain the increase in national medical expenses, counterbalancing the increase in medical spending for the elderly is emerging as a significant policy task to enhance the sustainability of the national medical security system and to guarantee the quality of life of senior citizens continuously.

Korea is not free from the burden of health and medical expenses, mainly stemmed from senior medical spending due to the ageing of the population structure and increase in chronic diseases. The ratio of senior citizens' population in Korea rose from 6.9% in 2001 to 9.2% in 2007, while the medical spending for them snowballed from Won 3,493.8 billion (19.0%) in 2001 to Won 9,508.1 billion (29.5%) in 2007. Korea has been facing the problem of ageing acceleration since the ageing of the society began in 2000. In particular, the population of elderly people in their 70s, 80s and older is rapidly expanding, seemingly becoming the cause of increasing national medical expenses. The ageing phenomenon in Korea is very serious because in addition to the pace of ageing, it is expected that by 2030 Korea will surpass the level of industrialized nations that have already become seriously aged countries and by 2050 it will be the most aged country in the world.

In the case of Korea, a single insurer, the National Health Insurance Corporation (NHIC), is covering all Korean people with a nationwide medical insurance system. In this context efficient management of medical expenses for elderly people paid by the health insurance is critical and the pattern of medical service utilization of elderly people plays an important role in managing the overall medical spending for the elderly. Increase in medical expenses for the elderly is due to natural causes such as increasing population of the aged and changes in disease structure. It may, however, be slowed down through innovation in systems or more efficient management and operation of the health insurance programme.

This article attempts to suggest an effective method to manage medical expenses for elderly people – an absolute cause of the rising national medical expenses – through comprehensive research and analysis of the current state and pattern of medical treatment for elderly people covered by the health insurance. First, by using the data about medical bills filed with the NHIC from 2001 to 2007, we analysed the characteristics and amounts related to high-cost medical treatment costs and major age-related illnesses as well as total amount of medical spending for the elderly, per capita medical treatment costs, and the ratio of medical spending for the elderly to total health care costs. Then, by using the management organization of the health insurance, we studied and analysed the pattern of the elderly people who frequently received medical treatments in using medical services. By doing so, we tried to provide information based on which efficient schemes may be devised to manage medical expenses for elderly people in the future.

Trends in Health Insurance Spending for Senior Citizens

Data and Analysis Framework

In order to analyse the characteristics and trends of health insurance expenditure incurred for senior citizens, we established a database on people's behavioural patterns in using medical services based on the data of entire medical services billed to the NHIC from 2001 to 2007. By doing this, we identified the amount of medical spending for elderly people by age, by type of medical institutions, and by reason of cost generation (hospitalization, outpatient treatment, or pharmacies) as well as the characteristics of high-cost medical treatment expenses (figure 2).

Figure 2: Framework for analysing health insurance expenditure for senior citizens

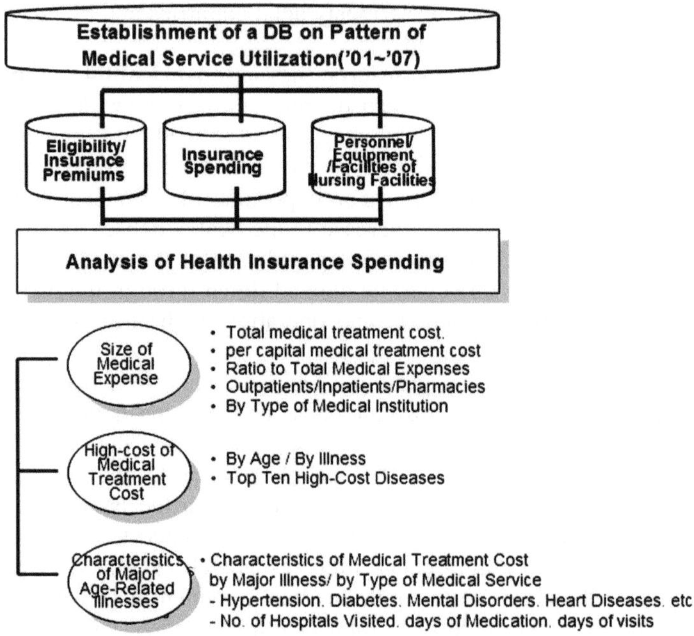

Furthermore, in order to clarify the medical treatment expenditure by type of medical services for major age-related illnesses, we set up a database on illnesses [1] that were frequently found among the aged, by researching those aged 65 or older who have used the health insurance in 2007 and have never filed for health insurance coverage on rare and hard-to-cure diseases or renal failure. Types of medical services are categorized by the number of medical institutions, days of medication, and days of hospital visits. Those among the top one per cent are categorized as the 'excessive' group and those, who are 'normal' in all three categories, are defined as the control groups.

1 High blood pressure, diabetes, heart diseases, cerebro-vascular diseases, nervous system disorders, other chronic obstructive pulmonary diseases, osteoporosis, arthritis, frozen shoulder syndrome, abdominal sickness, stomach-ache, gastritis, diseases of upper respiratory tract and vertebra.

Trend of Medical Spending for Senior Citizens

From 2001 to 2007 the ratio of the number of aged people to total population rose approximately 1.3 times from 6.9 to 9.2%, while during the corresponding period, the amount of total medical spending for them snowballed approximately 2.7 times from Won 3,493.8 billion to 9,508.2 billion, continuing the trend of annual increase. The ratio of medical spending for the elderly to total medical spending rose from 19.0 to 29.5%, and per capita medical spending almost doubled from Won 1.14 to 2.14 million (figure 3). From 2005 to 2007, total medical spending of pharmacies increased the most, from about Won 1,980 to 2,820 billion whereas hospitalization and outpatient costs remained almost the same.

By type of medical institutions, in 2007 per capita average medical treatment costs were the highest at nursing hospitals (Won 3.01 million), and were followed by general hospitals (Won 1.55 million), pharmacies (Won 660,000) and hospitals (Won 650,000). In particular, in the case of nursing hospitals, among all users, the number of elderly people accounted for about 36.6% but they incurred 83.4% of total medical treatment cost of nursing hospitals.

Figure 3: Trends in medical spending for senior citizens paid by the health insurance from 2001 to 2007

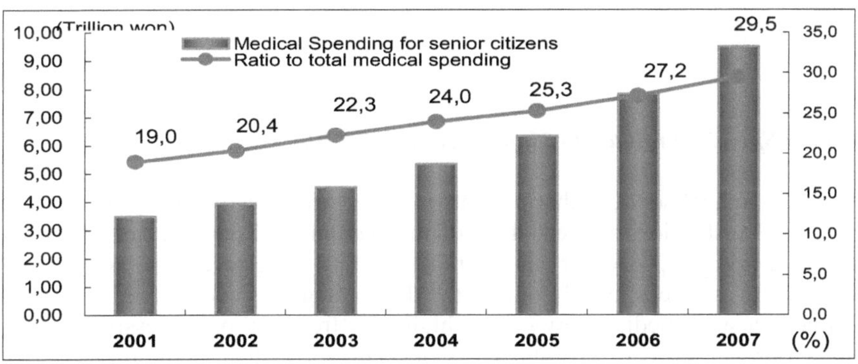

High-Cost Medical Treatments

Among those who spent 5 million Won or more per annum, those younger than 50 accounted only for around one per cent, and those in their 50s and 60s accounted for about two per cent and over five per cent respectively. Particularly, the proportion of high-cost medical treatment costs for those in their 60s or older soared year by year (4.9% in 2005 to 7.3% in 2007; figure 4).

Meanwhile, in the top 10 illnesses in terms of amount of total medical treatment costs, essential hypertension (Won 686 billion) topped the list, followed by cerebral infarction (Won 398.9 billion), gonarthrosis (Won 376.6 billion), diabetes (Won 337.7 billion), senile cataracts (Won 228.4 billion), angina pectoris (Won 204.3 billion), dorsalgia (Won 151.1 billion), other spondylopathies (Won 134.2 billion), other intervertebral disc disorders (Won 105.3 billion) and hyperplasia of prostate (Won 101.1 billion).

Figure 4: Distribution of high-cost medical treatment patients from 2005 to 2007

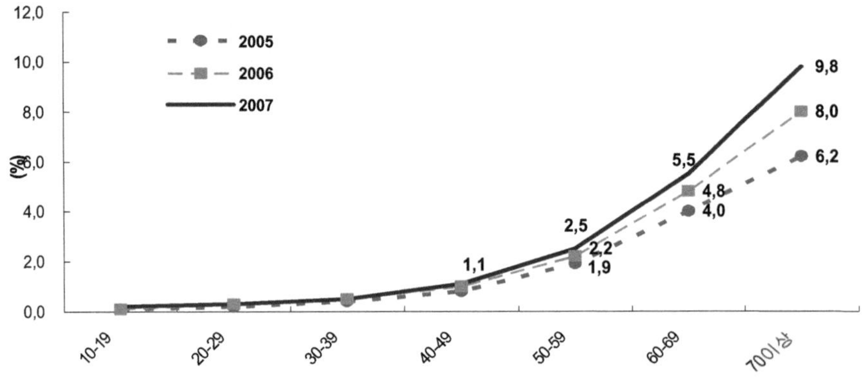

Medical Spending related to Major Age-Related Illnesses [2]

Types of medical services that patients received are categorized by the number of medical institutions visited, days of medication, and days of hospital visits and those in the top one per cent were defined as 'excessive'. If a person used 'excessively' services in only one of the three categories above, total per capita treatment cost by medical service was higher in 'frequent' or 'excessive medication' groups in terms of hospital visits or medication, than in 'multiple institutions' group in terms of the number of medical institutions visited. In addition, if 'excessive' in two or more categories, total treatment costs were highest in 'frequent' and 'excessive medication' groups.

2 High blood pressure, diabetes, heart diseases, cerebro-vascular diseases, nervous system disorders, other chronic obstructive pulmonary diseases, osteoporosis, arthritis, frozen shoulder syndrome, abdominal sickness, stomach-ache, gastritis, diseases of upper respiratory tract and vertebra.

Medical Service Utilization Patterns of Senior Citizens

Methodology

In order to identify the irrational behavioural patterns of elderly people in using medical services and the reasons behind such patterns, based on the health insurance database of 2007, we selected 1,543 people befitting the criteria for our research among: 1) excessive medical service users, 2) physical therapy recipients, and 3) long-term inpatients. First, among the health insurance beneficiaries, 65-year old people who have never billed for cancers, rare and hard-to-cure diseases, or renal failures [3] were selected for research. Among excessive medical service users and physical therapy recipients, outpatients who ranked in the top one per cent in terms of the number of medical institutions visited, days of hospital visits, and days of medication were chosen. As for the excessive medical service users, those with metal disorders were set aside as 1), and those with only one kind of age-related illness were classified as 2) in the simple illnesses group, and those with two or more illnesses were classified as 3) in the complex illnesses group (figure 5).

Figure 5: Selection process of research subjects

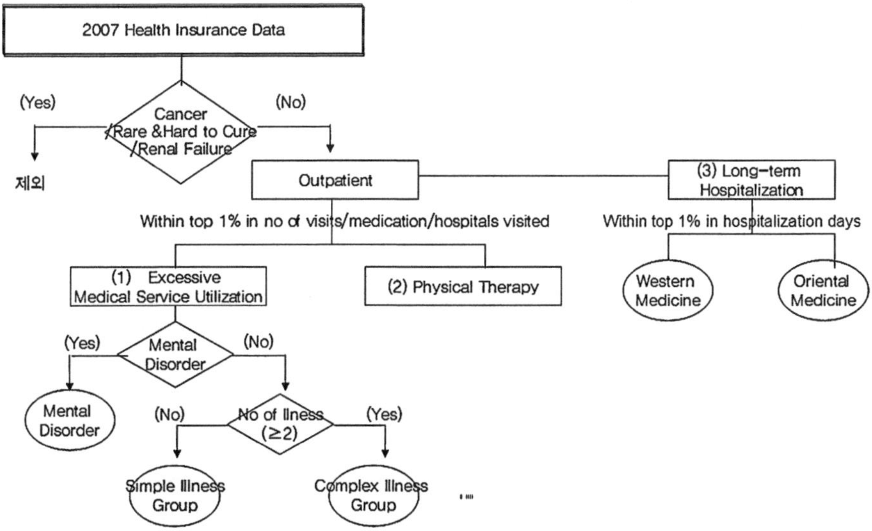

Details of the research were divided into consumer and supplier factors and were varied by research types (table 2). This research was carried out through one-on-

3 To exclude critically ill patients

one interviews led by specially trained employees of 178 branch offices of the NHIC in January 2009.

Table 2: Details of research by research type

Type Details	Excessive medical services	Physical therapy	Long-term hospitalization
Consumer factors			
Use of multiple institutions	○	○	
Redundant, excessive medication	○	○	
Long-term hospitalization etc.			○
Supplier factors			
Exemption/discount of patient expense	○	○	
Convenience service	○	○	
Over-treatment	○	○	○
Physical therapy		○	

Results

The number of people who have completed the research was 1,546 [4] (completion rate: 100.2%), the number of excessive medical service users was 728 people (99.1%), physical therapy recipients 312 people (101.3%), and long-term inpatients 506 people (101.2%). In general, women (64.9%), urban residents (medium and small cities/large cities: 79.5%), over 75 year olds (41.8%) showed high percentages.

Consumer Factors

Of the 1,040 excessive medical service users and physical therapy recipients, 91.8% answered that they visited medical institutions a lot to their recognition. Their reason of using medical services was mainly to treat their illnesses (81.3%) but there were psychological factors as well – some people felt their symptoms got better if they went to hospital often (11.7%) and others had an anxiety over the possibility of getting worse (3.9%).

40.8% of those who went to 'multiple institutions' [5] answered that they visited many hospitals because their illnesses did not get much better, 16.5% quoted other people's recommendation, 11.6% said because they did not know

4 The goal of research was 1,543 people. About seven times more research respondents applied.

5 This group is the top one percent in terms of the number of visits to medical institutions of outpatients by major diseases of senior citizens (801 people).

which one was more competent institution, 5.0% said they tried to find more affordable hospitals etc. (figure 6).

As to drug taking, about 20% of all people have taken multiple drugs at the same time. The main reason of multiple drug taking was because the "drugs were not very effective or not effective at all" (70%), but in 17.7% of the cases patients were not well aware of its effect to their health and in 6.6% patients thought it helpful for their illness. Accordingly, this research result suggests that appropriate education on drug taking is needed. Meanwhile, more than half of the respondents (54.1%) took five or more drugs together. A whopping 15.0% of those taking five to nine drugs answered that they were not taking too many drugs by their own judgment. 11.4% of the respondents said there were prescription drugs that they were not taking (the percentage was high among high frequency and excessive visit groups), and it was because "their body was troubled" in many cases. So, more attention should be paid to ensure that prescription drugs are appropriate for the physical condition of the patients. It was also suggested that intensive care is needed for the elderly who said they "forget to take" medicine (table 3).

Figure 6: Reasons of using medical services a lot [1] and reasons of visiting multiple medical institutions [2]

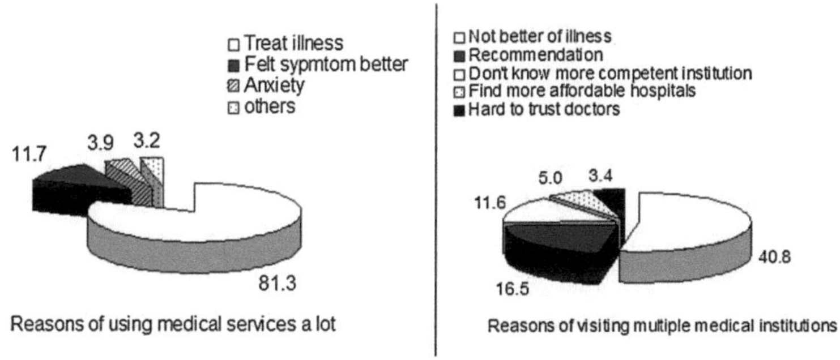

Notes: 1) Among those who answered 'very often' and 'often' to the question of frequency of visiting medical institutions (888 people). 2) Among those who visited multiple medical institutions (801 people) gave multiple answers.

Approximately 10% of long-term inpatients chose long-term hospitalization, because there was no place to go despite their attempts to transfer to long-term care facilities for the old. 84.6% said they would continue to be hospitalized even if they could be discharged and receive treatment as outpatients. In this case, 50% of them said it was because nobody could take care of them at home. Just 13.3% were discharged from hospital due to recovered health and 80.9% answered that they would remain in hospital even if the hospital fees go up in the future.

Table 3: Drug taking pattern (%)

Drug taking	*Total (1,040 people)*	*Excessive medical services (728 people)*	*Physical therapy (312 people)*
Have taken multiple drugs together	19.9	21.8	15.4
Effect to health			
Good	6.6	5.3	10.9
Bad	42.4	39.5	52.2
Different depending on drugs	28.8	32.9	15.2
Don't know	17.7	17.1	19.6
etc.	4.5	5.3	2.2
Kinds of medicines currently taken			
None	5.2	4.9	5.9
1-4 kinds	40.7	40.4	41.5
5-9 kinds	42.5	42.3	42.9
10 or more kinds	10.6	11.5	8.3
Prescription drugs			
Not taking now	1.8	1.1	3.6
Taking some of them	9.6	10.1	8.4
Reasons of not taking prescription drugs			
I adjusted the dose because my body is troubled	30.1	25.7	41.4
It is difficult to take drugs on time	25.2	28.4	17.2
It feels that the drug is not effective	15.5	17.6	10.3
I feel I recovered fully	7.8	8.1	6.9
I adjusted the dose to spare drugs	2.9	4.1	0.0
Others	18.4	16.2	24.1

Supplier Factors

Research on Exemption and Discount for Patient Expense

Among the 1,040 patients who have received excessive medical services and physical therapy, 7.0% have experienced free medical care during the past year, especially physical therapies, and 5.1% have received discounts on expenses (figure 7). In the future in the relation between out-of-pocket expenses and medical services, 52.1% said they would use medical services less if it is not free, and 30.8% said they would use less if it is not discounted.

Figure 7: Percentage of those having received free or discounted services

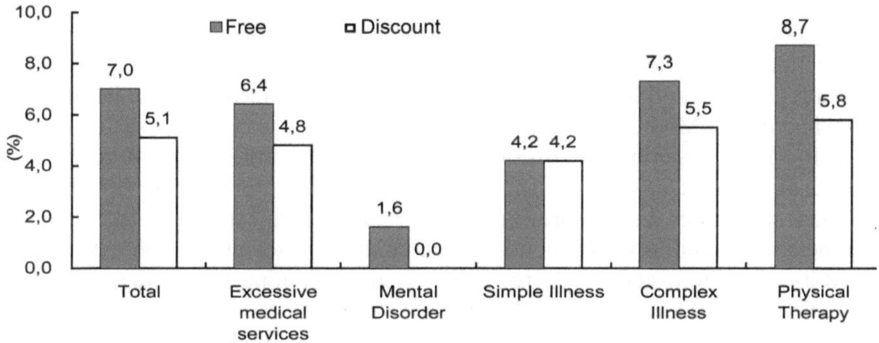

Note: Excessive medical services include mental disorders, simple illnesses and complex illnesses.

Convenience Services

71.7% of respondents said they used medical services after using convenience services provided by the medical institutions, highlighting the correlation between convenience services and medical services. In about 30% of cases, the medical institutions concerned even sent their vehicles for patient transportation.

Physical Therapy

Out of the 312 people categorized as physical therapy recipients, most people answered that their therapy was to treat specific diseases, while about 10% gave a psychological reason. 15.9% of total respondents rarely saw doctors when they received physical therapy. Moreover, about 9.3% of the recipients received a discount for, or were exempted from, treatment cost at the time of physical therapy. 51.4% answered that they would not receive physical therapy or reduce the number of therapy sessions in the future if not discounted or charged free, which suggested that the rate of out-of-pocket expenses needs to be adjusted more appropriately.

Medical Service Utilization by Senior Citizens and Methods of Medical Expense Management

Policy Framework for Managing Medical Expenses for Senior Citizens

In order to draw up countermeasures to deal with the rising medical expenses for senior citizens caused by the ageing population structure and increase in chronic illnesses, various efforts are needed to reform the medical security system in addition to disease prevention and health enhancement. Various policies are already being implemented in many countries, led by advanced nations. The introduction of long-term care insurance in Japan back in 2000 was not unrelated to such policies, and in the United States many policy measures are being tried, focusing on the Medicare programme.

In Japan, targeting the insurance subscribers from the age of 40 to 74, specific health check-up and specific health education is provided as part of an insurance subscriber disease prevention and health enhancement project focusing on metabolic syndrome. Reduction of the number of hospitalization days is pursued as a medium- and long-term policy goal concerning the average hospitalization days in order to optimize the medical expenditure. Since 2006, Japan has been adjusting the scope and details of medical insurance spending. In addition, in 2008, it created the old-old age medical programme under which the elderly aged 75 or older pay 10% of the financial resources of the programme as their insurance premiums.

The United States is running various programmes to improve the drug treatment system for chronic patients in old ages and to cut the prescription drug expenses of Medicare by means of prescription drug insurance and drug treatment management service. The method of paying hospitalization and treatment expenses of Medicare has been changed from per treatment payment based on the treatment cost of each medical institution to the Prospective Payment System (PPS), which is per treatment payment based on national average treatment cost. For reduction of medical spending for the elderly and financial stabilization, it is pursuing to enhance the portion of medical expenses charged to the patients and the insurance premiums for high-income individuals.

In Korea, where the national health insurance programme is covering 97% of all Koreans, management of health insurance spending is very important to ensure the financial sustainability of the national medical security. Accordingly, as a means to contain the increase in medical expenses for the elderly, management of medical treatment costs for the aged paid by the health insurance is essential. The results of the research of trends in medical treatment costs for elderly people and the research and analysis of medical services used by elderly people illustrate that it is necessary to come up with policies largely divided into those on the consumer side targeting the behavioural pattern of the elderly covered by the health insurance programme and those on the supplier side targeting the treatment practices of medical institutions for the elderly. Improvement of insurance expense management for efficient management and operation of the health insurance system, and medium- and long-term system improvement should be carried out as a basis for such policies. Means to contain the increase in medical expenses for the elderly covered by the health insurance can be summarized in figure 8 below.

Figure 8: Policy framework to contain medical treatment costs of the health insurance for the elderly

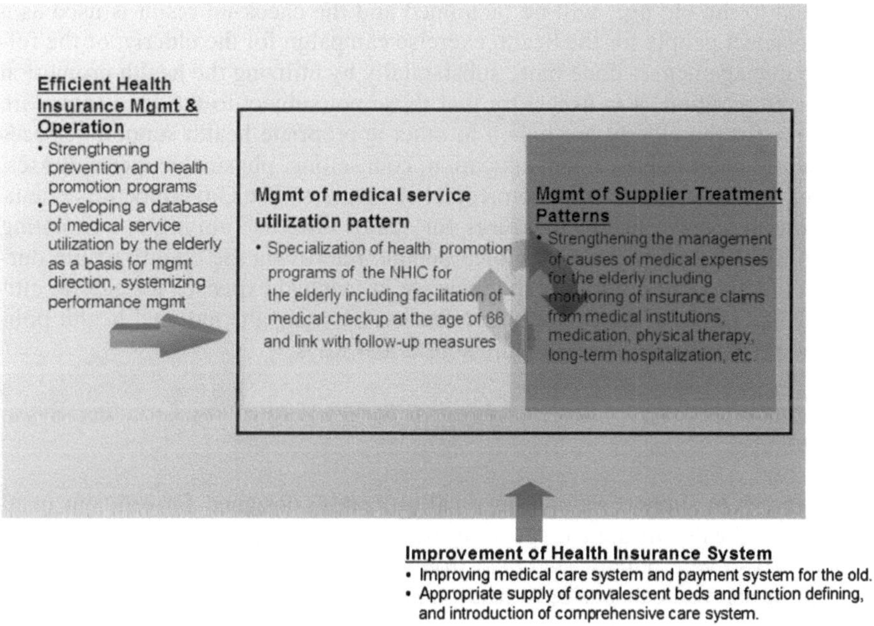

Improvement of Medical Service Utilization Pattern of Consumers

Expansion and Enhancement of Preventive Measures for Age-related Diseases

As chronic diseases that are becoming the main culprits of rising medical expenses of the nation are closely related not just with the lifestyle habits of the elderly but also with the habits prior to the aged period, health education throughout the entire life-cycle and health promotional measures are crucial.

The NHIC is expanding and strengthening the health promotion campaigns for efficient management of its finances and more effective health security for its subscribers. Furthermore, it has been almost a year since the long-term care insurance for elderly Koreans was introduced in expectation of curbing the escalating medical expenses for the elderly. Along with the introduction of the long-term care insurance, the age-related diseases prevention was added to the business of the NHIC. As a result, it is increasingly needed to revamp the whole gamut of health support programmes ranging from medical check-up to disease prevention, follow-up after medical check-up, appropriate medical support and health promotion and prevention by focusing on the reduction of medical expenses for the elderly.

It is gaining attention as very efficient measures that the medical check-up programme for transitional ages provided at the age of 66, which is considered a threshold to the old age, will be facilitated and the check-up result is used as a basis to select people for the health exercise campaign for the elderly, or the follow-up management is done more substantially by utilizing the health promotion centres. In addition, it is necessary that those not subject to the long-term care insurance for the elderly are linked to other appropriate health support services such as life habit improvement education, counselling, physical exercise classes, etc., so, that they do not become medical consumers. The Government is pursuing "comprehensive health measures for senior citizens" aiming at preventing serious illnesses, minimizing disabled people, improving the quality of life during the old age, and mitigating the increase in medical expenses for elderly citizens. Cooperation of insurance subscribers concerning the national health policies should also be rendered in more substantial ways.

Programmes to Support Rational Medical Service Utilization Targeting Senior Citizens

Programmes to support rational medical utilization designed for efficient management of health insurance spending needs to be enhanced, targeting elderly people. To solve problems stemmed from excessive medical service utilization, evident in the medical service utilization patterns of the elderly, and make desirable changes, it is an imperative to provide elderly people with education programmes and information on medical service utilization. Moreover, medication patterns of the elderly are pinpointed as the main reason of wasting medical expenses, and it is confirmed to a certain degree in the results of this research. In this light, the damage of excessive or multiple drug taking and potentially serious side effects of drugs should be taught and publicized to the people. In addition, supportive measures for rational medical service utilization are urgently needed, including publicizing the appropriate treatment periods for each illness and educating excessive physical therapy recipients who are increasing in parallel with the rising demand for physical therapy due to chronic degenerative illnesses of the elderly. As a supplementary arrangement against excessive medical service users, in case of physical therapy recipients, it may be considered to introduce systems that put a limit on the number of sessions covered by insurance spending, or raise the amount of costs charged to the patients. These measures can be utilized as crucial bases for performance management after being developed as evaluation criteria for support programmes for rational medical service utilization targeting senior citizens.

Management of Treatment Pattern of Suppliers

For the improvement of treatment patterns on the medical service supplier side, management and regulation of excessive medical services related to solicitation practices is meaningful. It seems that after analysis of the annual treatment records, management of outliers by illness groups is necessary for appropriate medical service utilization by the elderly. This means that policies need to be supplemented, so that medical services can be used by the elderly in such a way that their illness is continuously managed by a medical service provider in the form of a regular doctor or family doctor. It also means that the number of hospital visits and medications is appropriately managed. In particular, some autonomous municipal agencies and medical institutions allow the exemption of patients from out-of-pocket medical expenses, resulting in an increase in medical service utilization of the elderly. In order to fix this loophole, the out-of-pocket expense system needs monitoring and management guidelines.

Efficient Management and Operation of the Health Insurance and System Improvement

Establishment of an Information System on Medical Service Utilization of Senior Citizens and the Development of a Management Index

To systemize the management of health insurance spending more effectively, it is a prerequisite to substantiate the management basis of medical expenses for the elderly, including a database related to medical service utilization of the elderly. To this purpose, the treatment data of practicing hospitals should be fully utilized, and other information related to medical security for the elderly, as found in 'the senior citizens panel' operated by several research institutions, may be appropriately utilized. Based on the established database, management indices for medical expenses for the elderly may be developed and performance management within the corporation may be systemized, contributing to the containment of the increasing medical expenses for the elderly.

System Improvement for Management of Medical Expenses for Senior Citizens

As a medium- and long-term approach to the issue of medical expenses for the elderly, system improvement is needed. As the most significant method, introduction of a family doctor system for elderly people should be pursued to enhance the primary care and gatekeeper function. It is desirable to connect the system with measures of improving the chronic illnesses management system for the elderly. In addition, multiple and excessive medical service utilization by the elderly as well as medical care provision should be regulated and ways to improve the payment system – including introduction of a comprehensive medical fees system for age-related illnesses – should be actively sought after to streamline the management of health insurance spending.

Meanwhile, in order to cope with the reasons of increase in medical expenses for the elderly in relation with the out-of-pocket expense system, the out-of-pocket expense system needs improvement. Some of the potential methods of improvement include raising the bar for insurance premium reductions from the current 65-year old to 70- or 75-year old phase-by-phase to discourage the use of unnecessary or non-urgent medical care; and increasing the out-of-pocket expenses payable by long-term inpatients to curb the increase in medical expenses caused by the increase in 'social hospitalization' such as long-term hospitalization of aged patients who do not need medical treatment. and encourage them to use long-term care facilities or home care services. To contain the increase in medical expenses due to meaningless medical services at the end of their life, it will be useful to systemize home care and hospice palliative care for terminal patients.

Defining the Function of Nursing Hospital and Review of Comprehensive Care System

It is necessary to pay attention to the increase in hospitalization fees at nursing hospitals as one of the reasons of medical expenses for the elderly. In particular, after the introduction of the long-term care insurance programme, due to regionally unbalanced distribution of senior nursing facilities and system glitches, some of the demand for senior nursing facilities is transferred to nursing hospitals, materializing the potential demand for medical services and eventually giving rise to the medical expenses for the elderly. In this context, review of the roles and functions of nursing hospitals and senior nursing facilities is urgent. To this aim, it is needed to define the function of nursing beds by adjusting the supply quality of nursing beds for long-term hospitalization based on an appropriate supply plan for nursing hospitals and senior nursing facilities, devised in consideration of the demographic and sociological characteristics of each region. In addition, in order to help enable appropriate judgement on the demand for medical and long-term care, a comprehensive screening tool for health conditions of elderly people should be developed to establish the gatekeeper function for comprehensive care, and the foundation to characterize the roles and functions of nursing institutions and senior nursing facilities should be prepared.

References

Hong Seung-Yeon; Lee Ae-Kyung; Park Il-Soo & Soo-Ra Seo (2008), *The Analysis of the Effects of Health Support Programmes of the National Health Insurance Corporation.* Seoul: The National Health Insurance Corporation.

Jones, R. (2008), *Public Social Spending in Korea in the Context of Rapid Population Ageing.* Paris: OECD Economics Department Working Papers, No. 615.

Keehan, S.; Sisko A.; Truffer, C.; Smith S.; Cowan C.; Poisal, J.A. & M.K. Clemens (2008), 'National Health Expenditure Accounts Projections Team. Health Spending Projections Through 2017: The Baby-Boom Generation is Coming To Medicare', *Health Affairs,* vol. 27 (2): pp. 145-155.

Kuo, G.; Leal, S. Nichol, A. & J. Zive (2004), *Understanding Medicare Reform: What Pharmacists Need to Know.* Washington, D.C.: The American Pharmacists Association.

Meara, E. et al. (2004), 'Trends in Medical Spending by Age, 1963-2000', *Health Affairs,* vol. 23 (4), pp. 176-183.

Noh Yeon-Sook (2006), 'Meanings and Implications of the Introduction of Medication Therapy Management Services in the U.S.', *The Korea Institute for Pharmaceutical Policy Affairs*, vol. 1 (1), pp. 144-160.

OECD (2008), *Health Data.* Paris.

Poisal, J.A. et al. (2007), 'Health Spending Projections Through 2016: Modest Changes Obscure Part D's Impact', *Health Affairs*, vol. 26 (2), pp. 242-253.

Park Jong-Yeon; Kang Im-Ok; Kim Kyung Ha; Soo Soo-Ra & Ji-Yeon Shin (2005), *How to Improve Korea's Medical Security System for Senior Citizens.* Seoul: The National Health Insurance Corporation.

The Cabinet Office (2008), *White Paper on the Ageing Society*. Seoul.

The Korea National Statistical Office (2006), *Population Projections*. Seoul.

Yoon Seok-Won (2004), *Trends of Medical Security Innovation in the U.S. (Medicare Reform Bill): Suggestions for Prescription Drug Coverage*. Seoul: The Korea Institute for Health and Social Affairs.

Zuvekas, S.H. & J.W. Cohen (2007), 'Prescription Drugs and the Changing Concentration of Health Care Expenditures', *Health Affairs,* vol. 26 (1), pp. 249-257.

Internet

Document on the Proposal for Structural Reform of the Medical System.
http://www.mhlw.go.jp/topics/2005/10/tp1019-1.html.
http://www.census.gov/population/www/projections/2008projections.html.
http://www.cms.hhs.gov/NationalHealthExpendData/downloads/2004-age-tables.pdf.

Part V

11 The Financial Crisis and its Impact on the Pension and Retirement Income System

Jhinyoung Shin

Introduction

The current financial crisis, sparked by the collapse of the sub-prime mortgage market in the U.S.A. in 2007 is still ravaging global financial markets and economies. Stock markets in all over the world suffered one of the worst falls in history and still stumble to recover. Major financial institutions including once venerable Lehman Brothers, AIG, Citibank, RBS, to name a few are either bankrupted or barely survive with massive injection of capital from Government under mounting losses from sub-prime related financial securities and contracts, which happened to be the milking cows of astronomical amount of profits just a few years ago.

Governments and central banks are juggling every possible fiscal and monetary measure to prevent their financial systems and economies from sliding into the one of the worst recessions since the Great Depression. As housing prices fall freely, many homeowners, who financed their purchase of houses at very generous mortgage terms, are now struggling to avoid foreclosures while desperately hanging on their jobs.

The year 2008 is arguably the worst year for pension plans as the financial crisis has devastated global financial markets and economies. It is estimated that the plunge in prices of stocks and other financial securities wiped out $ 5 trillion from pension funds, as worldwide pension assets were reduced from $ 25 trillion to $ 20 trillion, a decrease of 19%, as *Reuters* reported. Some notable anecdotes of developed countries including Canada, U.S.A., the Netherlands and U.K. are following. Sponsors of defined benefit pensions in Canada believe that the current financial crisis would threaten not only the financial health of the pensions but also the sponsoring companies and eventually the Canadian economy.

"An overwhelming majority of Canadian senior executives believe defined-benefit pensions have become a crisis for the companies that have them, threatening to sap corporate resources already under stress from the downturn in the economy, according to a survey by the global consultancy Watson Wyatt: 'These plans can be very large, and the amount of money they have to put in can become a drain on the company, limiting the amount they have left for capital investment and expansion.' Mr. Markham (director of pension innovation at Watson Wyatt) said without some form of Government funding relief for pension sponsors, the crisis could have a domino effect on the rest of the Canadian economy, reducing demand for other company's goods and services and pushing down employment." ('Pension Funding Crisis', *Financial Post*, April 20, 2009.)

Due to its biggest size accounting for 61% of global pension assets, U.S. pension plans are hardest hit by the current crisis.

"$ 7 trillion worth of shareholder wealth evaporated in 2008 as the stock markets in US lost all of its gains earned from the prior six years. Company sponsored defined benefit plans that have heavily invested in risky asset are under-funded by the amount of $ 409 billion at the end of 2008, while U.S. retirement accounts lost $ 2 trillion worth of asset value. Some anecdotes are following.

- Colorado's largest pension fund lost $ 11 billion, or 25% of its assets, affecting more than the 413,000 current and former Government workers.
- North Carolina's state pension fund, which covers 820,000 state employees, lost 17% of its value in the past year.
- In Jacksonville, Fla., a police union is threatening to sue the city if it doesn't live up to its pledge to provide a steep increase to the police pension – although city officials say the money just isn't there anymore." (*Retirement Blues: Financial Crisis Pulls Billions from Pension Plans, Crimping Consumers' Dreams and Corporate Profits* by Mike Caggeso from moneymappress.com, April 29, 2009.)

Pension funds in the Netherlands cannot escape the fallouts of the financial crisis.

"The four biggest Dutch pension funds announced that they no longer met the obligatory 105% coverage ratio. All four funds are freezing pensions this year. The coverage ratio of civil service pension fund ABP, one of the biggest pension funds in the world, has written off € 22 billion because of the financial crisis. Health service pension fund Zorg en Welzijn, which has some 2.1 million clients, lost € 16 billion and its coverage ratio dropped from 126% to 92% in the fourth quarter. The Association of Industry-wide Pension Funds called on the Dutch central bank to give pension funds more time to get their investments in order." (*Dutch pension funds hard hit by financial crisis*, <www.chinaview.cn>, January 30, 2009.)

Britain's pension system is not an exception in the long list of victims of the financial crisis.

"In 2008, the London stock market has fallen by nearly 40% and deficits in U.K. occupational pensions in the top 100 corporations have leapt from £ 40 billion a year ago to more than £ 122 billion in October of 2008. The majority of final salary pension schemes did not have enough assets to cover their pension commitments in October, with 6,468 (84% of the total) in deficit and only 1,273 (16%) still in surplus. This contrasts with 3,121 in surplus a year ago. Their collective deficit stood at nearly £ 100 billion, an increase of nearly £ 20 billion on the month before. At the same time last year, the schemes had a surplus of £ 84 billion." (*Britain: Financial crisis threaten pensions and retirement plans*, by Jean Shaoul from www.wsws.org, December 15, 2008.)

Many soon-to-be retirees suffer most from this crisis. Their retirement income account has lost substantial amount of value in the nick of time as crisis has swept financial markets. The price of their house, which is a life-time accumulation of their savings, plunges, leaving even smaller amounts for their retirement. Those who are still a couple of years away from the completion of their mortgage payments are forced to work longer than they planned, even taking second jobs. Their dream of retiring in their fully paid home with a fat retirement account is forever lost. Young workers, who struggle to keep their jobs or to look for new ones, are shivering at the idea of retiring in poverty.

Pension and retirement income systems of developed countries cannot escape the fallouts of the financial crisis. Their burgeoning pension systems are hard hit by the knockdown of their assets values, and struggle to gear their systems to the right direction while recuperating from the sudden and massive loss.

This article examines the impact of the current financial crisis on pensions and retirement incomes, and reviews policy measures to keep this crisis from developing into a pension crisis. In section 2, causes and consequences of the financial crisis are briefly reviewed. Effects and the extent of the current crisis on different pensions and retirement income systems including defined contributions, employer sponsored defined benefits, pay-as-you-go systems are investigated in section 3. Short-term and medium-term policy measures to minimize the spill over of the financial crisis into pension systems while bolstering financially stable pension and retirement income systems are discussed in section 4. Conclusions and summary are provided in section 5.

Brief review of causes and consequences of financial crisis

It is a general consensus that the collapse of the US sub-prime mortgage market in 2007 triggered devastating chain reactions leading to the current crisis. Those who blame the rise and fall of the US housing market for the crisis point out three major causes: 1) The rapid growth and subsequent collapse of U.S. house prices; 2) a general decline in mortgage underwriting standards, reflected in a growing proportion of home purchases financed by non-prime mortgages; and 3) widespread mismanagement of financial risks by firms engaged in originating, distributing, and investing in mortgages, mortgage-backed securities, and derivative financial instruments.[1] However, root causes of the financial crisis are still debated among academicians, the press and policymakers, and full assessment of the causes are still tentative at this stage.[2]

Although it appears that problems arising from one segment of the US housing market rapidly developed into a fully blown global financial and economic crisis, various factors have interacted with each other, at least for ten to fifteen years still contributing to the evolvement of the crisis.[3]

1 *What caused the financial crisis*, http://timeline.stlouisfed.org/index.cfm?p=faq.
2 26 possible causes are listed in Jickling 2009.
3 Causes of the financial crisis are summarized by Financial Services Authority of the U.K. 2009, and the World Bank, November 2008.

Many experts agree that macroeconomic imbalances lie at the bedrock of the current crisis. Large current account deficits of the U.S.A., U.K. and other developed countries have been financed by capital inflows from oil-exporting countries, Japan, China, and some other East Asian emerging developing nations for the last ten years in the context of international financial market integration. Current account surpluses accumulated by China and other countries are invested in almost exclusively risk-free or close to risk-free Government bonds, or Government guaranteed bonds. Thanks to this spending binge on risk free bonds, real risk free rates of interest of the U.S.A. and the U.K. are driven down to the historically low level of less than 2% or at times as low as 1%.

Abundant liquidity and very low real interest rates have resulted in two effects: First, credit extension in some developed countries, particularly but not exclusively for residential mortgages in the U.S.A. and the U.K. has rapidly grown, being assisted by lax credit standards. Mortgage finance was the chief beneficiary of this extension of credit, which has contributed to a bubble in global real estate prices. Figure 1 shows the steady increase in household debt in major developed countries, which has been heavily invested in real estate. Considering very low interest rates and generous mortgage terms along with an optimistic view on future housing price increase, many households rush to borrow as much as possible to buy their homes.

Figure 1: Household debt as proportion of the GDP

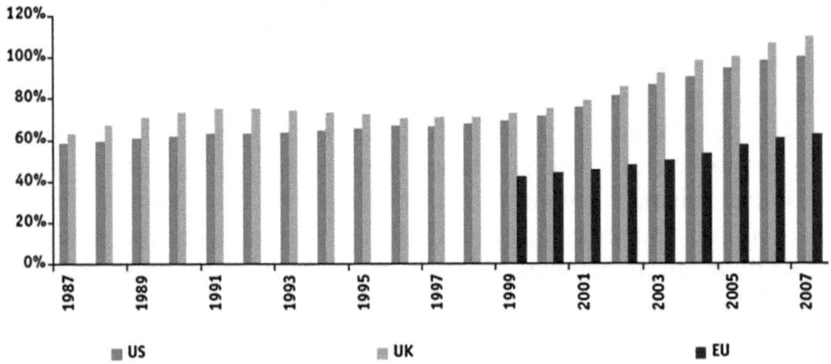

Sources: ONS, Federal Reserve, Eurodata, Bureau of Economic Analysis, FSA calculations; Financial Services Authority of the U.K. 2009.

Secondly, they have forced investors to be engaged in a ferocious 'search for yield' – a desire to invest in securities to gain as much as possible spread above the risk-free rate, to offset the declining risk-free rate. Any products that appear to be adding 20 or 30 basis points to very low yield, without adding too much risk, have looked very attractive. This trend results in general under-pricing of risk by investors.

Financial innovations have exacerbated the systemic vulnerability of the financial system in a couple of ways. The accelerated growth of the origination, packaging, trading and distribution of securitized credit instruments helped the expansion of mortgage markets, while being supported by financial innovations in structured finance and credit derivatives as well as by active secondary markets for mortgage related securities. Figure 2 displays the drastic increase in ABS and other securitized assets, mostly related to mortgage financing. Favourable economic conditions, coupled with fierce competition among financial institutions and ever growing asset prices encouraged financial institutions to loosen up their risk management by lowering credit underwriting standards, and investing in highly complex credit and mortgage related derivative securities, of which prices and risk are not fully understood.

Financial institutions in every sector, including traditional banking and insurance, venture out to riskier trading activities with maturity mismatches, while relying too much on sophisticated mathematical models.[4] For instance, AIG is hanging on the life line provided by U.S. Government due to their humongous loss from credit default swap trading, which has nothing do with its traditional insurance business. Investors ought to share the blame by reducing the monitoring of risks and vetting of their investment while aggressively 'search for yield'.

Inadequate regulation and oversight on financial institutions and system is another major culprit for the current crisis. It has been more than ten years since Governments have to compete against each other in relaxing regulations on financial markets. The Gramm-Leach-Bliley Act of U.S., which was passed in 1999 by repealing part of the Glass-Steagall Act of 1933 is criticized for having contributed to widespread use of opaque and complex financial instruments. Market discipline, which is the pillar of efficient financial systems, has been weakened by inappropriate accounting rules, inadequate disclosures and poor corporate governance of financial institutions, worsened by sheer greed of managements. Prudential oversight by financial regulatory and supervisory agencies became lax, effectively allowing poor credit standards, inadequate capital buffers and excessive leverage of financial institutions via a 'shadow banking system'.

4 Maturity mismatch means funding of longer term investment using shorter term financing.

Figure 2: Growth of securitized credit

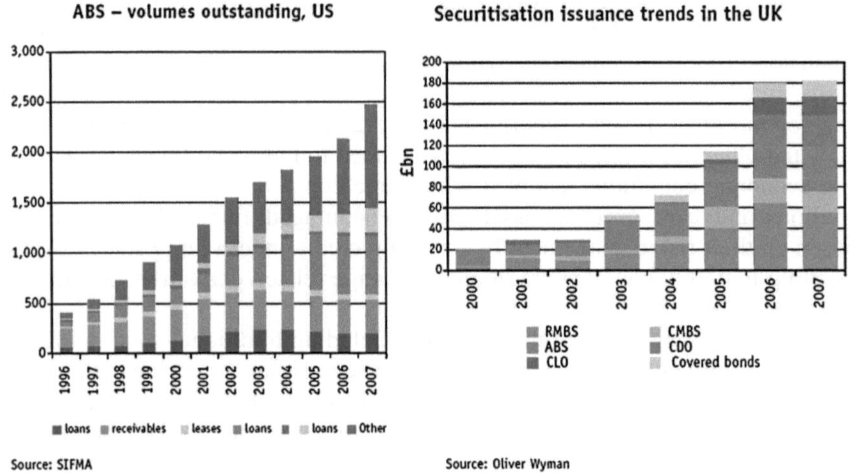

Source: Financial Services Authority of the U.K. 2009.

In mid-2007, however, these trends of abundant liquidity and ever increasing asset value ceased and then went sharply into reverse, which unravels the excess of the last decade in vengeance. The origins of this reversal of trend lay in the U.S. housing market, where excessive credit extension and weak credit standards had resulted in rapidly rising credit losses, and thereby the free fall of the price of many mortgage related derivative securities. This initial stimulus then triggered a self-reinforcing set of effects, progressing through the stages outlined in table 1.

As is displayed in figure 3, stock markets all over the world lost its gains earned in the last five to six years in a very short span of time from 2007 to 2008. Once the decade of excess was detonated by the collapse of the sub-prime market, financial markets and economies have been falling in a downward spiral in vicious circles, as the insolvency suffered from financial institutions were spreading to the real economy. The shock to the banking system has been so great that its impaired ability to extend credit to the real economy has played and is still playing a major role in exacerbating the economic downturn, which in turn undermines banking system strength in a self-reinforcing feedback loop.

Market value accounting and capital requirement stipulated by regulatory agencies are partly blamed for aggravating financial crisis creating negative feedback loop. Financial institutions, particularly commercial banks are mandated to regularly update their asset value based on fair market value, and to maintain their risk capital ratio,[13] at or higher than required level. As crisis unfolds, asset values tumbles while the risk of assets jumps up. Assets owned by financial institutions are reassessed at lower market value and higher risk, and consequently their risk capital ratio decreases. To maintain their required risk capital ratio, financial institutions dump their assets to the market, which reinforces the downward pressure on already reduced asset values. This vicious circle of de-

Table 1: Stages of the crisis 2006-2009

2006 – Summer 2007 Localised credit concerns	Rising defaults in US subprime and Alt-A loans. Falling prices of lower credit tiers of some credit securities. Expectations of property prices fall.
Summer – Autumn 2007 Initial crack in confidence and collapse of liquidity	Failure of 2 large hedge funds. Spreads in inter-bank funding and other credit products rise sharply. RMBS funding and inter-bank funding for second tier banks dries up. Northern Rock faces retail run.
Autumn 2007 – early Summer 2008 Accumulation of losses and continuation of liquidity strains	Severe mark-to-market losses in trading books. Collapse of commercial paper markets: SIVs brought back on balance sheet. Funding strains in the secured financing market. Worries about liquidity of major institutions Government assisted rescue of Bear Stearns.
Summer 2008 Intensification of losses and liquidity strains	Mark-to-market losses and liquidity strains continue to escalate. Housing market problems recognised as widespread in UK, US and other countries, as house prices fall and supply of credit dries up. Fannie Mae and Freddie Mac increasingly reliant on US government support. Funding problems of UK mortgage banks intensify.
September 2008 Massive loss of confidence	Bankruptcy of Lehmans breaks confidence that major institutions are too big to fail. Credit downgrade of AIG triggers rising collateral calls, requiring government rescue. Mix of credit problems, wholesale deposit runs and incipient retail deposit runs lead to collapse of Washington Mutual, Bradford & Bingley, and Icelandic banks. Almost total seizure of interbank money markets; major banks significantly reliant on central bank support.
October 2008 Government recapitalisation, funding guarantees and central bank support	Exceptional government measures to prevent collapse of major banks; explicit commitments that systemically important banks will not be allowed to fail.
November 2008 → Feedback loops between banking system and economy. Further government measures to offset feedback loop risk.	Impaired bank ability to extend credit to real economy produces major globally synchronised economic downturn. Recession threatens further credit losses which might further impair bank capital. Tail risk insurance – Asset Protection Scheme.

Source: Financial Services Authority of the U.K. 2009, Box 1.

creased asset value and market sell-off is very hard to contain, once it is kicked in, and current accounting standards and regulatory frameworks are rightfully blamed for at least partly.

Figure 3: Major stock market performance

Source: Thomson Financial Datastream. OECD, December 2008.

Financial institutions with their solvency and liquidity tightened up refuse to roll over old loans and give out new loans, and start to increase interest rates for existing loans. This results in financial distress of firms in the real sector, and as dreaded by everyone, problems started in the financial sector spread to the real sector causing global recession.

Although the crisis may have started in financial markets of developed countries, including the U.S.A. and the U.K. – particularly by obscure mortgage related structured financial instruments, it has been spreading rapidly and extensively to emerging developing countries via integrated global financial markets, which distinguished the current crisis from previous ones.

The initial blow was delivered to the direct exposure of emerging market financial institutions holding sub-prime related financial securities. However, such an impact was relatively minor, which cannot cause serious damage to the financial markets and economies of emerging countries. However, the next round of effects has been more damaging and severe, since they resulted from the deleveraging process and the reversal of capital flows, which is still in progress.

Many emerging market countries, which have enjoyed rapid economic growth, have benefitted from cross-border bank lending, particularly in countries where foreign banks play an important role in their financial sectors. The current crisis significantly tightens up once, abundant credit provided to emerging market countries. Interbank or corporate credit lines from international banks to domestic banks and companies suddenly reduced and stopped. This credit crunch exposed pre-existing domestic problems that used to be covered or overlooked while the economy was growing rapidly. The financial crisis is still in progress, and in many countries – regardless of being developed or emerging developing countries – every aspect of their societies is gravely affected. The next section discusses the impact of the current crisis on pension and retirement income systems.

Impact of the financial crisis on pension and retirement income systems

Pension funds have lost their asset values dramatically in 2008 – mainly due to the declining stock prices as is displayed in figure 3. OECD weighted average return in -22%, and pension funds in nearly all countries in figure 4 suffered negative real returns with the exception of very few countries including Korea. The size of loss varies, depending on how much is invested in equity and other risky assets.

Table 2 demonstrates that even in the midst of one of the worst financial crises, pension funds that have invested more conservatively fare better than others, whose portfolio has been geared toward riskier investment. For instance, Chile's retirement income is mostly drawn from a mandatory defined contribution system, but its conservative portfolio did not suffer loss, while its risky counterpart lost almost half of its asset value.

Table 2: Real pension fund return in 2008 under different portfolios

Per cent	*Portfolio*		
	Risky	*Balanced*	*Conservative*
Australia		-27.0	
Chile	-46.1	-23.1	0.0
Estonia	-30.5	-20.9	-9.7
Hungary	-35.0		-18.0
Iceland		-25.0	
Israel		-8.0	
Mexico	-8.3	-6.0	-0.5
Poland		-17.4	
Slovak Republic	-12.4	-10.3	-2.0
Sweden		-17.0	
Switzerland		-14.0	

Source: OECD 2009.

The impact of the financial crisis on pension and retirement varies depending on the systems, individual's age and other economic conditions, and the social safety net provided by the Government. Defined contribution systems, particularly provided and managed exclusively by the private sector might suffer most from the current crisis, but scale and severity of impact depends on a couple of factors.[5]

Figure 4: Nominal average annual pension fund returns over 5, 10, and 15 years

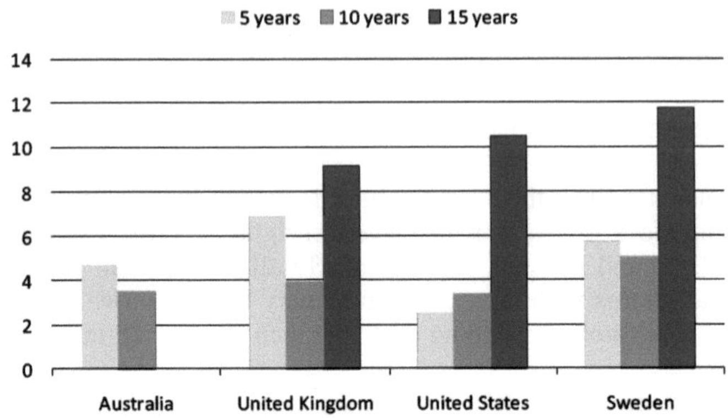

Source: OECD 2009.

Asset price recovery over the medium and long term

Although the short term effect of the financial crisis on the pension fund return is unbearably painful, pension funds' performance, by its critical nature, should be evaluated on a long term horizon. The current crisis is not the only major crisis suffered by financial markets and economies. Stock price decline during the 2000-2002 period after the burst of the dotcom bubble was as severe as in 2008, although the latest one has been much swifter. As is demonstrated by figure 5 on the long term pension fund returns of selected countries, in spite of the severity and proximity of the two major market downturns, pension fund returns are resilient enough to have respectably positive returns in the last ten years up to October 2008, and rather healthy ones in over a fifteen year period.

Proportion of pension wealth supported by funded individual account under defined contribution system

Funded individual accounts are a part of multi-pillar pension and retirement systems, and it only accounts for part of the overall retirement package. The multi-pillar pension system can be highly resilient under the pressure of severe financial and economic downturn. It incorporates elements of zero pillar of well-targeted social pensions or minimum guaranteed benefits to ensure broad protec-

5 Discussion on the defined contribution system is summarized from World Bank, December 2008, and OECD 2009.

tion against old age poverty, the first pillar is based on sustainable earnings, and the second pillar individually funded. If a substantial portion of retirement income is generated from zero and the first pillar, then the reduction in the value of retirement account may not seriously be hurt the welfare of retirees. Percentage of income from financial assets accumulated in individually funded account varies across countries, less than 30% in Hungary and Lithuania, but close to 100% in Chile and Peru, and the impact of crisis on retirement income obviously varies depending on the portion of income from defined contribution plans.

The presence of minimum social pensions or guarantees integrated into the pension system

Although decline in asset prices still reduces overall retirement income and benefit, the provision of minimum pension guarantee can prevent poverty during retirement even when asset values of defined contribution account are heavily exposed to the fluctuations in the value of invested assets. Average value of this guarantee is approximately 30% of the average economy wide income.[6]

Only a small number of workers will retire during the crisis period, in which the value of their funded accounted would be reduced due to the knockdown of asset prices

Those who face most dire consequences of the current crisis on their retirement income are the ones, who have to retire in the midst of the crisis. Particularly those who are mandated to turn their accumulated retirement savings into an annuity are effectively locked up their retirement benefits at substantially depressed value without being given any chance to recoup the value as financial markets recover. However, there are relatively few with a large reliance on funded account for their retirement income, who will be retiring in the short term. For instance, even in Chile with the oldest funded system, only 5% of the members of the system will retire in the next five years. Young workers many years away from retirement might be the main beneficiaries of the current crisis, since they have the opportunity to amass assets in their account at depressed price, which can generate handsome return as the market recovers from the crisis.

The long term nature and generational differences inherent in defined contribution systems are worthwhile to be discussed further. Van Derhei (2009) analyses the impact of the financial crisis on the 401(k) retirement plan, and demonstrates how individual participants are affected by the crisis, is largely determined by their account balance, age and job tenure. The U.S.A. has been

6 Please refer to Whitehouse (2007) for the calculation.

hardest hit by the current crisis, and S&P500 has decreased by 45% in 2008, which consequently reduced the value of most 401(k) accounts, heavily invested in stock and other risky assets. However, the impact of the crisis on the members of 401(k) varies substantially depending on their individual situation.

Those with less than $ 10,000 in the account balance had an average growth of 40% during 2008, since contributions had a bigger impact than investment losses. But, those with more than US$ 200,000 in account balances had an average loss of more than 25%.

Figure 5: Change in account balances from January 1, 2008 to January 20, 2009 by age and tenure

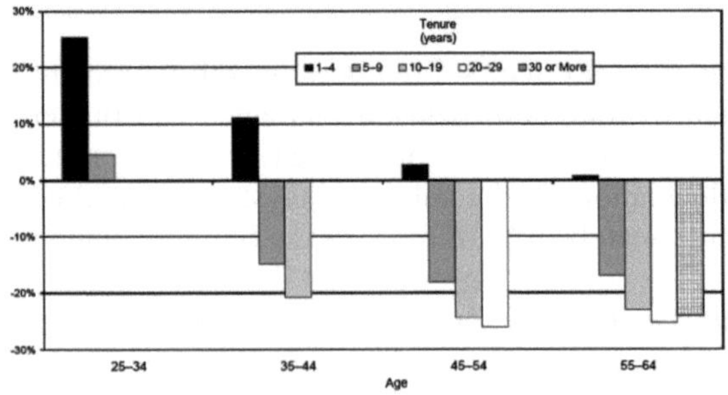

Figure 6 clearly displays strikingly different impact of the current crisis on 401(k) participants depending on their tenure on the same job and age. Participants on the verge of retirement aged between 56 and 65 suffered more than 20% loss in their account value. The current crisis hurt most those who have stayed in the same job over an extended period. Anyone with a tenure longer than ten years had borne more than 20% reduction in his account value. However, young workers, who recently joined the current job fare much better as those aged between 25 and 34 with less than four years of tenure actually gain more than 25% in their account value in the midst of turmoil.

Another important aspect to be investigated is how long it might take for end-of-year 2008 401(k) balances to recover to their beginning-of-year 2008 levels before the drastic stock market plunge. Van Derhei (2009) analyses through simulation with different assumptions on future market returns. Obviously higher returns of equity speed up the recovery back to the pre-crisis value. Consistent with the previous results, those who have stayed in the same job in longer period require longer time for recovery, as is displayed in figure 6.

Although it is based on the U.S. system, this study clearly demonstrates strikingly different effect of the financial crisis on the members of defined contribution systems. Old participants on the verge of retirement with long tenure in the same job are casualties of the current crisis without being given any chance to recuperate the loss of their life time savings while young workers can go through the crisis without scathe even seizing the opportunity to earn higher returns as market recovers.

Figure 6: Time needed to recover from 2008 loss with a non-equity return of 3.15% [7]

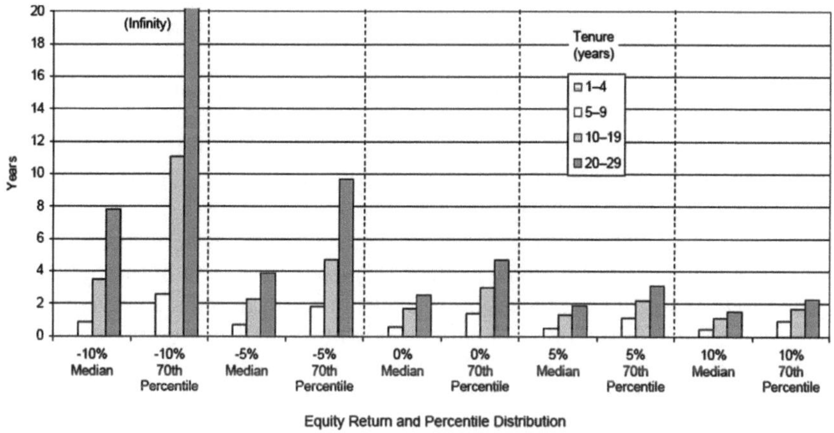

Beneficiaries of employer sponsored defined benefit plans and public pay-as-you-go (PAYG) or fully funded systems may not be affected immediately by the current crisis. However, if the crisis deepens and it takes longer time for financial markets and economies to recover, they might not be able to escape the fall-out of the turbulence of the current crisis.[8]

The major distinction between defined contribution and benefit plans lies in, who bears the investment risk: In defined contributions, members are the ones, who bear the risk, while the sponsor carries the risk in defined benefit plans. In employer sponsored defined benefit plans, employers are required to step in to make up shortfalls between the pension liabilities they expect to pay and their assets with extra contributions to the plan. However, employers already under pressure from recession might be tempted to reduce the generosity of benefits in an attempt to minimize the extra contribution. Some may even close their defined-benefit scheme and switch to defined-contribution provisions in an attempt to escape from the burden of bearing the investment risk. As is illustrated in section 1, many U.K. and Canadian sponsors are underfunded and struggle to make up the shortfalls in the midst of recession.

The worst possibility is the bankruptcy of the employer, while the pension fund's shortfall is not fully replenished yet. However, some countries with wide-

7 Median and 70th percentile means time needed for 50% and 70% of the participants in the same cohorts to recover to the pre-crisis level, respectively.

8 Discussion on defined benefit and public pension systems are drawn from OECD 2009, and World Bank, December 2008.

spread defined-benefit occupational plans have established special funds to protect benefits in these circumstances. The Pension Benefit Guarantee Corporation (PBGC) in the United States is one example. The problem is that the finances of the PBGC are already stretched and some call on the public purse may be necessary. The same might apply to the Pension Protection Fund in the United Kingdom, which was established more recently than the PBGC.[9]

Multi-employer pension funds are generally more robust to the collapse of a sponsoring company than single-employer plans. However, as is discussed in section 1, many multi-employer pension funds including ABP are underfunded due to massive losses from their highly risky investments, and they might need Government rescue if the crisis continues.

Earnings related pay-as-you-go pension systems will be affected in a less immediate way due to the crisis, since the investment risk is borne by the Government. However, global recession is likely to result in reduced revenue, while increasing the benefit claims: Economic downturn will reduce the contribution revenue to the system as a result of decrease in employment or reductions in the level of earnings, on which contributions are levied, and concurrently expenditures from such schemes will likely increase as more individuals retire from the labour force and seek pension benefits in the face of an economic downturn.

The extent of the financial impact depends significantly on the maturity of the scheme. Most countries maintain the pension fund reserve to meet the expenditure. Countries, which will face the greatest pressures from the current crisis, are those where revenue flows from contributions and investments are less than expenditures for benefits. They might need to reduce cash balances temporarily and/or draw on pension fund reserves, which have not been accumulated enough due to their short existence. However, it should be possible to repair the effects and replenish the reserve once the crisis has passed.

The effects on members will depend on how Governments deal with the shortfall in revenues. Governments facing shortfalls have a couple of options. They could finance deficits in full. Alternatively, they might partially default on pension promises, by delaying pension payments or failing to index benefits, for example. The balance between the two options will be politically determined as pensions are just one of a range of competing demands for limited public resources. Countries that have overall fiscal deficits and rely on external debt financing should deal with the most difficult situation as it becomes increasingly difficult to refinance with the global credit crunch.

9 However, there is a growing concern that the PPG itself might be underfunded. The Financial Times reported that the PPF deficit has been updated to £ 155 billion as at the end of November 2008, an increase of £ 30 billon in one month and three times what it was last year. Woolworths, which recently collapsed, has a pension deficit of £ 250 million, and The Financial Times revealed that Lehman Brothers, which collapsed in September 2008 with a widely reported £ 100 million pension fund deficit.

In some cases as recently occurred in Argentina, countries that have introduced funded defined contribution schemes may be tempted to roll back the portion of the payment to the defined contribution system that was previously levied to pay-as-you-go schemes back to the public schemes. Although this might be a short term remedy for cash flow problems of PAYG system, it does not improve the overall net-liability of retirement income owed by the Government, and furthermore it risks having negative long term consequences on the individual benefit position on a couple of grounds. First, it diminishes the diversification of the overall retirement system and might place workers at the risk of future benefit reductions if the system cannot remain fiscally viable over the long term with the increased liabilities. Second, this will also close funded accounts when asset values are at very low level, and thereby locked in losses and preclude members from the opportunity to benefit from any recovery in prices.

The current crisis has very widespread and different effects on diverse pension and retirement income systems. Retirees and would-be retirees might suffer not only from the decreased pension income but also from the reduction in their personal wealth and non-pension income. As is shown in figure 1, household debt accumulated before the commencement of the crisis might haunt them as they are sitting on large amounts of debt borrowed to finance their housing, whose value has fallen substantially. The next section discusses possible policy measures to cope with the crisis and build up more fiscally healthy and stable pension and retirement income systems.

Policy measures

With plunging asset prices, declining economic growth and mounting unemployment rates, Governments all around the world are scrambling to wield any possible policy measures in an attempt to rescue their financial markets and economies. Although the current crisis dealt a serious blow to the pension and retirement income systems, the degree of shock is not as serious as the one suffered by other sectors of the society and economy.

Many countries, particularly emerging developing countries, where old age pension – whether it is private or public – is a relatively new system, are in the process of establishing them. Some of them that already had public pension systems are scaling back public pensions, rapidly switching to private pensions. The financial and economic crisis might provide a right incentive and impetus for Governments to re-examine the design and implementation of policies to best achieve the objectives of the pension and retirement income systems. The short term political pressure on Governments to take action is enormous. However, it is imperative not to have any expedient responses that might threaten the long-term stability, financial health and sustainability of the whole pension and retirement income systems. The following is part of policy recommendations for the improvement of pension and retirement income systems.[10]

Avoid short term reversal of pension system reform

Many countries were in the process of pension system reform by which part of the pension provision was being shifted from public pay-as-you-go schemes to privately defined contribution systems, and they are pressured to allow people to switch back into the public system. The Government of Argentina even nationalized its mandatory private pension funds. This is not desirable in that moving back to public schemes limits the members to make contributions to the funded system, when they can purchase assets at relatively low prices and thereby accrue large potential gains in their retirement. Reversal back to the public system is clearly destructive for stability and sustainability of retirement-income provisions for two reasons. First, demand for policy changes will recur whenever the economic and social environment changes. Second, as people switch back to public scheme, they buy back their public pension using the decreased asset value in their private plan. This might give boost to the public finances in the short term, but it will turn into Government's increased burden as costs to the public pension spending will be greater in the medium and long term horizon in exchange for short term gains.

Do not underestimate the potential positive effects of pensions on the financial system and ultimately employment and economic growth

In many emerging markets pension funds become major institutional investors, and significantly contribute to the development and stability of their financial markets. There is increasing evidence that pension funds are moving into loan markets, previously dominated by commercial and investment banks, as is witnessed in Chile and the Netherlands. Well established pension systems would help develop financial markets and thereby contribute to the economic growth of many emerging developing countries.

Use the safety net to protect the benefits of low income workers

Low income workers might be the ones who will be affected most by the crisis. Countries should address issues related to unemployment and poverty, which arise from the current financial crisis, primarily via their publicly funded safety nets including unemployment insurance and minimum income provisions. Fig-

10 Policy recommendations are drawn and summarized from OECD 2009; World Bank, December 2008, and November, 2008.

ure 7 shows that gross replacement rates in public pension plans are widely different between countries, and the OECD warns that there is a risk of elderly poverty in some countries with insufficient safety nets. This crisis highlights the importance of a basic safety net, provided by the Government, for those who cannot afford enough retirement income.

Figure 7: Gross replacement rates in public pension plans

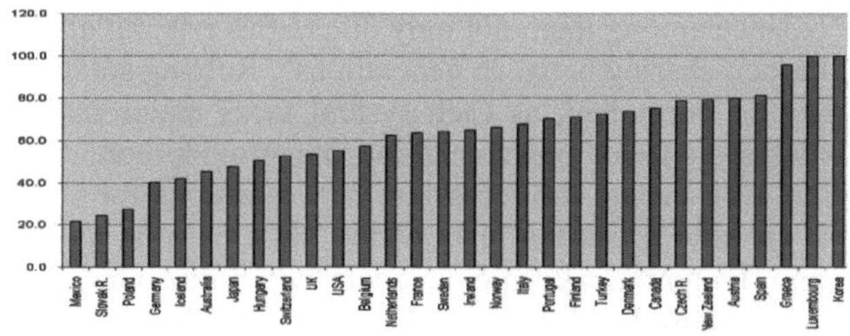

Sources: OECD 2007, *Pensions at a Glance*; Antolin & Stewart 2009.

Governments could consider options to provide maximum protection for them facing declining salaries by offering flat-rate minimum pensions and full indexation of benefits combined with unemployment insurance and other social safety nets.

Help people make informed choices

It is utmost important to help people make informed decisions on their pensions and retirement income schemes, and to educate them on investment risks associated with these schemes. People might have to make decisions on their retirement income schemes, choosing between public and private programmes, the range of competing pension managers or different investment portfolios. The current crisis highlights the significance of effective disclosure by pension scheme providers including Government, and broad financial education that will help people make informed decisions on their retirement benefit schemes.

Establish a framework for phased or deferred annuitization

The individuals most hurt financially from the rapid decrease in asset values are those close to retirement, who are potentially forced to lock up with the large declines, when they convert their savings in their retirement accounts into an annuity. Allowing for phased withdrawals and the gradual purchase of annuities can provide them with opportunities for eventual recovery from the loss by not requiring the liquidation of invested assets until their value has some time to recover.

Diversify the pension and retirement income systems

The best approach to pension and retirement income provision is to diversify sources of retirement income, including both public and private, as well the two main forms of financing, pay-as-you-go and funded pensions. The report on *Maintaining Prosperity in an Ageing Society*, published by the OECD, stresses that "each of the elements of the system has its own strengths and weaknesses and a flexible balance among them not only diversifies risk but also offers a better balance of burden-sharing between generations". Relying solely or largely on one scheme may be imprudent, as each system faces major risks of different sorts. Multi-pillar systems of retirement income provide core benefits to the broad population even during the recession. Key questions for Governments to resolve will be: (I) how to set the level of the basic pension and its eligibility conditions to; and (II) how to allocate the contribution rate between the first pillar, which is more exposed to labour market risks, and the second pillar, which is more exposed to financial risks.

Improve the financial risk management of the pension portfolio

The current crisis should renew the public attention on the importance of well-established risk management and governance standards, and integrating these into the regulation and supervision of pension funds. Mechanisms to better protect retirees from the impact of drastic volatility of pension account values immediately before retirement should be explored. For instance, as is analysed by Van Derhei (2009), although many asset allocation models and financial advisors may suggest that extreme concentrations in equities for the young cohorts would be acceptable, few would recommend it for those approaching retirement. Nevertheless, the 2007 asset allocation shows that almost a quarter (22%) of the oldest 401(k) participants (ages 56-65 in 2007) had 90% or more of their 401(k) assets in equities. Another 10% had 80-90% in equities, and 11% had 70-80% in equities. Target-date funds with automatic rebalancing and a 'glide path' ensuring 'age-appropriate' asset allocation are likely to become much more common after the full implementation of the Pension Protection Act of 2006 (PPA) in the U.S.. Investment choices between portfolios with different risk-return characteristics should be allowed in schemes, where members bear investment risks. But there should also be a default portfolio pattern based on the lifecycle approach to put investments on automatic pilot for those individuals, who do not want to manage their portfolio actively. This lifecycle investing, which requires low and middle income workers to switch part of their balances to less risky investments – as they get closer to retirement –, can reduce investment risks over the career without the sacrifice of financial returns from a broader portfolio at younger ages.

Integrating unemployment savings and insurance options into an overall social insurance system

Pension systems can become de facto unemployment insurance systems in periods of economic disruptions as workers, who lost their jobs, seek to claim retirement or disability benefits when other alternatives are not available. Some countries need to consider stronger restrictions on disability claims and early retirement, while strengthening the income-protection systems for workers, who lose their jobs. Policy options include combinations of unemployment insurance and unemployment individual savings accounts that can be accessed during spells of unemployment.

Diversify portfolio based on risk-return trade-off

Diversification in investment portfolio properly taking into account risk-return trade-off is essential. Although conservative portfolios with more weight on bonds perform better in the current crisis, equities have historically delivered higher investment returns than bonds. As is shown in table 3 and in the appendix, investment returns of major public funds demonstrate that those with higher portfolio weight on equity generally generate higher returns, although their performance in the recent crisis are mostly negative. Munnell, Webb and Golub-Sass (2008) show that in the financial markets of developed countries a diversified portfolio of assets would result in a higher level of retirement savings over nearly all time periods – despite significant variations in rates or returns due to market volatility. Some public funds have moved asset allocations to less risky financial assets – such as short term Government debt – to placate members with diminishing accounts. However, such portfolio rebalancing as a response to the current crisis will severely limit the opportunities for higher retirement benefits as financial markets recover from the crisis, and should not be enacted hastily.

Proper regulation on defined benefit plans

Governments generally impose funding or solvency rules on employer sponsored defined-benefit schemes. These rules are designed to ensure that the assets currently held in the pension funds will be sufficient to meet the stream of future liabilities. A couple of rules need to be adjusted considering crisis situations. Defined benefit plans are in general required to adopt the mark-to-market valuation of the assets. In spite of improved transparency and disclosure, strictly imposing this rule in the midst of the current crisis proves to be counterproductive. Regulators and supervisors may reconsider relaxing mark-to-market valuation, when extreme short term price movements occur. Some smoothing of valuation in periods of extreme volatility – like in the current crisis – reflect the true underlying values more accurately, and can possibly avoid adverse reactions to large changes that turn out to be very short term. One response to the current crisis might be to allow temporary extensions in the recovery periods, during which sponsors must replenish pension-fund deficits. Extending recovery periods makes most sense in an economic recession, in which company profitability is declining and access to credit is heavily restricted. Companies' cash-flows are already being constrained, and so forcing employers to increase contributions to their underfunded pensions may only make matters worse. It may even threaten the solvency of sponsoring companies, which is obviously not in the interest of beneficiaries. Regulatory agencies in some countries do not allow funds to sit out a crisis and wait for values to rise again. They have to sell to maintain assets to liability ratios, and given the major role pension funds play in some markets, this drives prices down even further. This type of rule – although intended to protect participants of defined benefit plans – may actually make things worse by reinforcing the downward spiral in asset values, and should be reconsidered.

Table 3: Investment returns and sizes of major public funds

Pension		*CPP (Canada)*	*AP 2 (Sweden)*	*GPIF (Japan)*	*CalPERS (U.S.A.)*	*APG (The Netherlands)*	*NPRF (Ireland)*
Size		CAD 108.9 billion	SEK 173.3 billion	JPY 95.2 trillion	USD 183.3 billion	EUR 173 billion	EUR 16.4 billion
Equity % (2007)		65%	61%	24%	60%	51%	72%
Return (%)	2008	-13.7 (April-Dec.)	-24.0	-3.0 (April-Sept.)	-23.1	-20.2	-29.5
	2007	-0.3	4.8	-6.10	10.2	3.8	3.3
	2006	12.9	13.0	4.6	15.7	9.5	12.4
	2005	15.5	18.7	14.4	11.1	12.8	19.6
	2004	8.5	11.6	4.4	13.4	11.5	9.3
	2003	17.6	17.8	13.0	23.3	11.0	12.8
	2002	-1.5	-15.3	-8.6	-9.5	-7.2	-16.1
	2001	4.0	-3.2	-2.7	-6.2	-0.7	4.4

Conclusion

The current financial crisis was sparked by the collapse of the sub-prime mortgage market of the U.S. in 2007, and financial markets and economies are still in severe turbulence. Governments and central banks are desperately implementing every possible fiscal and monetary measure to prevent their financial systems and economies from sliding into one of the worst recessions since the Great Depression.

Pension and retirement income systems cannot avoid the fallout of the crisis. It is estimated that the plunge in prices of stocks and other financial securities wiped out $ 5 trillion from pension funds, as worldwide pension assets were reduced from $ 25 trillion to $ 20 trillion, a decrease of 19%. Many people are forced into retirement as they lose their jobs. They are not only concerned about the security of their retirement pension but also they are left with substantially decreased personal wealth, mostly invested in housing whose price has plunged due to financial crisis.

Although the impacts of the financial crisis are diverse – depending on differences in pension systems and individual characteristics of the members – the effects of the crisis on pension and retirement income systems is not so severe as on the financial markets and economies. The current crisis might provide a right incentive and opportunity for Governments to re-examine the framework and implementation of policies to best achieve the objectives of the pension and retirement income systems. Although short term political pressure on Government to take action is enormous, it is imperative not to have any expedient responses that might threaten the long-term stability, financial health and sustainability of the whole pension and retirement income systems.

References

Antolin, P. & F. Stewart (2009), *Private pensions and policy response to the financial and economic crisis*. Paris: OECD Working Papers on Insurance and Private Pensions No. 36

Financial Services Authority of the U.K. (2009), *Turner Review: A regulatory response to the global banking crisis*. London, March.

Jickling, M. (2009), *Causes of the financial crisis*. Washington/D.C.: Congressional Research Service, January 29.

Munnell, A.; Webb, A. & A. Golub-Sass (2008), *How much Risk is Acceptable*. Boston: Center for Retirement Research at Boston College, November, No. 8-20.

OECD (2008), *Pension Markets in Focus*. Paris: December, Issue 5.

OECD (2009), *Pensions in a financial crisis*. Paris: February 20.

Van Derhei, J. (2009), *The Impact of the Recent Financial Crisis on 401(k) Account Balances*. Employee Benefit Research Institute, Issue Brife No. 326.

Whitehouse, E.R. (2007), *Pensions Panorama: Retirement-Income Systems in 53 Countries*. Washington/D.C.: World Bank.

World Bank (2008a), *The unfolding crisis: implications for financial systems and their oversight*. Washington/D.C.: Working Paper 464830, November.

World Bank (2008b), *The financial crisis and mandatory pension systems in developing countries*. Washington/D.C.: December.

Appendix: Asset allocations of major public funds

Japan: GPIF

	2003.3		*2004.3*		*2005.3*		*2006.3*		*2007.3*		*2008.3*	
	Amount	*%*	*Amount*	*%*	*Amount*	*%*	*Amount*	*%*	*Amount*	*%*	*Amount*	*%*
Domestic Bonds	162,269	51.35	252,012	54.99	322,115	54.99	349,242	48.36	441,997	52.01	569,443	62.37
Domestic equities	73,818	23.36	120,019	21.21	124,234	21.21	189,789	26.28	190,676	22.44	137,923	15.11
Foreign bonds	25,458	8.06	39,520	9.89	57,923	9.89	75,515	10.46	90,694	10.67	96,641	10.58
Foreign equities	44,676	14.14	59,255	13.91	81,500	13.91	107,617	14.90	126,376	14.87	109,057	11.94
Short-term assets	9,766	3.09	9,804	0.01	49	0.01	13	0.00	10	0.00	9	0.00
Total	315,988	100.00	480,610	100.00	585,820	100.00	722,176	100.00	849,753	100.00	913,073	100.00

Canada: CPPIB

	00.3.31	01.3.31	02.3.31	03.3.31	04.3.31	05.3.31	06.3.31	07.3.31	08.3.31	08.12.31
Canadian equities	1,954	5,025	9,969	11,561	22,572	27,669	29,138	29,174	28,891	19,368
	81.7%	70.2%	69.8%	66.2%	68.6%	47.1%	32.8%	25.2%	23.5%	17.8%
Non-Canadian equities	438	2,130	4,149	5,510	9,326	20,882	32,568	46,390	48,159	43,289
	18.3%	29.8%	29.0%	31.6%	28.4%	35.6%	36.6%	40.0%	39.2%	39.7%
Real return assets	-	-	145	313	634	1,010	8,499	11,756	14,353	19,955
			1.0%	1.8%	1.9%	1.7%	9.6%	10.1%	11.7%	14.7%
Nominal fixed income	-	-	27	69	363	9,161	18,801	28,664	31,374	30,305
			0.2%	0.4%	1.1%	15.6%	21.1%	24.7%	25.6%	27.8%
Total	2,393	7,155	14,289	17,453	32,894	58,722	89,006	115,984	122,777	108,917
	100.0%	100.0%	100.0%	100.0%	100.0%	100.0%	100.0%	100.0%	100.0%	100.0%

The Netherlands: APG (Previously ABP)

	08.12.31	07.12.31	06.12.31	05.12.31	04.12.31	03.12.31	02.12.31	01.12.31	00.12.31
Bonds	77.5	95.0	91.2	88.5	74.5	69.6	73.7	75.1	75.2
Bonds	44.8%	43.4%	43.2%	46.4%	44.3%	46.3%	54.0%	50.9%	50.0%
Equity and AI	84.6	112.7	107.8	97.7	86.2	79.7	62.4	72.6	72.6
Equity and AI	48.9%	51.5%	51.1%	51.3%	51.3%	53.0%	45.0%	49.2%	48.3%
Others	10.9	11.1	12.1	4.4	7.3	1.0	-0.5	-0.3	2.7
Others	6.3%	5.1%	5.7%	2.3%	4.4%	0.7%	-0.4%	-0.2%	1.7%
Total	173	218.8	211.1	190.6	168.1	150.2	135.6	147.3	150.3
Total	100.0%	100.0%	100.0%	100.0%	100.0%	100.0%	100.0%	100.0%	100.0%

AI: Alternative investment

U.S.: CALPERS

	01.06.30	02.06.30	03.06.30	04.06.30	05.06.30	06.06.30	07.06.30	08.06.30	08.12.31
Cash	3.5	2.7	1.3	1.1	0.3	0.7	1.7	2.90	15.2
	2.22%	1.88%	0.88%	0.67%	0.18%	0.32%	0.68%	1.2%	8.3%
Domestic bonds	40.0	34.6	32.9	38.2	49.8	46.5	55.5	54.2	40.4
	23.69%	24.41%	22.77%	22.96%	26.38%	22.16%	22.25%	22.6%	22.0%
Foreign bonds	5.0	5.5	5.0	4.8	4.5	5.5	5.7	4.9	4.2
	3.23%	3.84%	3.50%	2.87%	2.39%	2.63%	2.28%	2.1%	2.3%
Domestic equities	63.1	53.8	58.5	68.9	76.0	85.0	100.6	71.7	40.1
	40.43%	37.92%	40.57%	41.39%	40.26%	40.41%	40.30%	30.0%	21.9%
Foreign equities	27.7	26.4	27.6	33.6	38.8	44.9	49.1	52.5	34.7
	17.75%	18.64%	19.13%	20.19%	20.5%	21.49%	19.67%	22.0%	18.9%
AI	7.1	6.6	7.4	7.7	9.8	12.1	16.8	24.8	24.0
	4.59	4.67%	5.12%	4.66%	5.21%	5.74%	6.73%	10.3%	13.1%
Real estate	12.6	12.3	11.6	12.1	9.6	15.2	20.1	28.3	24.7
	8.09%	8.64%	8.03%	7.26%	5.06%	7.25%	8.06%	11.9%	13.5%
Total	156.0	141.8	144.3	166.5	188.9	209.9	249.6	253.0	183.3
	100.0%	100.0%	100.0%	100.0%	100.0%	100.0%	100.0%	100.0%	100.0%

12 Korean National Pensions: Facts and Functions in 2009

Jun-Ho Bae

Introduction

While the number of beneficiaries of a National Pension (NP) has been steadily increasing in recent years, one of the noteworthy developments is the faster increase of perfect pensioners (i.e. pensioners who had contributed over 20 years). Starting from 2008, perfect pensioners had started to emerge and their number reached 12,798 at the end of 2008, which was equivalent to 0.6% of the total of old age pensioners (2.06 million) and 5.3% of new pension beneficiaries, respectively, in 2008. In 2009, the number of perfect pensioners reached 16,429 at the end of February, which was equivalent to 0.6% of total old age pensioners (2.11 million) and 8% of the new pensioners, respectively.

The reason why we should pay close attention to the increasing number of perfect pensioners is that their monthly pension amount is very high at Won 722,000 which is four times higher than the special old age pension (Won 172,000) and 3.2 times higher than the monthly average pension of old age pensioners (Won 224,000). The significance of the perfect pension is that, unlike other old age pensions, this pension can contribute substantially for old age income protection. The amount of this pension is 92% of the minimum cost of living for a two-member family (Won 784,000), which is announced by the Ministry of Health, Welfare and Family and used as the basis of low income support programmes. Since the cash portion of the minimum cost of living is Won 657,000, the perfect pension amount is equivalent to 110% of the cash component.[53]

Some of the pensioners of a NP may have additional income and transfer income from children or friends as a typical case. Some other pensioners may even have earned income by working and have financial income from interests, dividends and rentals, which can allow them to live a comfortable life. However, most of the elderly are living on the verge of poverty. Accordingly, the Government has introduced the Basic Pension Scheme, a public assistance pro-

53 Compared to 2009 the minimum cost of living (Won 836,000 for a two-member family), this pension amount is equivalent to 86% and 105% of the cash component. As old age pensions are adjusted every April to reflect changes in the consumer price index (4.7% raise in 2009), it is better to use the 2008 figures to analyse the February pension.

gramme in nature, to provide income protection to 70% [54] of the elderly. Under this pension, a monthly pension of Won 84,000 (Won 134,000 for a couple) is paid in 2008, the pension amount was increased to Won 88,000 (Won 148,000 for a couple) from April 2009. Since the amount of the Basic Pension is so small, there may be many elderly, who are still suffering from poverty.

Furthermore, the economic recession of Korea in the aftermath of the world financial crisis adversely affected elderlies' employment and their earnings. If the current trend continues, the number of the elderly population aged over 65 is projected to increase by more than 190,000 persons every year. As their employment and income decline, the financial burden to look after them falls to their children or the Government budget. In the meantime, 20,000 additional pensioners are being produced every year by the NP and other public pension schemes.

As the number of beneficiaries from the Basic Old Age Pension increases while employment of elderly would be drastically reduced, income disparities between elderly pensioners and other elderly may be further widened. This argument cannot be verified due to the lack of data. The inequality in consumption levels among the elderly population has been continuously reduced for the past ten years thanks to the Government's efforts to provide income support for elderly through public pension schemes and public assistance programmes (Lee So-Jung 2009).[55]

It may be worthwhile to think about what the NP should do during this economic recession with its huge amount of reserve funds with respect to a flexible fund operation to maximize returns or to use its reserve to reactivate the economy. Several key issues, that can be seriously considered, include whether the NP should continue its operations of collecting contributions and pay pensions to 2.59 million pensioners (as of February 2009) as defined in its Act, or whether the NP could provide some kind of loans to its participants within their contributions to ameliorate their economic hardship or whether the NP should return contribution amounts to unemployed participants. All these issues are interesting subjects but there was no discussion in the NP at all. The answer is quite clear. The NP is an institutional scheme committed to protect long term income of the elderly, disabled and surviving dependents, and a counter-cyclical policy is not NP's concern.

---

54 As of March 2009, it is paid to 3.48 million elderly. Since the beneficiaries of the Basic Livelihood Guaranty System (about 400,000) must forfeit the corresponding amount if they receive the Basic Old Age Pension, therefore, most of them give up the basic Old Age pension.

55 So-Jung Lee (2009) maintains that – based on the analysis of panel data of the Korea Labor Institute – inequality in gross consumption levels of elderly households were continuously reduced since 1998 (in 2001, 2003, and 2005).

Given the size of the NP fund reserves that exceeds 25% of the GDP, it may be possible to consider to use part of it to boost macroeconomic consumption or investment, since the purpose of fund reserve operations could include the maximization of returns as well as the promotion of participants' life through economic stabilization. At present, the NP appears to be concentrating to enhance investment returns, and there seems to be no discussion about using funds to boost the investment demand.

In the following section, I want to review the current status of old age income protection in Korea as well as NP revenues and expenditure. In the next section, NP fund operation methods during the period of declining income would be reviewed, while the changes in consumption levels during the period of declining income will be analysed from the perspective of equalization of consumption and the role of pensions in the last but one section. The institutional and policy improvements regarding NP and old age income protection will be briefly described in the last section.

Retirement Income and NP Benefits

Composition of the Retirement Income

According to a survey (KIHASA 2005) on the living standards of elderly, 37.4% of elderly households had a household income, which was lower than the minimum cost of living. As to the characteristics of households, 59.8% of single elderly households and 38.7% of elderly couple households and 21.9% of elderly households living with children were living with an income below the minimum cost of living (2003 income basis). About 60% of single elderly households were living in poverty, and 90% of them had transfer income from public sources, 73% of them received transfer income from private sources, which implied that they were living with income support from neighbours. It was also reported that 30% of the households had some income from work and business, and 15% of them had even financial income.[56] Public transfer income included NP, (old) Elderly Pension, (old) transport allowance and the Basic Livelihood Guarantee Fund. Since there were not so many beneficiaries of NPs and the

56 According to the elderly statistics of the National Statistics Office (2006), elderly households are composed of single elderly (18.1%), elderly couple (33%) and elderly with children households (48.3%). Their total monthly income was 1.16 million Won and the total monthly outlay was 1.13 million Won, respectively. The sources of income were transfer income (54.6%), income from work (10.2%), business income (8.4%) and others (26.8%). Income of elderly couples was equivalent to 38.7% of non-elderly households (3 million Won). On the other hand, the income composition of Jang Ji-Yeon (2008) was as follows: contribution of other household members (29.4%), private transfer (28.2%), work income (23.6%), public transfer (13.9%) and income from assets.

Basic Livelihood Guarantee Fund at that time, most of them received an (old) Elderly Pension and (old) transport allowances.

The core of the problem was that pensions from the NP were not sufficient enough to protect old age life. As of February 2009, the average amount of monthly pensions from the NP was Won 224,000 (old age pension), Won 722,000 (perfect pension), Won 360,000 (disability pension) and Won 204,000 (survivor pension) respectively. Considering that the minimum cost of living in 2008 was Won 463,000 (cash benefit, Won 388,000) for single household and Won 784,000 (cash benefit, 657,000Won) for a couple household, the pension amounts were far below the minimum cost of living. Even assuming that elderly households may use slightly less expenses, it is quite obvious that they cannot live only with a NP pension. In good contrast to this dismal picture, the average monthly pension of Government employees amounted to 1.88 million Won (2007 retiree basis), which was over eight times higher than the old age pension and 2.5 times higher than the perfect pension. With this level of pension, one can live quite comfortable.

Public pensions in other OECD countries provide much higher coverage than the NP. In the case of the U.K., elderly in the 65-74 age bracket depend upon their living on public pension (36%), private pension (32%), work (16%), public assistance (9%) and other sources (8%), while the elderly in the 75-84 age bracket depend upon public pension (43%), private pension (28%), work (7%), public assistance (14%) and others (8%). It is quite clear that the public pension plays the core role in providing old age income protection in the U.K.[57] In the U.K. gender discrimination seems to be present in the basic pension. Though the pension amount depends on many factors such as length of contribution, 87% of male retirees were eligible for pension, while only 46% of women over 60 years of age were eligible for pension and women's pension amount was far lower than males'.

Regarding old age income protection in Korea, I am concerned by the low effective participation rate of the NP. The nominal participation rate [58] of public pensions, including NP, exceeded 92% at the end of 2007, which was almost the same as the other OECD countries. However, if we exclude those who are exempted to contribute and those who had overdue premiums, the effective participation rate would be 57.5% of the economically active population in the age

---

57 BBC 2008. Diamond (2005) argued that earnings-related pension privatization was not inefficient and that indexing basic pensions with the consumer price index will make old age life miserable by reducing pensions.

58 Kim Sung-Sook et al. (2008, p. 241) estimated that the participation of the 19-59 years age group to the NP, Government employees pension, military and private school teachers pension was 91.7%. This rate would increase a little bit if we exclude the economically active group aged 18-19 years.

group 20-59 years. Consequently, some elderly may face serious difficulties in living, because they would not receive a pension at all.

As the NP matures, it is expected that its function to protect old age income would be further strengthened. However, the problems of those elderly without any pension benefits including elderly women, and the low pension problem will remain unresolved for some time.

NP Benefits: Number of Pensioners and Benefits Amount

For the first time in 11 years, the GDP and per capita GNI in Korea are expected to decline in 2009. Despite the macro-economic downturn, some 240,000 pensioners are expected to be added to the NP in 2009. As the NP enters its 21st year of business in 2009, it is expected to have quite a few perfect pensioners in 2009 unlike the preceding years. As the perfect pensioners will be paid monthly pensions of Won 720,000, they can enjoy quite a comfortable old age living without looking for another job. As the rate of elderly employment declines, and the proportion of pensioners' increases, it is possible that the decrease in consumption inequality among the elderly, which had been sustained since 1998, could be continued (see Lee Soo-Jung 2009).

Figure 1 shows the number of NP pensioners by type since 1993. The number of pensioners exceeded the 200,000 mark in 1998 (10th year of operation), and surpassed 2.5 million by 2008. As to the old age pension, which is eligible for 55 years old or older, there were more than 150,000 pensioners in 1989, and the number of old age pensioners exceeded 2 million in 2008. Even though their pension amount is rather small, they accounted for 27% of the elderly population in 2008. If we include pensioners receiving other public pensions such as Government employees, military and private school teacher pensions, the ratio of public pensioners accounted for 31% of the elderly population.

Classified by pension types, the largest number of pensioners was old age pensioners, followed by survivors and disability pensioners. Among the old age pensioners, the largest group was the special old age pensioners, followed by the reduced, early old age, perfect and split pensions. As the increasing rate of special old age pensioners is expected to decline, the shares of perfect pensioners and reduced pensioners are expected to increase substantially.

Figure 2 shows the amount of pensions paid by the NP. The pension amount increased rapidly, surpassing 300 billion Won in 1998 (10th year) and 5,800 billion Won in 2008 (20th year), respectively. The growth rate of the pension amount was higher than that of pensioners, because highly paid pensioners became numerous in later years. The monthly pension amounts by types are presented in figure 3.

Figure 1: Number of pensioners by benefit types

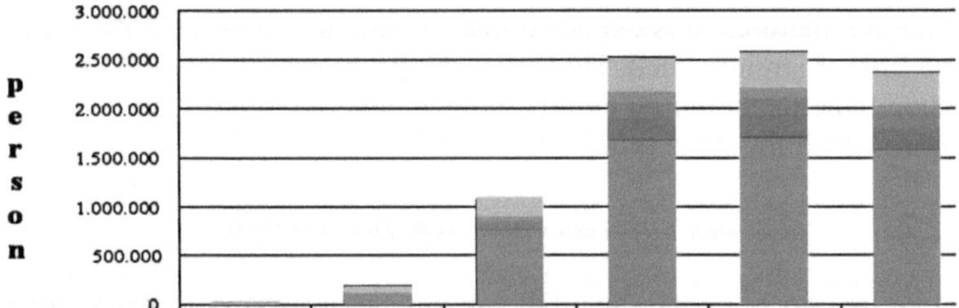

	1993	1998	2003	2008	2009.2	2009.2
survivor	20.637	74.334	207.626	372.352	378.654	345.771
disability	4.012	14.870	48.439	100.776	102.332	66.470
age,split	0	0	182	2.425	2.578	2.269
age,early	0	0	67.219	159.202	166.361	156.009
age,reduced	0	0	25.884	216.084	223.469	217.243
age,20years+	0	0	0	12.798	16.429	16.061
age,special	10.971	112.946	759.065	1.673.576	1.700.876	1.575.315

Source: NPS.

Figure 2: Annual benefits amount (billion Won)

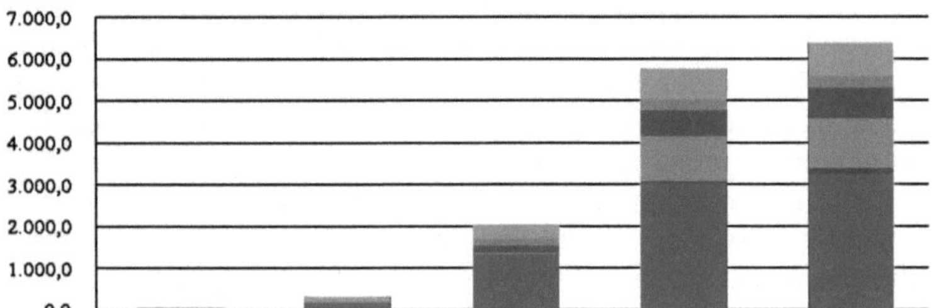

	1993	1998	2003	2008	2009estimated
survivor	43,8	100,1	352,7	731,4	787,1
disability	9,8	38,1	153,9	268,1	276,5
age,split	0,0	0,0	0,2	3,2	4,1
age,early	0,0	0,0	170,1	619,7	721,6
age,reduced	0,0	0,0	34,3	1.057,7	1.202,2
age,20years+	0,0	0,0	0,0	49,6	127,5
age,special	6,4	171,4	1.329,0	3.035,4	3.253,5

Note: 2009 estimated by author; *Source*: NPS

Figure 3: Monthly benefits to pensioners by types (as of February 2009)

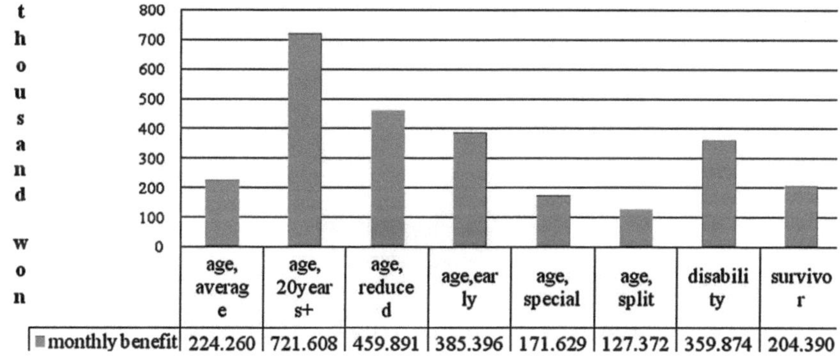

Source: NPS

Operations of the NP during the recent recession

In this section, we would like to summarize various complaints and demands filed by NP participants on the wake of the financial crisis, which became evident in November 2008, and a series of policy measures and responses taken by the Ministry for Health, Welfare and Family Affairs (MIHWAF) and the NPS.

Complaints of Participants

During November and December 2008, when the downturn in the domestic economy was evident, over 900 complaints and demands were filed with the NP every month. If we analyse the 934 complaints filed in December 2008 (and 906 complaints filed in November 2008 in brackets), the complaints on eligibility, collection, pension benefit and fund topped the list with 395 cases (344 cases) accounting for 42% (38%) of total complaints, followed by complaints regarding the pension system such as the benefit level and contribution rates that accounted for 23% (24%), telephone inquiries 17% (16%), attitudes of NPS employees 12% (17%) and EDI 6% (5%), respectively, as shown in figure 4. There were some monthly fluctuations in the number of complaints, but the majority of complaints were regarding the treatment of the pension business and pension system which accounted for more than 60% of complaints.

Figure 4: Participants' complaints and demands (December 2008)

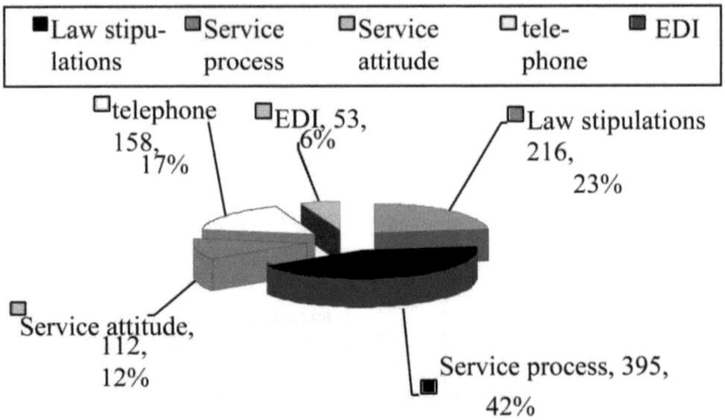

It is noteworthy that about 20% of complaints were on the basic structure of the NP. Most of the complaints were on the introduction of one time withdrawal payments (27%), high contributions (23%) and low pension benefits (15%) that are difficult to accommodate. For example, the introduction of one time withdrawal cannot be accommodated, because of the nature of the NP that is committed to provide lifetime protection. Moreover, complaints on the high contribution rate cannot be accommodated for the sound financial position of the NP that needs higher contribution rates, and complaints on low pension benefits were baseless, because most of the pensioners were special old age pensioners,[59] and the remaining pensioners were composed of reduced pensioners, early old age pensioners and split pensioners.[60] There were very few perfect old age pensioners.

It is important to note that the number of complaints started to increase rapidly from June 2008, when the economic downturn became evident. Up to May 2008, the number of complaints was less than 120 per month. In June 2008, the NPS received 230 complaints, and the number of complaints filed with the NP reached 290 cases per month in August and September 2008. Since then, the number of complaints showed a declining trend, though the demands for one-time withdrawal payments and loans within the contribution amount are consistently increasing, reflecting the hardship facing many participants of the NP during the recent recession (see table 1).

59 Special old age pensioners are those, who contributed for 5-10 years and there were 1.57 million special old age pensioners in February 2009 that accounted for 80% of the total old age pensioners (1.967 million).

60 In February 2009, there were 16,000 perfect old age pensioners (0.8%) and the shares of reduced pensioners, early old age pensioners and split pensioners were 11.0%, 7.9% and 0.1%, respectively.

Table 1: Participant demands and complaints: Pension system (2008)

	Complaints & Demands	Mar.	Apr.	May	June	July	Aug.	Sept.	Oct.	Nov.	Dec.	Total
Pension system	Low pension amount	51	44	49	53	78	64	47	40	53	28	507
	High contribution	38	27	15	35	36	40	32	25	38	41	327
	Forced participation	-	7	17	28	18	39	45	25	14	15	208
	Lack of withdrawal	-	3	7	53	24	59	75	40	33	48	342
	Imposition of late payment penalty	4	5	10	39	18	43	50	23	18	20	230
	Fear for fund depletion	26	17	17	18	12	20	23	6	17	14	170
	Contribution criteria & loan facility	-	1	4	12	4	23	23	19	21	15	122
	Total	119	104	119	238	190	288	295	178	194	181	1,906

Source: *Voice of Clients*, NPS, 2008.

During the first three months of 2009, complaints from participants continued to be filed with the NP, which were mostly on the introduction of the withdrawal system (94 cases, 4.8%), loan facilities within the contribution amount (34 cases, 1.9%), low pension amounts (82 cases, 4.2%), high contribution rates (25 cases, 1.3%) and unilateral imposition of late payment penalties (32 cases, 1.7%; see table 2).

Table 2: Complaints and demands of participants: Pension System (January-March 2009)

	Subject	Complaint & Demands	Cases (%)
System	Benefit	Introduce withdrawal system	94 (4.8%)
		Low pension amount	82 (4.2%)
	Fund	Lack of loan facility	34 (1.9%)
	Collection	High contribution rates	25 (1.3%)
		Imposition of late payment penalty	32 (1.7%)

Source: NPS, *Voice of Clients*, 2009.

Responses from the Authorities

In response to the growing complaints from NP participants, the Ministry of Health and Welfare and the NPS have tried to respond. Due to the nature of the NP, in which flexibility of policy implementation is not incorporated, their hands are tied and their responses have been minimal.

Ministry for Health, Welfare and Family Affairs (MIHWAF)
The responses from the policy-making authority, the MIHWAF, have been on two subjects: reduced contributions for some participants and expansion of loan facilities and financial services.

Firstly, it was decided to allow lower contributions for some participants, whose income was reduced significantly. The National Pension Deliberation Committee (chaired by the Deputy Minister) decided to allow temporary reductions of the contribution rate for those participants, whose income dropped more than 20% by applying the current year income (rather than the previous year income) as basis for the contribution rate calculation with the consent of the participant concerned (MIHWAF February 27, 2009).

Since the basis for calculating the contribution rate is the income of workplaces of the preceding year [61] this policy to reduce the contribution rate is intended to reflect the lowered income of those workplaces, where revenues are substantially reduced due to structural adjustment and job-sharing movements.

The employer should submit his request to adjust contribution rates by submitting complete documents to prove the reduced income, including payroll reports and written consent of participants, to NPS during March. Once the request is approved, the reduced rate will be applied from April to June of the next fiscal year, when the new rate will be determined. If the income of the employee will be increased considerably during this period, the employee's adjusted income will be applied.

The next subject is the total financial services for low income participants (Ministry of Health and Welfare, Press Release, May 4, 2009). This service aims to provide a complete set of advisory and to arrange financing from Korea Asset Management Co. (KAMCO) for those participants who are facing bankruptcy starting from November 2008. First, a debt clinic will be organized by private financial consultants,[62] who would provide detailed assistance to reduce debts.[63] Starting from May 2009, the household interest on loans would be reduced by arranging substitute loan facilities provided by KAMCO.[64]

61 Income of the previous year filed with National Taxation Service (NTS) before March 10 of the current fiscal year.

62 This is Podo Financial Designers. Eligible participants are those with monthly income of less than 3.7 million (for four member households) with credit rating of 6-10 grades.

63 Based on survey of 300 persons (158 males and 142 women), who had debt consultant advice, it was found that monthly household deficit of 590,000 Won was reduced (from Won 740,000 deficit to Won 130,000) by mostly reducing spending. The household debt was reduced from Won 54.1 million before consultation to Won 40.7 million after consultation.

64 The household debts amounted to 688 trillion Won at the end of 2008 recording an increase of 57.6 trillion Won (9.1%) in a year. The ratio of defaulters was estimated at 5.7% of general households (KIHASA 2008) while this default ratio was 1.5 times higher for low income households (8.4%) (MIHWAF, Press release, dated April 9, 2009).

The MIHWAF signed a Memorandum of Understanding (MOU) entitled "Joint Public and Private Sector Agreement on Comprehensive Assistance to Low Income Financial Defaulters" on April 9, 2009 with the Social Welfare Joint Fund Raising Society, KAMCO, Korea Legal Aid Corporation and Credit Counselling and Recovery Service (CCRS) in order to carry out the total financial services. Based on this MOU, the "Sound Financing Total Solution Consulting Center" will be operating to provide services to about 3,000 persons on a pilot scheme basis with a view to expand this operations if the pilot scheme turns out to be feasible. For details, you may refer to press releases of the MIHWAF.

National Pension Service (NPS)

The NPS received some 533 complaints and demands regarding the pension system during the first three months of 2009, of which NPS referred 47 cases (8.5%) to its Advisory Committee for their deliberation. For the remaining cases, NPS intends to respond by participants' better understanding by persuasion (53.7%), and close monitoring of consumer satisfaction (37.8%, see table 3).

Table 3: Voice of client responses (System improvement, January-March 2009)

	Items	*Cases (%)*	*CS monitoring*	*IPCC VOC*	*Reporting unkind*	*Advisors group*	*Review request*
System improvement	Benefits	290 (52.4)	133	126	-	4	27
	Funds	57 (10.3)	17	35	-	5	
	Eligibility	94 (17.0)	45	42	-	6	1
	Collection	112 (20.3)	14	94	-	1	3
	Total	553 (100.0)	209 (37.8)	297 (53.7)	-	16 (2.9)	31 (5.6)

Source: NPS, *Voice of Clients*, 2009.

Table 4 summarizes the NPS's responses to complaints of participants. In case of complaints on system improvement, promotion of better understanding through dialogue with participants, reporting of unkind responses and referral to the Advisory Committee will be handled by the NPS Head Office while monitoring of consumer satisfaction will be undertaken by its branch offices.

Though the NPS responses have been somewhat passive in nature, its measures taken at the outset of the economic downturn such as temporary withdrawal return system, delayed contribution and voluntary (continued) participation brought some positive results (NPS, Press Release, April 21, 2009). The temporary withdrawal return system is a system in which participants, who withdrew from the NP, can restore eligibility by returning the withdrawn amount within a certain time period. The delayed payment system allows participants to defer actual payment while the voluntary participation system is intended to attract participation of someone with no income such as housewives, and continued participation allows participants to stay with the NP after reaching 60 years of age.

Table 4: Responses to voice of clients (January-March 2009)

		Cases	*CS monitoring*	*IPCC system*	*Unkind correction*	*Advisory group*	*Review request*
System improvement		553 (28.5)	209 (15.3)	297 (61.6)	-	16 (64.0)	31 (100)
Others	*Head office*	638 (32.9)	466 (34.2)	169 (35.1)	-	3 (12.0)	-
	Branch offices	693 (35.7)	647 (47.5)	6 (1.2)	40 (100)	-	-
	others	57 (2.9)	41 (3.0)	10 (2.1)	-	6 (24.0)	-
Total		1,941 (100)	1,363 (100)	482 (100)	40 (100)	25 (100)	31 (100)

Source: NPS, *Voice of Clients,* 2009.

In 2009, the number of applicants for the temporary withdrawal return system and delayed payment system has increased by 68% compared to 2008, due largely to the Consulting on Successful Ageing (CSA) scheme which was actively promoted by NPS from April 2008. The number of applicants for voluntary (continued) participation has increased by 42% (see table 5).

Table 5: Withdrawal return, additional and voluntary contributions

	2006	*2007*	*2008*	*2009*
Withdrawal return	632	927	1,753	2,961
Additional contribution	435	694	778	1,310
Voluntary (continuous) contribution	2,234	2,772	3,219	4,572

Source: NPS.

It is noteworthy that the renewed interest on the NP has been occurred in the middle of the economic downturn, which reflects the changing perception on retirement planning. With the introduction of the temporary withdrawal return and additional contribution systems, which were promoted by the NPS from February 2009, many persons who were not eligible for pension due to lack of contribution period could now be eligible for pension.

For example, a certain Mr. K was not eligible for pension with only a contribution period of 92 months. However, Mr. K was able to restore 105 months by returning withdrawal money to the NPS under the new measure, and he is now entitled to a monthly pension of 600,000 Won. NPS plans to intensify these programmes in order to attract women and low income groups, who would be vulnerable in the ageing society.

Change in Private Sector Consumption in the Recent Recession: Effects of Equalization and Pension

It is expected that many countries including the OECD countries would record negative economic growth due to the world financial crisis in 2009. The Korean economy is projected to record negative growth in 2009, 11 years after its negative growth recorded in 1998. It is generally believed that the downturn in economic growth is preceded by a decrease in consumption and investment expenditures. This implies that negative growth in 2009 was able to forecast with changes in 2008. Park Jong-Kyu (2009) mentioned that decrease in consumption expenditures in the second quarter of 2008 had a similar pattern with the decrease in consumption experienced in the fourth quarter of 1997, after tracing changes in private consumption for 120 quarters after the third quarter of 1978.[65] During the two quarters under review, consumers reduced expenditure for eating outside and increased in-house eating. Households had saved for precautionary motives for the future by behaving adequately.

As pointed out by Park Jong-Kyu (2009), consumers rarely reduce their consumption except for a certain period, in which the sense of economic crisis was heightened such as 1980, the financial crisis of 1997, the 2002 credit card crisis and the world financial crisis of 2008, when the decrease in private consumption lasted more than a single quarter. Though there were three temporary declines in consumption, their impact was not as severe as those longer term decreases.

The reason why household consumption shows stable patterns regardless of changes in income was because household consumption tends to maintain a certain level. This is due to the so-called lifetime cycle-permanent income hypothesis (LCPIH). According to the LCHIP, the consumption level is maintained at a stable level throughout life time regardless of changes in income during working period and even after retirement.

This was cross breeding of Modigliani's lifetime cycle hypothesis (Modigliani 1954, 1963) and permanent income hypothesis of Friedman (1957). This hypothesis was proven valid through empirical studies in many countries, espe-

---

65 According to Jong-Kyu Park (2009) and the Bank of Korea (2009), out of total 122 quarters between fourth quarter of 1978 and the first quarter of 2009, there were 13 quarters, in which household final consumption expenditure (private consumption) declined: of which temporary decrease (only one quarter decrease) occurred three times and continued decrease happened ten times. Temporary decreases were in Q3 of 1996, Q1 of 1997 and Q4 of 2008, and continued decreases were recorded in Q1-Q4 of 1980, Q4 1997-Q1 1998, Q4 2002-Q2 2004 and Q2-Q4 2008 (4 times). I considered Q3 of 2008 as a decrease quarter, when it recorded 0% growth for the convenience of analysis.

cially the changes in income were very substantial and predictable.[66] According to Browning and Crossley (2001), the households with limited rationality tend to adjust their consumption level, when changes in income are substantial and predictable, while they tend not to adjust consumption if changes in income are unpredictable (reject LCHIP).[67]

To summarize our presentation, consumption levels in Korea had gone through severe decrease four times since 1978 whenever it was confronted with economic downturn. Since the changes in income during this period were not so big [68] and irregular, it was difficult to predict. In most other cases, the hypothesis can be validated when the change in income is big and regular.

There are different views on the impact of the introduction and expansion of public pension on national saving and consumption. There was a theory that public pension (forced saving) will reduce the voluntary saving of households, and empirical evidences from this theory differed depending on the country. While Feldstein (1974, 1995), Gale (1998) and Attanasio and Brugiavini (2003) argued that public pension reduces household savings, Barro (1978) and Leimer and Lesnoy (1981) argued otherwise. In Korea, some believe that it has some impact (Kim Sang-Ho 2005; Kang Sung-Ho & Lim Byung-In 2005), while others believe otherwise.[69]

It is quite obvious that consumption expenditure of elderly had increased and stabilized due to stable income during the retirement period with the introduction of public pension. As pointed out by Lee So Jung (2009), the continued decrease in consumption inequality among elderly observed during 1998 and 2005 can be attributable to the general income level improvement of the elderly population caused by the expansion of public pensions and public assistance programmes. The introduction and expansion of the pension system had greatly contributed to equitable life time consumption from the perspective of providing predictable and regular income rather than precautionary motives.

In the following section, the article will review the increase in pension benefits and consumption followed by the effect of pensions on equalization of household consumption and stable household consumption expenditure.

---

66 The degree of household consumption equalization, which was anticipated under LCHIP is still being debated. Though income estimates were reviewed and the focus has been on identifiable changes in income, debates are still going on. Some researchers believe that predictable changes in income had an impact on consumption levels, while others do not believe this theory.

67 Though the degree of effect of predictable changes in income on consumption is varied depending on analysis, there is consensus that consumer behaviour would be patterned so as to increase utility loss.

68 The degree of decrease during economic downturn is usually smaller than the degree of increase in income during an economic growth period.

69 Lim Gyung-mook & Mun Hyung-Pyo (2003) argued that the impact was verified in participants of occupational pensions but not in participants of the NP.

Increasing Pensioners and Elderly Consumption

Most of elderly joining the elderly class of 60s are born after 1945 (liberation) and before the outbreak of the Korean War (1950). They are the main players during the high development period (1970s and 1980s) of the Korean economy. As such, quite a few of them made large assets during the real estate boom, and they can afford to enjoy a comfortable old age life without pension. As the elderly pension benefits increases and bigger amount of pensions are paid to this group of elderly, the share of elderly consumption has been increasing, and this has stabilized consumption expenditure.[70]

As the elderly population is expected to increase rapidly in the early part of the 2010s, when a large number of baby boomers retire and join the elderly pool. These baby boomers are also an affluent group with sizable real estate holdings and financial assets as well as perfect old age pensions. Therefore, these new elderly pensioners are expected to lead elderly consumption expenditure.

At present, the share of elderly pensioners receiving public pension remains low at 31%, causing serious problems of elderly poor.[71] At the end of June 2008, the number of elderly pensioners (60 years old +) was 1.928 million,[72] which was equivalent to 27.4% of the total elderly population (7.029 million).[73] In addition to that, there are some 260,000 pensioners, who are receiving occupational pensions.[74] If we add public and occupational pensioners, the share of elderly pensioners will increase to 31%. As most of retirees who join the elderly group (over 60 years old) are eligible for public pension, so the pension coverage ratio for elderly would be raised steadily.

The pension coverage ratio of Korea is relatively low compared to major OECD countries. The pension coverage ratio of elderly over 65 years of age (23.1%) in Korea is far too low compared with the U.S., U.K., Canada and Japan where the ratios exceeded 90% (see table 6). Though the basic old age pension, which was introduced in 2008, has a very broad coverage but its impact is very low due to low pension. One noteworthy fact is that the effort to increase coverage ratio in Korea has limited impact because the share of self-employed is too high in Korea. Their income is very hard to estimate and their contribution record is rather poor.

70 The statistics on the share of elderly in gross household consumption are not published.

71 In terms of households, over 50% of elderly households received public pensions.

72 Male – 1,248,000 (64.5%), female – 684,000 (35.5%).

73 Male – 41.4% of 3,006,000, female – 17.0% of 4,022,000

74 In case of civil service pension, there were 267,000 pensioners at the end of June 2008, of whom retirement pensioners were 239,000. The share of elderly over 61 accounted for 165,000 pensioners (69% of total pensioners).

Table 6: Public pension coverage in some OECD countries: Over 65 years old

Country [1]	*Population (A) million*	*Public pensioners (B, C)*		*Public assistance & basic old age pension (D)*	*Ratio, %*		
					B/A	C/A	D/A
Korea	5.09	NP + occupational pensions		Basic old age pension	23.1	-	60.0
		1.00+0.18 = 1,17 [2]		3,05 [2]			
U.S.A.	35.5	OASI		SSI	97.1	-	5.6
		34,47		2,00			
U.K [3]	12.18	National pension (basic + second tier)		Pension credit	98.4	-	20.5
		11.98		2.73			
Canada [4]	4.42	OAS(B)	CPP(C)	GIS	98.7	90.5	33.9
		4,37	4,00	1.50			
Japan	26.40	Basic pension	Welfare Pension	(livelihood protection) [7]	95.5	54.2	5.7
		25.20 [5]	14.32 [6]	(1.51)			

Notes: 1) Base year; Korea: 2008; U.S.A.; 2006; U.K.: 2007.11; Canada: 2007.7; Japan: 2007.3. 2) Base: April 2008. 3) Since women can be eligible at 60 years of age, this figure represents the ratio of pensioners against total eligible participants. If pension credit is included, total pensioners will be 3.34 million and the ratio 27.4%. 4) 5.7% of OAS are reduced pensioners. CPP 3.36 million, survivors 0.74 million, both pension 0.1 million reach to 4.0 million. 5) Pensioners of basic pension reach to 12.73 million. 6) Welfare pensions 11.98 million, cooperative pensions 2.34 million, and other welfare pensions 20,000. 7) In Japan, there is no public assistance but there is livelihood protection, similar to the basic old age pension in Korea.

Sources: Sung-Sook Kim et al. 2008, p. 307; Japan, Ministry of Welfare and Labour, home page.

Table 7: Self-employed in labour market participants in some OECD countries (in %)

U.S.A.	7.6	Japan	14.9
U.K.	13.6	Turkey	49.2
France	8.8	Portugal	25.9
Germany	11.8	Mexico	37.0
Canada	9.5	Korea	34.0
OECD average		17.4	

Note: This ratio represents self-employed to private employees.

Source: OECD Factbook 2006.

Equalization of Consumption: Review of Empirical Analysis Using Pension Income

The increase in elderly population and pensioners has a positive impact on the economy during an economic downturn by mitigating the severity of business cycles. Since there is no strong incentive to save for the elderly population, elderly have a high propensity to consume. Even without the increasing number of the elderly population, there would be pressure to equalize consumption levels during economic downturns. Here, I would like to review some empirical studies on the consumption equalization during economic downturns. I want to present the Russian case, in which pension payments have been delayed, and the Japanese case, in which public pensions were paid once every two months and its impact on consumption. The first case is related to consumption equalization with no reference to pension, while the latter two cases involved equalized consumption, which is directly related to pensions.

Zhang and Kang (2007) undertook a systematic study on how economic crises influenced consumption equalization. They have analysed the impact of the 1997-1998 economic crisis on consumption equalization by using our Daewoo panel data. They found out that risk on consumption expenditure is jointly owned by municipal Governments during the economic crisis, while risk on national level consumption expenditure is not jointly owned.[75] They argued that the unequal distribution effect on individuals, households and local Governments experienced during economic downturn are usually offset by private or public transfers and loans, so as to enable equalization of consumption.

Null (2003) analysed the impact of pension payment delay on household consumption expenditure by using income and consumption data of Russia during six years (1995-2000) and confirmed that household used only small part of pensions (1/6-2/5) for consumption, while the remaining amount was converted to financial transactions to equalize consumption. It was also shown that labour income is a substitute for pension income. She argued that households used unofficial risk aversion in addition to official resorts, such as official insurance, borrowings and loans, savings and asset depletion, labour income and agriculture in the course of consumption equalization.[76] Her model failed to explain how households selected financial transactions and why.

Stephens and Unayama (2007) had analysed the impact of the Japanese public pension, which is paid out once every two months on the consumption expenditure of households. They confirmed that household consumption of Jap-

75 The Joint ownership hypothesis of risk on national level consumption was rejected in many studies, e.g. Asdrubali, Sorenson & Yosha 1996; Attanacio & Davis 1996, Hayashi, Altoji & Koylikoff 1996.

76 The analysis method is to use simple equations using the endogenous characteristics of household financial transactions.

anese households was in line with LCPIH, confirming its validity in Japan. They found out that consumption on non-durable goods fluctuated within a 1% range, while consumption on leisure service fluctuated within a 16% range. Consumption on leisure was equivalent to 11% of consumption on durable goods and 7% of gross consumption, respectively.[77]

Stephens (2003, 2006) showed that, unlike the results obtained from Korea, Japan and Russia, predictable cyclical changes in income led to increased consumption on the basis of a study on U.K. data. Stephens (2003) also found that non-durable consumption in the U.S. increased by 10% during the week, when social security checks are mailed. Similarly, Stephens (2006) found that consumption on non-durable goods in the U.K. would be increased by 7% within a week after the monthly pay checks are mailed out. As to the validity of LCPIH, he thinks that further studies on the consumption patterns should be in order, while LCHIP itself cannot be verified even if liquidity constraints and precautionary saving are taken into accounts.

So far, we have confirmed that household consumption remained during economic downturns in Korea, Japan and Russia. As shown in the household consumption statistics in Korea since 1978, consumption levels will decline if the change in income is rather small and irregular. We can conclude – based on our study – that recent increases in elderly population and pension coverage ratio would contribute to mitigate the severity of economic downturns by maintaining consumption levels.

Concluding Remarks

The number of perfect old age pensioners, which started to emerge from 2008, reached the 16,000 mark in February 2009, and their number is expected to reach the 35,000 level by the end of 2009 as they are increasing at the rate of 2,000 a month. Given their high pension amount which is four times higher than the old age pension, the impact of the NP on old age income protection would be greatly enhanced. During this time of economic downturn, the increased income of elderly would contribute greatly for protecting elderly living standards and for eliminating consumption inequality.

If the current trend would be continued, it is highly likely that, after 2030, more than 40% of the elderly population and 20% of elderly households would be left out without any pension protection. Though half of them could be protected through the basic livelihood guarantee scheme, there could be large number of elderly, who cannot escape from poverty trap.

---

77 First, the effect of monthly pensions on consumption was analyzed. Later, the impact of pension differences among households on consumption was investigated. The first effect was that non-durable consumption fluctuated in the 1-2% range. The second effect confirmed that fresh food fluctuated widely in the 1-16% range.

Even among the households receiving pensions currently, quite a few of elderly households are living on the verge of poverty, because the level of pensions is too low to sustain a comfortable living. Though the number of perfect pensioners is increasing, 40% of today's pensioners are depending on special, reduced, early and split pensions.

Consequently, the NPS should put their best efforts to enhance effective participation to rate up to 70% of the economically active population. As to the participants with overdue contributions or those, who were exempted from contribution, we must have a clear fundamental solution such as the payment of contributions from the Government budget.[78] It is also worthwhile to change the mode of operation of the Basic Old Age Pension (introduced in 2008) with a view to transform it as a subsidiary pension scheme supplementing the NP.

It is worthwhile to consider to raise the contribution rate in a gradual manner so as to enhance the financial position of the NPS with the consent and support from participants and other stakeholders. In this regard, it is imperative to restore the lost confidence of the NPS.

Concurrently, we should promote the expansion of retirement allowances and individual pensions. Voluntary pensions would be very attractive to most Koreans, who abhor forced participation, under the condition that stronger tax incentives are provided, and the scheme would be well designed to satisfy the needs of potential participants.

It is also urgently necessary to devise policy measures to remedy the wide difference in pension benefits between the NP and occupational pension schemes. The current level of benefit differences, in which the average pension in occupational pension schemes is 2.5 times higher than the perfect pension of the NP and eleven times higher than the special old age pension, is outrageous and should not be tolerated. Urgent actions to correct this imbalance should be undertaken without any further delay.

Lastly, it is suggested to formulate an econometric model to analyse the repercussion effects of the recent economic downturn on income and consumption inequality of the elderly population.

78 The reason why so many participants are involved in this situation is that the share of self employed is so high and their economic capability is very much limited. The income gap between workplace participants and self employed is being widened as time passes. This is a structural problem of the Korean labour market. As such, it is a very difficult and time consuming task.

References

in Korean and Japanese

Jang, Ji-Yeon et al. (2008), *Comparative study on the Mid-elderly Labour Market.* Seoul: KLI.

Kang, Sung-Ho & Lim Byung-In (2005), 'Empirical Study on Effect of Public Pension on Private Saving', *Economic Analysis,* vol. 11 (2), Bank of Korea, Institute for Banking and Finance.

Kim, Sang-Ho (2005), 'Influence of Pension Assets on Household Saving: Theoretical Empirical Study on the Substitution Effect', *KYUNG JE HAK YON GU*, vol. 53 (4), pp. 47-65.

Kim, Sung-Sook et al. (2008), *Understanding Public Pension.* Seoul: NPS Research Institute, December.

KIHASA/Korea Institute for Health and Social Affairs (2005), *Survey on Elderly Living Status & Welfare Needs*. Seoul.

Lee, So-Jung (2009), 'Analysis of Consumption Inequality of Elderly Households', *Social Welfare Studies,* vol. 40 (1), pp. 235-260.

Lim, Kyun-Mook & Moon Hyung-Pyo (2003), 'Effects of Public pensions on Household Savings, in Choi Kyung Soo et. al. (eds.), *The Economic Effects of Ageing and Policy Issues (1),* Seoul: KDI.

Ministry for Health, Welfare and Family Affairs, ROK/MIHWAF (2009), *Press releases*: February 27, April 9, May 4. Seoul.

Ministry of Welfare and Labour, Japan, Pension Bureau: *Home page*.

NPS/National Pension System (2009), *Internal Document*. Seoul: Press Release April 21.

NSO (2006), *Statistics on Elderly*. Seoul: October 10.

Park, Jong-Kyu (2009), *Changes in Composition of consumption Expenditure and its Policy Implication.* Seoul: Korea Finance Institute, March.

The Bank of Korea (2009), *Press Release*. Seoul: April 24.

in English

Ando, Albert & Franco Modigliani (1963), 'The Life -Cycle Hypothesis of Saving: Aggregate Implications and Tests', *American Economic Review,* March.

Asdrubali, P.; Sorenson, B.E. & O. Yosha (1996), 'Channels of risk sharing: U.S. 1963-1990', *Quarterly Journal of Economics*, vol. 111, pp. 1081-1110.

Attanasio, O.P. & A. Brugiavini (2003), 'Social Security and Household Savings', *Quarterly Journal of Economics*, vol. 118, pp. 1075-1119.

Attanasio, O.P. & S. Davis (1996), 'Relative wage movements and the distribution of consumption', *Journal of Political Economy,* vol. 104, pp.1227-1262

Barro, R.J. (1978), *The Impact of Social Security on Private Saving: Evidence from the U.S. Time Series.* Washington/D.C.: American Enterprise Institute for Public Policy Research.

BBC (2008), *The Future of Pensions in Depth.* http://news.bbc.co.uk/1/shared/spl/hi/pop_ups/05/business_pension_report/html/2.stm.

Browning, Martin & Thomas F. Crossley (2001), 'The Life Cycle Model of Consumption and Saving', *Journal of Economic Perspectives,* vol. 15 (3), pp. 3-22.

Browning, Martin & Annamaria Lusardi (1996), 'Household Saving: Micro Theories and Micro Facts', *JEL,* vol. 34 (4), pp. 1797-1855.

Diamond, Peter (2005), *Reforming Public Pensions in the U.S. and the U.K.* [a longer version of a lecture given at the London School of Economics and Political Science on May 18].

Feldstein, M. (1974), 'Social Security, Induced Retirement, and Aggregate Capital Formation', *Journal of Political Economy,* vol. 82 (5), pp. 905-926.

Feldstein, M. (1995), 'Social Security and Saving: New Time Series', *National Tax Journal,* vol. 49 (2), pp. 151-164.

Friedman, Milton (1957), *A Theory of Consumption Function.* Princeton/N.J.: Princeton University Press.

Gale, W.G. (1998), 'The Effects of Pensions on Household Wealth: A Revaluation of Theory and Evidence', *Journal of Political Economy,* vol. 106 (4), pp. 706-723.

Hayashi, F.; Altonji, F. & L. Koylikoff (1996), 'Risk sharing between and within families', *Econometrica,* vol. 64, pp. 261-294.

Modigliani, Franco & Richard Brumberg (1954), 'Utility Analysis and the Consumption Function: An Interpretation of Cross-section Data', in K. Kurihara (ed.), *Post-Keynesian Economics,* Piscataway/N.J.: Rutgers University Press.

Null, Clair (2003), *Methods of Consumption Smoothing: Coping with Pension Arrears in Post-Soviet Russia.* DARE UC Berkeley, mimeograph.

Stephens, Melvin Jr. (2003), ' '3rd of the Month': Do Social Security Recipients Smooth Consumption Between Checks?', *American Economic Review,* vol. 93 (1), pp. 406-422.

Stephens, Melvin Jr. (2006), 'Paycheque Receipt and the Timing of Consumption', *The Economic Journal,* vol. 116, issue 513, pp. 680-701, August.

Stephens, Melvin Jr. & Takashi Unayama (2007), *Consumption Smoothing and Periodic Income: Evidence from Japanese Public Pensions* <http://harrisschool.uchicago.edu/programs/beyond/workshops/ppepapers/fall07-stephens.pdf>.

Zhang, Qiang & Sung Jin Kang (2007), 'Crisis and Consumption Smoothing', *Annals of Economics and Finance,* vol. 8 (1), pp. 137-154.

The Authors

Prof. Peter Abrahamson, is professor of social policy at Seoul National University, Seoul, Republic of Korea. His research interests revolve around comparative studies of welfare state issues: poverty, social exclusion, activation, spatial differentiation, regional integration. From 2006 to 2008 he lived in and worked on Central America, before he worked on Europe, based at the University of Copenhagen, Denmark. He is co-author of *Welfare and Families in Europe* (Ashgate 2005) and co-editor of *Understanding Social Policy in Europe* (Casa Verde Publishing 2008) and *New Social Partnerships in Europe* (The Copenhagen Centre). He published recently in *Global Social Policy, Journal of Comparative Policy Analysis, Comparative Family Studies, International Journal of Urban and Regional Research, Acta Sociologica, Journal of European Social Policy* and *Social Policy and Administration*. He received a Ph.D. in sociology from the University of Copenhagen and a Ph.D. in public administration from Roskilde University. He has been a visiting scholar at Boston University, UC Berkeley, UC Davis, Sorbonne, Consejo Superior de Investigaciones Científicas/Madrid, University of York, University of Mannheim, University of Nantes, and Ritsumeikan University/Kyoto.

Prof. Karen M. Anderson is Associate Professor in the Department of Political Science, Institute for Management Research, Radboud University, Nijmegen/The Netherlands. She received her Ph.D. in political science from the University of Washington (Seattle). Her research focuses on comparative political economy of the welfare state, particularly the role of unions and social democratic parties in welfare state restructuring processes. She is the editor (with Ellen M. Immergut & Isabelle Schulze) of the *Handbook of West European Pension Politics* (Oxford University Press 2007). Her work has also appeared in *Comparative Political Studies, Comparative Politics, Zeitschrift für Sozialreform, Canadian Journal of Sociology*, and the *Journal of Public Policy*. She is currently completing a book about social policy in the European Union.

Prof. Jun-Ho Bae is Japan Professor at the College of Social Science, Hanshin University, Osan City, Republic of Korea. He received a Ph.D. in Economics from Hitotsubashi University and is currently member of the law-regulation committee, Ministry of IHWAF and of the military pension reform committee, Ministry of Defence; before he had been a member of the civil servant pension reform committee, MOPAS.

Prof. Gary Burtless holds the John C. and Nancy D. Whitehead Chair in Economic Studies, The Brookings Institution, Washington, D.C., U.S.A. He is also a research associate of the Center for Retirement Research at Boston College. His research focuses on issues connected with public finance, ageing, saving, labour markets, income distribution, social insurance, and the behavioural effects of government tax and transfer policy. He is co-author of *Globaphobia: Confronting Fears about Open Trade* (1998), *Five Years After: The Long Term Effects of Welfare-to-Work Programs* (1995), *Growth with Equity: Economic Policymaking for the Next Century* (1993), and *Can America Afford to Grow Old? Paying for Social Security* (1989). He was also editor or co-editor and contributor to *Aging Societies: The Global Dimension* (1998), *Does Money Matter? The Effect of School Resources on Student Achievement and Adult Success* (1996), *A Future of Lousy Jobs? The Changing Structure of U.S. Wages* (1990), *Work, Health and Income Among the Elderly* (1987) and *Retirement and Economic Behavior* (1984). Burtless has also written many scholarly and popular articles on the economic effects of Social Security, public welfare, unemployment insurance, and taxes. Burtless received his undergraduate education at Yale University in New Haven, Connecticut, and in 1977 obtained a doctoral degree in economics at the Massachusetts Institute of Technology (M.I.T.) in Cambridge, Massachusetts. Before coming to Brookings in 1981, he served as an economist for the U.S. Secretary of Health, Education, and Welfare and for the U.S. Secretary of Labor. In 1993 he was visiting professor of Public Affairs at the University of Maryland, College Park.

Dr. Yong Chan Byun, is Senior Research Fellow at the Korea Institute for Health and Social Affairs, Seoul, Republic of Korea. Dr. Byun's research interest covers population policy and welfare for the disabled and for the elderly. He received his doctorate in Sociology from Utah State University.

Rah-Il Hwang, received her doctoral degree in Nursing from Korea University. She is now Associate Research Fellow at the Health Insurance Research Center, Seoul, Republic of Korea. Her research focuses on comparison of health insurance systems in different countries.

Jinsoo Kim, Jinsoo Kim is Research Fellow at the Korea Institute for Health and Social Affairs (KIHASA). Before joining KIHASA, he has served as Research Fellow at the Health Insurance Research Center. Dr. Kim received his Ph.D. in economics from the University of Houston. His research interest lies in health economics.

Kyungha Kim, Researcher, National Health Insurance Policy Research Institute, National Health Insurance Corporation, Seoul, Republic of Korea.

Prof. Yongha Kim, is President of the Korea Institute for Health and Social Affairs, Seoul, Republic of Korea. His Ph.D. is from Sungkyunkwan University, Seoul, Korea. An economist by training, Dr. Yongha Kim has written extensively on social security and pension reform.

Min Jung Ko is Associate Research Fellow at the Health Insurance Research Center. Prior to joining the Center, she worked as Senior Researcher at the Korea Institute for Health and Social Affairs. Dr. Ko received her doctorate in Epidemiology from Seoul National University, Korea.

Dr. Takanobu Kyogoku, Director General, The National Institute of Population and Social Security Research, Tokyo, Japan. He was born in 1942 in Tokyo. He completed the Graduate School of Economics, University of Tokyo, in 1975 (Ph.D.). He has been in the present position after having been an Associate professor at the Japan College of Social Work, a Technical Official of Social Welfare at the Ministry of Health and Welfare, and is Professor and President of the Japan College of Social Work since 2005. He was a member of the Advisory Council for Social Security, and he is now the chairman of the Central Council for the Promotion of Measures for Disabled Persons. He has a great deal of scientific publications, which include the inclusive edition of Takanobu Kyogoku (2003), Social Security and Japanese Economy (2007), Home Medical Care and Social Work (2008), The Issues of the Law for the Support of Persons with Disabilities (2008) and others.

Chong Yon Park, Jun Tae Han and Jin-Hee Kwon, are researchers at the Health Insurance Research Centre, The National Health Insurance Corporation, Seoul, Republic of Korea.

Prof. Martin Seeleib-Kaiser is reader in Comparative Social Policy and Politics, Fellow of Green Templeton College, University of Oxford/U.K. His research focuses on the political economy of welfare states, with special foci on the role of political parties and the shifting boundaries between 'public' and 'private' social policies. He is the U.K. independent expert on social protection for the EU Commission. His book publications include: Party Politics and Social Welfare – Comparing Christian and Social Democracy in Austria, Germany and the Netherlands (2008, co-authored with S. v. Dyk & M. Roggenkamp); Welfare State Transformations – Comparative Perspectives (2008), The Dual Transformation of the German Welfare State (2004; co-authored with P. Bleses) and *Globalisierung und Sozialpolitik* (Globalization and Social Policy, 2001). His journal articles have been published in the *American Sociological Review,* the *British Journal of Industrial Relations, Social Policy and Administration* and *West European Politics.* Martin Seeleib-Kaiser received his master's degree (1989) and his doctoral degree in political science from the Geschwister-Scholl Institute, Ludwig Maximilians University, Munich (1993). In 2000, he obtained his *Habilitation* with a *venia legendi* in political science at Bremen University. Before joining Oxford University in 2004, he held appointments at the universities of Bielefeld and Bremen (Germany) as well as at Duke University (Durham, USA). In 2008, he was a visiting professor at the Centre for Comparative Welfare Studies, Department of Economics, Politics and Public Administration, Aalborg University, Denmark.

Prof. Jhinyoung Shin is Professor of Finance at the School of Business, Yonsei University in Korea. He started his academic career as an Assistant Professor at the Department of Finance, Hong Kong University of Science and Technology in 1993. Prior to joining Yonsei University, he had been an Associate Professor of Finance of Ajou University in Korea from 1999 to 2002. He was also Visiting Senior Fellow of School of Business, National University of Singapore during the summer of 2006 and 2007. Professor Shin's main areas of research cover corporate finance, market microstructure, industrial organization, and investment. He has published in major finance and economics journals. Professor Shin has been extensively involved in policy advisory works for the Financial Services Commission, the Ministry of Finance and Economy, the Ministry of Planning and Budget, the National Pension Service, Korea Exchange, the Korea Deposit Insurance Corporation, and the National Tax Service. He has written numerous policy reports on the deposit insurance system, the Korean security markets, the asset management of National Pension Service, and the reforms on state owned banks. He is currently serving as a member of Financial Market Development Committee of Financial Services Commission, and Performance Evaluation and Compensation Committee of National Pension Service. He is also a non-executive director of Mirae Asset Security Corporation, one of the leading brokerage companies in Korea. Professor Shin graduated from Seoul National University in 1985 with a B.A. degree and an M.A. degree in Economics in 1987. He received a Ph.D. in Finance from Carnegie Mellon University in 1993, while he was a recipient of Sloan Foundation Fellowship.

David Stanton, TD, Chair of the Indicators Subgroup of the EU Social Protection Committee, Coppingerstown, Ireland. David Stanton qualified at Oxford and the London School of Economics. He started his career as an ODI Nuffield Fellow working of the Uganda Government. Returning to the UK he was a lecturer at Brunel University before joining the UK Government Economic Service. He worked in Transport, Housing and the Treasury before a secondment to the Hong Kong Government. Back in the UK David worked for the then Employment Department becoming Chief Economist in 1987 and then moved in 1992 to the Department of Social Security as Chief Economist. His last post before retiring in 2002 was Chief Economist at the Department for Work and Pensions. Since retiring, he has worked as economic consultant to the Turner Commission on Pensions. He has been Chair of the EU's Social Protection Committee's Indicators Sub Group since 2001.

Prof. György Széll, Professor emeritus of Sociology, Department of Social Sciences, University of Osnabrück/Germany and Institute of Economic Research, Hitotsubashi University, Tokyo, Japan. Born in Budapest/Hungary; several times Dean of the Faculty of Social Sciences; Vice-president of the University from 1995 to 1997; Member of the Executive Committees of the International Sociological Association/ISA (1990-1994) and of the International Association of French-Speaking Sociologists (1978-1988); visiting professor in more than 60 universities in 30 countries world-wide; expert to the European Commission and numerous scientific bodies. Studied at the universities of Frankfurt a.M., Münster, Aix-en-Provence, Cologne and Algiers; degrees: Diplom-Soziologe (1965); Dr.sc.pol. (1967, both University of Münster, Germany). Main Publications: *The Injustice at Work – An International View on the World of Labour and Society* (2002); *Environmental Challenges for Germany and Japan* (2004); *Corporate Social Responsibility in the EU and Japan* (2006); *European Social Integration – A Model for East Asia?* (2009); *Social Innovation, the Social Economy and World Economic Development. Democracy and Labour Rights in an Era of Globalization* (2009); *Quality of Life & Working Life in Comparison* (2009); (Co-) Editor of several international book series and scientific reviews; altogether more than 300 scientific publications.

Prof. Zheng Gong-Cheng, Renmin University of China (RUC), Peking, China, Deputy Director of the Faculty Committee of the RUC, Commissioner of the Academic Committee of the RUC, Chair Professor of Social Security. Deputy Dean of the School of Labour and Human Resources (LHR) of RUC, Director of the Center for Social Security Studies of China of the RUC, Director of the Center for the Disabled, Member of the Standing Committee of the 11th National People's Congress, Member of the Internal and Judicial Affairs Committee of the 11th National People's Congress. As one of the key pioneers of social security, commercial insurance and related disciplines of China, Prof. Zheng's academic achievements, both theoretical and policy-oriented, had an extensive and far-reaching influence on the academic community and related government agencies, and many have also provided sound theoretical grounds for policy-making. Because of these excellent academic achievements, Prof. Zheng has earned many honours and awards, such as the title of 'Youth Specialist with Distinguished Contributions' and 'Distinguished Scholar Entitled Special State Council Allowance'. He has also been selected as one of the 'One Hundred Theorists for the 21st Century Project of Beijing' and 'New Century Excellent Talents in University of the Ministry of Education'. As team leader, Prof. Zheng has accomplished many research projects, among which many are supported and funded by the National Fund for Social Sciences (NFSS) (both the general and key programme), the Ministry of Education Fund for Social Sciences (MOEFSS), the Ministry of Labour and Social Security (MLSS), the Ministry of Civil Affairs (MCA), the National Development and Reform Commission (NDRC), the National Population and Family Planning Commission of China (NPFPC), the Ministry of Agriculture (MA), the Social Sciences Fund of Beijing and the Social Sciences Fund of Hubei Province etc.

Comparative Regional Integration Studies

Edited by György Széll and Woosik Moon

Vol. 1 Yongha Kim / György Széll (eds.): Economic Crisis and Social Integration. 2011

www.peterlang.de